Admiralty Salvage

Also by Tony Booth:
Cox's Navy

Admiralty Salvage

In Peace & War
1906–2006

Tony Booth

Pen & Sword
MARITIME

First published in Great Britain in 2007 by
PEN & SWORD MARITIME
an imprint of
Pen & Sword Books Ltd
47 Church Street, Barnsley, South Yorkshire, S70 2AS

Copyright © Tony Booth, 2007

ISBN 978-1-84415-565-1

A CIP catalogue record for this book is
available from the British Library

Typeset in 11/13 Sabon by Concept, Huddersfield, West Yorkshire
Printed and bound in England by Biddles Ltd

Pen & Sword Books Ltd incorporates the Imprints of
Pen & Sword Aviation, Pen & Sword Maritime, Pen & Sword Military,
Wharncliffe Local History, Pen & Sword Select,
Pen & Sword Military Classics and Leo Cooper

For a complete list of Pen & Sword titles please contact
PEN & SWORD BOOKS LIMITED
47 Church Street, Barnsley, South Yorkshire, S70 2AS, England
E-mail: enquiries@pen-and-sword.co.uk
Website: www.pen-and-sword.co.uk

In Memory of Michael Cobbold
21 January 1933–11 December 2000
Salvage and Mooring Officer

Who always believed this story should be told

'The work of the Salvage Organization has been beyond praise, and its value to the Allied cause, in terms of shipping and cargo saved, is incalculable.'

Admiral Harold Martin Borrough,
Naval Commander-in-Chief,
Allied Expeditionary Force, 1945

'the work of Naval salvage, a vital job whose achievements can all too easily be forgotten'.

Louis, Earl Mountbatten of Burma, 1965

Contents

Foreword

At a time in which the relevance of the maritime environment and its central role to the prosperity and security of the UK is perhaps less well understood than at any time in our recent history, I am delighted to have the opportunity to introduce this book. Benefiting from meticulous research, Tony Booth has distinguished the incredibly important role of Admiralty Salvage from the more romantic view of salvage perpetuated along the lines of films such as *Whisky Galore!* and the recent scenes at Branscombe Bay.

At its core remain the relentless and unforgiving nature of the sea and of the selfless, heroic and pioneering actions of men who first worked in this often harsh environment, particularly during the two world wars of the last century. However, the work of the Admiralty Salvage Section goes beyond these two conflicts through Suez, the Falklands and the 2nd Gulf War, often in highly dangerous circumstances and conditions, and invariably at the cutting edge of innovation and technology. As the book unfolds, the reader will soon discover that salvage comprises many different aspects, including recovery of cargo, food, ammunition, gold bullion and military equipment to name but a few.

What is absolutely clear is the critical role that the Section played during the world wars, and its part in keeping open the flow of vital supplies that separated this country from starvation and military impotence. It is not only a fitting testament to the officers and men involved, but a reminder of the importance of the sea to us all, and those who ply their trade upon it.

Admiral Sir Jonathon Band KCB, ADC
First Sea Lord and Chief of the Naval Staff
February 2007

Acknowledgements

I would like to thank the following organizations and individuals for images, quotes or interview material to ensure that this book could be completed. For his information and recollections as a Rescue Tug crew member during the Second World War, Deanne Wynne. Deanne served aboard Rescue Tugs during the North Atlantic convoys as well as in the D-Day operation, and is today the president of the Deep Sea Rescue Tug Association, whose many current members were involved in Operation Overlord and the towing of Phoenix units across to the Normandy beaches. To Birlinn, publishers in Scotland, for permission to quote from *The Great War at Sea* by Richard Hugh. Details from the book *Up She Rises* by Frank Lipscombe and John Davies, published by Hutchinson, are reprinted here by permission of The Random House Group Limited. Extracts from *The Path to Power* by Lady Margaret Thatcher are reprinted by permission of HarperCollins Publishers Ltd © Margaret Thatcher, 1995. The *Orcadian* newspaper for the use of some statistics regarding salvaged ships that they published in 1941. Lawrence H. Officer, 'Purchasing Power of British Pounds from 1264 to 2005', www.measuringworth.com, 2006, for accurate calculations of currency value based on the Retail Price Index. The National World War II Museum, for use of the D-Day oral history of Private G.W. Levers, from the Peter S. Kalikow Oral History Collection at the Eisenhower Center for American Studies, University of New Orleans.

Photographic archivist David Mackie at the Orkney Library & Archive for permission to use an image of the salvage vessel *Bertha*. ITN Archive/Stills for images of Suez and Commander Polland while salvaging the de Havilland Comet *Yoke Peter*. The National Oceanic and Atmospheric Administration/Department of Commerce (NOAA), for their image of the abandoned SS *Coulmore* in a raging sea. The Imperial War Museum for images H 393000, B 5225 and A 24130, covering D-Day. The National Archives, Kew, to quote from their files and the use of images covering the *Laurentic* salvage and the loss of the de Havilland Comet Yoke Peter. Jennifer Cochrane for her editorial advice. Mr Barry Carroll for his much-appreciated (more than he realizes) help in London. My wife, Virginie, for tolerating my long and often late hours at the keyboard. Jack and Hugo for being two little boys. Jane Westcott for never once complaining to anyone about giving me that one thing all writers crave: time. Susie Deflassieux, a mother-in-law in a million who ensured that I could make much-needed research trips. Please note, despite prolonged and exhaustive enquiries, tracking down certain copyright holders has proved impossible.

And finally I cannot thank enough the United Kingdom's current Chief Salvage and Mooring Officer, Morgyn Davies OBE. During one of Britain's worst heatwaves, in July 2006, Morgyn allowed me free access to the salvage files at the MoD establishment in Foxhill, Bath, in the middle of a particularly busy working schedule. That same week Israel was bombing southern Beirut and the Royal Navy was tasked with evacuating British subjects; a helicopter carrying the Albanian Deputy Prime Minister had crashed off Corfu killing all on board; three aging Russian nuclear submarines were about to be stabilized and moved to a safe location for breaking up. All these events were making him very busy indeed, either to actually deploy a salvage force or plan for such an eventuality. Still, whenever I had a question, needed specific files, images or answers to what must have sometimes seemed trivial questions, Morgyn always took the time to give me what I needed. Salvage is a specialized business, the mechanics of which are understood by very few, not least by a writer trying to fully comprehend the subject's largely forgotten impact on modern history. Morgyn's reading of the final manuscript, and valid comments, has made this a much better book than I could possibly have hoped for.

Introduction

On 24 June 1944 duty tug master Captain Victor Nichols received an urgent telephone call ordering him to render whatever assistance he could to a merchant ship adrift and burning half a mile south-east of Folkestone in Kent. He immediately set sail in the salvage tug *Lady Brassey*, arriving on the scene less than forty-five minutes later. Nichols said, 'At 4.20 pm we arrived close to the vessel, which had been abandoned by the crew, and drifting with head to the south-east, burning furiously from bridge to stern. The name of the vessel could not be ascertained as the name board had burnt away.'

She was in fact the 3,000-ton cargo ship *Empire Lough*, which was bound for Gold Beach, Normandy, with supplies for the post-invasion build-up. Earlier that afternoon German long-range guns on the French coast had shelled the vessel but – as yet – she was refusing to go down. Captain Nichols turned the *Lady Brassey* upwind of the *Empire Lough* to get in as close as possible to begin a standard foam fire-fighting procedure. Twelve minutes later the fire reached her Number One hold. Captain Nichols continued:

> At 4.32 pm, the fire was now raging very fiercely, with flames leaping to mast height, and ammunition exploding in all directions. At 4.45 pm the ammunition exploded much faster and I decided to lay off owing to danger of explosions, the foam having no effect on the fire, and not knowing the nature of the cargo the vessel was carrying, I considered it too dangerous to remain in close.

The *Empire Lough* was carrying 2,800 tons of cased petrol and government stores. Now well alight she was rapidly becoming a floating firebomb. Saving her was now hopeless, but neither could she remain out of control in such a busy shipping lane. At 4.50 pm Nichols got his first break when exploding ammunition eased off a little and, regardless of the burning petrol, he decided to risk going in much closer to get a line aboard and tow the crippled vessel to nearby Lydden Spout, a deserted rocky outcrop near Folkestone. He managed to get the *Lady Brassey*'s stern right under the *Empire Lough*'s starboard bow flare, but none of his senior crew members were able to get aboard and secure a towing wire. Nichols added:

> Sixteen-year-old Ordinary Seaman V. Brockman at once observed the difficult position, and entirely of his own initiative, without being requested to do so by me, climbed on board the burning vessel and made the tug's towing wire fast to the starboard bollard, after which he was taken back on board the tug and we commenced towing the vessel towards the shore at 5 pm.

At last Nichols had control over the *Empire Lough* and was able to get her clear of the shipping lanes.

Twenty minutes into their hour-long tow to shore the ammunition began exploding with far greater ferocity. Burning debris was hurled high into the air all around the *Empire Lough* with every fresh burst, much of it landing on her main deck, her superstructure and into the surrounding sea. Nichols refused to let his towline go and persisted in steaming for the shore with a burning ship that could ignite in one final and massive detonation at any moment. At 5.45 pm, with the explosions much more frequent, his towline on fire, because of its oil-impregnated rope core (or 'heart'), Captain Nichols ran the *Empire Lough* aground at Lydden Spout. He then slipped his towline and steamed away as fast as possible without waiting to recover the burning wire. Within three hours of being deployed, he was safely back at Dover and another major incident was logged.

Four days later, Captain Nichols, again aboard *Lady Brassey*, and Captain George William Holman aboard the salvage tug *Lady Duncannon*, were called out to another similar incident. The 874-ton collier *Dalegarth Force* was in a convoy en route from Tyneside to Poole when she, too, was hit by German batteries. By the time the two captains reached the *Dalegarth Force*, three of her crew had already been killed and all the remainder, except for her captain, had abandoned ship. She was well alight and while enemy shells were still raining down on the convoy, Captain Nichols put a line on the burning ship's deck bollards and took her in tow for Dover. Meanwhile, Captain Holman manoeuvred his tug alongside and started firefighting procedures immediately.

Under constant enemy shellfire, the two tug masters managed to get the *Dalegarth Force* out of the convoy and safely into Dover Harbour, by which time Captain Holman and his crew had extinguished the blaze. This time both the ship and her cargo were saved, the former going on to work as a cargo carrier until she was finally broken up in 1959. Within four days Captain Nichols had twice risked his life to salvage a distressed vessel. The following month the Commander-in-Chief, Dover, Admiral Henry Daniel Pridham-Wippell, recommended that Nichols should be decorated for his efforts to clear the *Empire Lough* from the Channel. Pridham-Wippell stated in his recommendation: 'While being towed the *Empire Lough* burned more fiercely and the vicinity became a miniature battlefield from exploding ammunition as many bullets and splinters fell on board *Lady Brassey*.' Captain Holman was also decorated for his efforts in putting out the fire aboard the *Dalegarth Force*. These two cases are far from unique in the day-to-day running of salvage under Admiralty control.

Three days before war was declared, the Admiralty Salvage Department went into business, its primary role being to recover disabled merchant convoy ships during Germany's U-boat offensive in the early war years. The salvage men sometimes steamed more than 1,000 miles into the North Atlantic to recover a disabled ship under appalling conditions. Some salvage missions seemed an insane risk of the highly skilled crews and their ships, but as an Admiralty spokesman said in 1941, 'We recover cargoes even when the expense is greater than the value, because it means lessening the tonnage required for the Battle of the Atlantic.'

The First World War was no easier on merchant ships plying the trade routes across the Atlantic, which were Britain's only thread-like lifelines for many years. In October 1916, Admiral of the Fleet Sir John Jellicoe was well aware of the danger to merchant shipping when he wrote from his flagship in Scapa Flow:

> The very serious and ever-increasing menace of the enemy's submarine attacks on trade is by far the most pressing question at the present time. There appears to be a serious danger that our losses in merchant ships, combined with the losses in neutral merchant ships, may, by early summer of 1917, have such a serious effect upon the import of food and other necessities into the Allied countries as to force us into accepting peace terms which the military position on the Continent would not justify and which would fall far short of our desires.

Jellicoe's prediction looked as though it would become a reality. By January 1917 shipping losses from unrestricted U-boat attack had reached an average of 153,000 tons a month; by June 1917 the figure had reached 417,000 tons – and would get much worse. The situation became so bad that at one point Britain was only six weeks away from running out of food. From its inception in 1915, until November 1918, the Admiralty Salvage Section, as it was known at the time, recovered hundreds of merchant ships which, had they been given up for lost, could well have tipped the balance against the Allies winning the first Battle of the Atlantic, and realized Jellicoe's fears.

The importance of marine salvage during armed conflict has been vastly underestimated since it became a vital arm of naval combat in the early twentieth century. In other major theatres of operation, such as the second Battle of the Atlantic, D-Day and the Allied advance on Germany, right up to the Suez crisis, the Falkland's conflict and even during Gulf War II, the same story can be told. In every major theatre of operations, salvage men slip into war zones to either recover valuable cargoes and equipment or clear the path for other combat forces to move on. All too often their courage, sacrifice and contribution to victory go unnoticed beyond the armed forces they serve.

Other branches of Admiralty salvage included the Wreck Dispersal Department, whose job it was to remove, in pieces if necessary, ships deemed unfit for full recovery. The Rescue Tug Service played another key role, often working hand in hand with salvage personnel on many operations. The Rescue Tug Service had originally come into being in May 1917 but was dissolved early in 1919. When the Second World War was declared the Service had only three civilian requisitioned vessels, but numbers grew rapidly as the war progressed. Twenty-seven of the Rescue Tugs were for Operation Overlord, the D-Day landings, towing Phoenix Units and components for Pluto, the trans-Channel fuel pipeline, necessary to keep the array of tanks and vehicles supplied for the Allied advance. However, between 1939 and 1945 nearly forty were lost to enemy action alone.

Admiralty salvage operations during peacetime have also made a major impact. When the Cunard liner RMS *Laurentic* was mined and sank with great loss of life towards the end of the First World War, the Admiralty Salvage Section set out to recover her cargo of more than £150 million (in today's value) of much-needed gold bullion for Britain's post-war recovery. In 1954 the first commercial jet airliner, the de Havilland Comet, was plagued with problems. Under direct orders from Louis, Earl Mountbatten of Burma, using new technology, the Department recovered debris from the best-known of these, code-named Yoke Peter, off Elba in the Mediterranean. Her salvage solved an enigma as to why several Comet jet airliners crashed, leading to changes in future airliner construction.

Today's Admiralty salvage has adapted to meet a variety of needs, both in peace and war. One operation assembled the resources to locate and survey Britain's biggest ever shipwreck, the MV *Derbyshire*, which mysteriously disappeared in the Pacific Ocean in 1980. Gulf War II included a variety of operations, further showing how salvage is continuously evolving to meet new needs. Transporting three derelict and fully fuelled nuclear-powered Russian submarines from their fifteen-year-old moorings to where they were safely broken up was another ground-breaking operation, which did more than just protect the environment from inevitable radioactive contamination.

A century has now passed since Admiralty salvage first began with a handful of civilian experts trying desperately to save one of Britain's most advanced battleships of the day, when bureaucracy was the greatest enemy. Although organized salvage as a legitimate naval arm only came into being during the First World War, and peaked during the Second World War, its roots can be traced back more than 200 years to the Royal Navy's worst ever peacetime warship disaster.

Chapter 1

'Grope, Grub & Tremble'

On a balmy Sunday morning late in August 1782, HMS *Royal George* was anchored at Spithead, near the Isle of Wight. She was the first Royal Navy warship to gross more than 2,000 tons and was the eighteenth-century equivalent of a weapon of mass destruction. Although she was HMS *Victory*'s sister ship, the *Royal George* was slightly better armed, packing 108 assorted guns on three deck levels compared to the *Victory*'s 100 mixed weaponry. The *Royal George* lived up to her reputation as a mighty man-of-war, having distinguished herself many times during her thirty-year life. In 1759 she sank the French warship *Superbe* after only one broadside during the Battle of Quiberon Bay. In the same battle she helped run ashore the French flagship *Soleil Royal*, which was then burned.

HMS *Royal George* had been laid up for many months, but now her decks and holds were a flurry of activity. Within two days she was due to join the Grand Fleet in the Mediterranean and resume her combat career as the flagship of Admiral Richard Kempenfelt, who had seen action against both the French in the East Indies and during the American War of Independence. Six months' stores had already been loaded, as well as many tons of powder and shot ready to feed her massive armament. Through fear of desertion by members of the crew so near to sailing, all shore leave was cancelled, making her normal company of about 1,000 officers and men swell to nearly 1,400, including hundreds of women and children. A number of merchants were also on board selling food, clothing and trinkets. One contemporary writer described the *Royal George* as resembling a large floating market as traders and prostitutes vied for business among the hundreds of seamen about to leave England for an uncertain future.

Admiral Kempenfelt was then about seventy years old and, although a tall, thin and stooping man, he had lost nothing of his spirit as a fighting mariner. While the bustle and bargaining was going on around

1

the ship, Kempenfelt stayed in his cabin where his personal barber gave the Admiral his morning shave. The *Royal George*'s master, Captain Martin Waghorn, ordered all her lower gun ports to be left open to speed the loading of the last few remaining stores in time for the Tuesday morning tide. Some small repairs were also in hand, including replacing the *Royal George*'s water cock, which had been leaking for some time. Waghorn then handed his ship over to a junior officer who could oversee the myriad preparations needed before setting sail, and retired to his cabin.

A water cock was used to pump the open sea up from about 4ft below the *Royal George*'s waterline to her main deck for washing down purposes. Being so far below sea level a technique called a 'parliament heel' was often used to access submerged areas, allowing the ship to be tipped over at a steep angle without the need for dry-docking. Aboard the *Royal George* was 24-year old Able Seaman James Ingram. Many years later he explained in detail the simplicity of what a parliament heel was, 'The whole of the guns on the larboard [port] side were run out as far as they would go, quite to the breasts of the guns, and the starboard guns drawn in amidships and secured by tackles, two to each gun, one on each side [of] the gun.'

While this standard manoeuvre was being carried out the 50-ton sloop, *Swallow*, owned and operated by three brothers, was lashed to the *Royal George*'s now low port side to unload casks of rum. Once she was secured Ingram and several other seamen were piped to clear the sloop of her cargo. The most effective way was to split the working party between unloading the casks from the sloop and loading them into the *Royal George*'s hold. Ingram continued:

> I was on the larboard side, bearing the rum-casks over, as some of the men of the *Royal George* were aboard the sloop to sling them. At first no danger was apprehended from the ship being on one side, although the water kept dashing in at the portholes at every wave; and there being mice in the lower part of the ship which were disturbed by the water that dashed in, they were hunted in the water by the men, and there had been a rare game going on.

At about 9.00 am a great many rum casks were on the *Royal George*'s main deck waiting to be stowed below, making her list creep further to port. Some of the more experienced seamen were concerned for the ship's safety until a carpenter advised the Lieutenant of the Watch to have the drummer beat the 'right ship' order, but the crew did not like or respect the Lieutenant. Ingram explained:

> His name I do not recollect. The men called him 'jib-and-foresail Jack', for if he had the watch in the night, he would be always bothering the men to alter the sails, and it was 'up jib' and 'down jib' and 'up foresail' and 'down foresail' every minute. He had an annoying habit of moving his fingers about when walking the quarterdeck, the men said he was an organ player from London.

The officer, Third Lieutenant Monin Hollingbery, flatly refused to listen to the carpenter, dismissed him and ordered the man to get below and continue his duties. About fifteen minutes later the carpenter's concern had turned to alarm and he again approached Hollingbery to express his fears. Hollingbery lost his professional cool, snapping back, 'Sir! If you can manage the ship better than I can you had better take command.'

Fear was now spreading among the men, somewhat fuelled by their lack of respect for Hollingbery. Ingram and a good many other seamen were at the ship's waist or in the gangways and heard Hollingbery's retort. Ingram recalled, 'We knew the danger and began to feel aggrieved, for there were some capital seamen aboard, who knew what they were about quite as well or better than the officers.' The carpenter decided to go over Hollingbery's head and tell Captain Waghorn what had happened. Within minutes Waghorn gave the order for the drummer to beat 'right ship'.

Ingram continued, 'There was no time for him to beat his drum, and I do not know if he even had time to get it. I ran down to my station, and, by the time I got there the men were tumbling down the hatch-ways and over [one] another to get to their stations as quickly as possible to right ship.' Ingram's station was the third gun from the ship's head on the lower gun deck, starboard side. Without waiting for the order, the men tried to loosen the guns and roll them out of the starboard gun ports as fast as possible to counter the list. Now the massive iron guns were at a steep angle on an ever-increasing sloping plain. Within seconds the cannon began breaking free. They careered across all three cramped and crowded gun decks, maiming and crushing the many hundreds of men trying in vain to hold them back. Their efforts were futile as splintered wood, cannon, shot and mangled flesh rushed to, and compacted against the rapidly submerging low port side. Waghorn rushed to Kempenfelt's cabin where the aged admiral was now writing a letter, but the extreme port list had caused his door to jam fast in its frame. Kempenfelt was trapped on the inside of his cabin and neither he nor Waghorn could prize the door free.

Below decks Ingram grabbed an eyebolt next to his gun port and climbed through on to the outside of the ship's starboard side. Once through it, Ingram remembered:

> I saw the porthole as full of heads as it could cram, all trying to get out. I caught hold of the best bower anchor [the larger starboard anchor], which was just above me, to prevent from falling back into the porthole, and seized hold of a woman who was trying to get out of the same porthole, and I dragged her out. I threw the woman from me, and saw all the heads drop back again in at the port-hole, for the ship had got so much on her larboard side that the starboard port-holes were as upright as if the men had tried to get out of the top of a chimney with nothing for their legs and feet to act upon.

Just before the *Royal George* sank, Ingram and many other survivors reported feeling a strong *whoosh* as air blew out through the open starboard gun ports while the water poured in. A widely reported contemporary eyewitness account came from a woman who was writing a letter overlooking Spithead just before the *Royal George* began to capsize. She was idly gazing at the mighty warship while composing a sentence in her head. The woman looked down to pen the sentence, and when she looked up again a few moments later the *Royal George* had fully capsized and the entire ship's number were fighting – many in vain – for their lives. Nearly 1,000 people, including 300 women and 60 children were killed.

After about ten days residents in and around Portsmouth saw the grizzly sight of bodies bobbing to the surface. Ingram well remembered how:

> Bodies would come up, thirty or forty nearly at a time. A body would rise and come up so suddenly as to frighten any one. The watermen, there is no doubt, made a good thing of it: they took from the bodies of the men their buckles, money, and watches, and then made fast a rope to their heels and towed them to land.

A contemporary writer recorded how 'When the time arrived for the buoyancy of the drowned persons, the individual penning this saw them towed into Portsmouth Harbour, in their mutilated condition, in the same manner as rafts of floating timber, and promiscuously (for particularity was scarcely possible,) put in carts, which conveyed them to their final sleeping place.' For many weeks afterwards the open carts were pulled through the streets of Portsmouth, full of recovered bodies, before they were placed in several mass graves along the Hampshire coast.

The surviving officers and some crew had to face a court martial. All were acquitted of negligence and her loss was officially recorded as the general state of the decay of her timbers. The carpenter who tried to warn Hollingbery was saved and taken along with many others to HMS *Victory* nearby. He was laid on the hearth before the galley, but all attempts to revive him failed. The woman Ingram hauled out of the gun port was also taken to the *Victory* and although very near death, she did survive. Captain Waghorn, who could not swim, also survived, but his son, a young lieutenant, was below decks and was killed. Third Lieutenant Monin Hollingbery survived, remained in the Royal Navy and was eventually promoted. Some said this was not so much for his seamanship, but his ability to keep quiet at the official inquiry. The sloop unloading rum casks was dragged down with the *Royal George* and two of the three brothers who owned her were lost. Admiral Kempenfelt never escaped from his cabin. Able Seaman James Ingram was one of only three to escape from below decks. He outlived every *Royal George* survivor before dying in 1851 aged ninety-three.

Within a year the Admiralty wanted the *Royal George*'s stores and weapons salvaged and, if possible, to recover the ship. An invitation went out to the general public for the best way to salvage her, an ambitious idea that had never before been made on such a grand scale, and more than 200 ideas were put forward before the Admiralty accepted engineer William Tracey's plan. Tracey adopted a classic and what was even then a well-trusted method called a 'tidal lift' – but with a few modifications. His idea was to place men-of-war on each side of the *Royal George* at low tide and make her fast to the vessels by wrapping copious ropes around her hull at low water; then he would use the rising tide to lift her clear of the seabed. He planned to use more than twenty strong ropes around key points of her hull to ensure she could be lifted evenly.

Since the tidal lift method was first used in medieval Venice, the problem always arose that if one rope parted then the strain on the remaining ones would be greatly increased, and thus a chain reaction of parting ropes might occur. Tracey's unique rope arrangement ensured this could not happen. The ropes were secured in a similar way to what sailors today call a 'barrel hitch', which means tied in a manner that the more pressure applied, the tighter they become. This was the first time such an ambitious idea had been tried. Once the *Royal George* was clear of the seabed, suspended between lifting craft, Tracey planned to tow her, still submerged, towards the shore. Then on each successive tide he would wind in the slack on the ropes and repeat the process until the *Royal George* was well above the high-tide line. In reality Tracey only managed to move her about 30ft. His plan failed for two reasons: she was too heavy, and only two lifting craft were provided, although he requested four. The Navy Board also refused to pay Tracey, so he was unable to make necessary alterations to his salvage plan. Some historians believe the Navy Board never wanted the *Royal George* salvaged from the very beginning – just in case her rotting timbers were found to be sound.

In the early 1820s two Deptford-born brothers, John and Charles Deane, patented the world's first ever smoke helmet, enabling fire-fighters to enter a burning building, fully protected with an air supply fed into a copper helmet. No one was interested in their new life-saving idea, but five years later they saw the potential to adapt the design for diving. The new diving, or 'open' helmet, was basically a miniature diving bell over the diver's head with an air supply fed down to him from the surface. The diver wore a short stiff canvas jacket that was also designed so that the air was trapped within, but still free to escape from underneath. In 1831 the Deane brothers gave a demonstration to the Chief Engineer to the Navy, Simon Goodrich, and the Admiralty at the entrance to Portsmouth Harbour. Goodrich was responsible for the management and installation of machinery in all naval dockyards, as well as inspecting new designs for possible incorporation into the Navy. He was also in close contact with some of the greatest engineers of the time, such as Henry Maudslay and Isambard Kingdom Brunel, whose great ocean liner the SS *Great Britain* would be launched thirteen years later. Goodrich's background and qualifications ideally placed him to assess the Deane brothers' new diving method. But Goodrich was unimpressed and refused to invest Navy funds in the new idea.

The following year the brothers gave another demonstration at Sheerness Dockyard before Sir James Beresford. He, too, was unimpressed and the brothers returned to Deptford without securing a naval contract. The *Royal George* had gone down right in the middle of the Navy's biggest and busiest anchorage and a large sandbank was gradually building up around the wreck, adding to the danger of the navigational hazard. For more than fifteen years after her loss, the *Royal George*'s masts were still well above sea level and she had already been run into several times. Although a British frigate ran down the last mast in 1794, parts of her decks were still visible at low spring tides until they, too, were consumed by the rising sand. In 1832 the Navy Board was abolished, clearing the way for another salvage attempt as her removal was now becoming urgent.

The Admiralty still had no dedicated salvage personnel. Since the mid-eighteenth century most diving was carried out from a submerged diving bell from which men would go out and work in short bursts on the seabed, with air fed from the bell. The method was cumbersome, limited by depth and no longer practical to deal with such complex salvage operations as the *Royal George*. Overwhelming pressure forced the Admiralty to act and finally give the Deane brothers the chance to prove their worth and attempt salvaging the wreck. They sailed out to the wreck site, dropped anchor and lowered their sturdy iron ladder down to the hulk. The brothers gingerly climbed down to the ship and thoroughly surveyed her condition, but they could only report back to the Admiralty that the *Royal George* was rotten throughout and beyond salvaging.

All that could be done was to recover the many bronze, brass and iron guns scattered about the wreck site. Altogether the brothers managed to recover twenty-nine weapons in two years, which, being from HMS *Victory*'s sister ship, were melted down and now form part of the interior base of Nelson's Column. On 16 June 1836, while re-covering the well-preserved weapons, John Deane came across another wreck he felt bound to investigate. The ship was soon identified as Henry VIII's sixteenth-century flagship, *Mary Rose*. Both brothers worked at the new wreck site for some time recovering guns, timbers and artefacts such as longbows. Once they returned to the *Royal George*, the final resting place of the *Mary Rose* was lost again until 1968.

Under such demanding conditions the Deane brothers' revolutionary diving suit began to show design flaws. A diver only had to lose his footing slightly for the fragile bubble to escape and seawater to gush in and fill his lungs. The brothers contacted German-born precision engineer Augustus Siebe, who had started as a metalworker in Berlin, making guns, watches and various engineering instruments before emigrating to London in 1816 to continue his work. The Deane brothers asked Siebe if he could improve their smoke-come-diving helmet and thus allow men to work deeper but more safely in the hostile underwater environment.

The first alteration Siebe made, which seems obvious now, was to enclose the helmet and suit around the diver to prevent sudden air loss should he lose his footing; he also added an air regulator, allowing the diver to have control over the volume of air in his suit. Divers could now work at depths of about 60ft – fully confident that if they fell while submerged, they had a much greater chance of survival. By 1839 the Admiralty was again under great pressure to have the *Royal George* removed, even though the Deane brothers had reported that she was far too rotten to salvage. Both naval and merchant ships were becoming bigger, deeper and faster and it was only a matter of time before a vessel, perhaps now steel built and steam driven, ploughed into the *Royal George* or the rising sandbank around her still solid hulk.

About 100 miles away in the River Thames, near Tilbury, a Royal Engineer colonel was conducting experiments into how to demolish two sunken wrecks with explosives. Scottish-born James Pasley had joined the Royal Military Academy in Woolwich aged only sixteen, first enlisting in the Royal Artillery and then the Royal Engineers. He saw active service during the Napoleonic Wars and in 1812, the Duke of Wellington appointed him as the first director of the Royal Engineer Training Unit in Chatham, Kent. In 1838, disregarding the Admiralty's views on diving, Pasley began personally looking into the possibility of making it a legitimate arm of the naval service. Until then he, like many other salvage workers, had used the established diving bell method, but this proved hopelessly inadequate when dealing with explosives. Pasley decided to experiment with the Deane brothers' 'open helmet' diving equipment and Siebe's 'closed helmet' version to determine if either could have a practical naval application beyond the scope of a theoretical demonstration. On 28 April 1838 he became the first service diver when he tested the equipment, before allowing other men to be trained in the new diving technique.

Now placing the explosive charges became a much simpler operation, as the diver had full mobility and much more time to select where to place the charges for maximum effect. After successfully demolishing the two Thames wrecks, Pasley and his team were asked to attempt to blast the *Royal George* out of the Royal Navy's main anchorage area. The technique for placing explosives involved a diver going down and securing two eyebolts into the ship's wooden hull. With a pulley system to the surface a large explosive charge was then lowered accurately into place. Once the divers were out of the water the explosive was detonated by a charge from a voltaic battery, very similar to today's car battery. Another innovation Pasley developed is nowadays better known in diving parlance as the 'dive buddy', a routine which recognized the importance of one diver shadowing another, should either become trapped or lost. The technique now forms the cornerstone of all modern dive training and operations.

After Pasley demolished the *Royal George*, which took several tons of explosives and more than four years to scatter her remains safely across the bed of the Solent, he was able to convince the Admiralty of the value of diving as a Royal Navy resource. Unlike a few years before, when the Deane brothers tried to sell their idea, the Admiralty now realized diving's true worth and a training school was opened shortly afterwards. On Pasley's recommendation the Siebe diving suit was favoured above the Deane brothers' for its 'public service'. Thirteen Royal Navy petty officers and seamen were the first men to be trained by one of Pasley's Royal Engineers. The diving school was set up at HMS *Excellent* in Portsmouth, near the Defence Training School, Whale Island, where military divers are still trained today. Siebe's diving suit was so successful that it was used virtually unchanged both commercially and in the Royal Navy from the late 1830s until 1989, and is still used extensively in the Far East today.

The Royal Navy salvage divers' motto 'Grope, Grub & Tremble' describes perfectly the difficulty and danger they have to face on a day-to-day basis. Quite often they have to *grope* in agitated silt or the dark to find their way around a sunken wreck, and get back out again. Then they need to *grub*, meaning to search for and pull up by hand. And finally *tremble*, due to the sudden, unpredictable danger that is part of their daily working lives.

Although Admiralty diving was borne out of this catastrophic marine tragedy more than 225 years ago, the first few pioneering divers commissioned to clear the *Royal George* were the seeds of what was later to become the Admiralty Salvage Section. And, as the Victorian era ended, the need for such a service was about to be tested to the limit in the most vicious and war-torn century since men first fought each other on the high seas.

Chapter 2

'War Risk'

On 26 February 1909, the main sea powers of Europe, together with those of the United States and Japan, met in London to agree the Declaration Concerning the Laws of Naval Warfare. The treaty listed seventy-one articles codifying international behaviour on the high seas, including twenty-one articles covering the blockading of enemy ports that Britain forced Germany to adhere to during the First World War. The Declaration also detailed the rights of warships to board and, if deemed appropriate, confiscate a merchant vessel and/or her cargo, or to destroy both if they appeared to assist the enemy. Regarding merchant ships, Article 50 stated: 'Before the vessel is destroyed all persons on board must be placed in safety, and all the ship's papers and other documents which the parties interested consider relevant for the purpose of deciding on the validity of the capture must be taken on board the warship.' Article 50 became known as the 'cruiser rules'. At first, both sides adhered strictly to the gentlemanly conduct, but by 1918 the war at sea had degenerated into a lawless and brutal struggle for supremacy where merchant ships constituted the main victims.

Even before hostilities began, the Admiralty was aware that the salvage of warships might be required, a decision that was derived from two very obvious events during the previous decade. Firstly, naval combat had changed beyond all recognition since the mid-nineteenth century, and secondly there were many more merchant vessels and warships steaming along the sea lanes around the British coast. The Admiralty did have highly skilled divers from HMS *Excellent* and a large amount of salvage plant – such as various pumps, hoses, cutting tools and a great deal of minor implements needed to recover very small vessels – but more often than not salvage meant recovering objects lost at sea. With no experience in wholesale ship recovery the Admiralty looked at recent history as a model on which to base their new department.

In 1904, during the Russo-Japanese War, Japan made a surprise naval attack on the unsuspecting Russian fleet anchored off Port Arthur, Russia – a valuable lesson the Japanese put to good effect at Pearl Harbour forty years later. Six major warships were sunk in the attack. Unable to afford replacement vessels, and since they lay in very shallow water, Russia decided to salvage them. Nearly 200 skilled workmen, including an engineer, a foreman, a draughtsman and about 190 mechanics from the St Petersburg shipbuilder, Baltic Yard, set out for the Russian west coast with five railway cars packed with pneumatic, electrical and steam-driven tools, as well as pumps, hoses and yards of timber. Due to the shallowness of the water around Port Arthur, they were able to recover all six warships using what is known as the 'cofferdam' method. The salvage operation greatly impressed the Admiralty who believed that Britain could achieve the same result, should the need ever arise.

The simple theory of a cofferdam method was nothing new, having been used for building the foundations for bridges over rivers and in harbour areas for centuries. A wooden or steel structure is built up from the vessel's damaged area to well above the high-water line. The water inside the structure is then pumped out so that workers can move freely in and around the damaged area without the need for diving equipment. After studying the Russian success story at length and reading excerpts from a handbook on salvage written by British salvage engineer Frederick Young, the Admiralty declared: 'If it be granted that ships of our fleet may be grounded round our coasts in circumstances under which the cofferdam method is the only resort, if they are to be restored to the fighting line, it seems prudent that materials and equipment in a readily transportable form be kept available for emergency.'

As orders were despatched to all naval bases around the United Kingdom to submit lists of their available salvage plant, the true amount of the Navy's equipment was beginning to look quite healthy. Bases like Sheerness, Portsmouth, Chatham and Devonport reported back an array of 6in to 15in pumps, some of which were oil, steam or electrically driven; cutting gear and portable boilers also seemed to be in abundance. Some bases like Portland and Pembroke had pumps ready built into tugs 'available in an emergency'. Sheerness even had two lighters with built-in steam pumps. (A lighter was a flat-bottomed barge normally used for loading and unloading cargo from a ship, but they had also been used for salvage work as a floating pontoon or pumping platform since the late nineteenth century.)

Captain Frederick Young was a skilled and resourceful ex-Admiralty diver who worked as Chief Salvage Officer for the Liverpool Salvage Association. Unlike other salvage companies the Association did not hold commercial gain as a priority, rather its main role was to protect the interests of insurance companies and shipowners. Its committee was made up entirely of marine insurance representatives and there were no shareholders. A separate bank account was opened for each vessel before recovery began and all invoices relating to the casualty were paid immediately. Not only did the Association recover distressed ships, but they also undertook every eventuality such as arranging bonds, storage of cargo, sales of damaged cargo, delivery, all legal issues and every incident right down to answering telephone queries. The Association made money by charging a commission on all disbursements and a fee at the end of each case for establishment and superintending charges. Any profit was ploughed back into the Association for upkeep and additions to their salvage plant.

Young began working for the Liverpool Salvage Association in 1906 and was without a doubt Britain's leading expert on ship recovery. His smiling eyes and quiet, unassuming manner were enhanced by his portly frame, handlebar moustache and King George V 'goatee' beard – but when it came to ship recovery his whole being seemed to change. Young's son, Desmond, joined his father on many salvage operations, the first when he was only four years old. Much later in life, and a successful salvage engineer in his own right, Desmond was able to sum up his father's character. 'At a wreck his mind was never away from the job and no detail was too small to escape his eye. He never took an unnecessary risk, but there was no risk that he would not take with ships, gear or men if he considered it necessary.'

Young was no stranger to the Admiralty. In the same year that he joined the Liverpool Salvage Association, he was invited to advise on the recovery of a stranded battleship, which had become a considerable embarrassment to the Royal Navy. The 14,000-ton Duncan Class pre-Dreadnought battleship HMS *Montague* (which was later renamed *Montagu* after being built) was the cutting edge in naval engineering. In 1906 the *Montagu* was testing new radio equipment in the Bristol Channel under Captain T.B.S. Adair and his navigating officer, Lieutenant J.H. Dathan. Part of the exercise included steaming up and down, testing wireless communication with Land's End. On 29 May she anchored just off Lundy Island in the Bristol Channel to continue tests. The distance was too far for the signal to reach the *Montagu*, so Adair weighed anchor and steamed towards the Isles of Scilly in the hope that transmission might be stronger. About four hours later, thick fog forced the *Montagu*'s return to her anchorage, however her reciprocal course was about 2 miles off its original track and the *Montagu* ran up Shutter Point, a rocky outcrop on Lundy's extreme south-west corner.

The Royal Navy still had no dedicated salvage arm at that time, so Frederick Young was employed in an advisory capacity to Admiral Sir Arthur Knyvet Wilson. He was at that time the Channel Fleet Commander better known for the quote that submarines were 'Underhand, unfair and damned un-English'. Unfortunately, he also saw himself as something of a salvage expert. Desmond later recalled, 'Admiral Sir A.K. Wilson took a keen interest in the salvage and was, by virtue of his position, in supreme control of it. Admiral Wilson had no experience of salvage. He had, however, a ready flow of ideas, most of which seemed to my father wrong, or impracticable, or both.'

Wilson employed hundreds of men who were ordered to remove some of the *Montagu*'s armoured plating and replace it with caissons to give her more buoyancy, but the caissons broke free in the slightest swell. His salvage attempt went on for six months until he eventually struck on the idea of filling the entire battleship with cork to give her enough buoyancy to lift her off on a spring tide. Young was not impressed when Wilson passed on the news. Desmond continued, 'When my father returned he went into his cabin and wept. For he knew that no pump would ever run again without choking and that it was too late for the *Montagu*.' There was now no chance to save this state-of-the-art, two-year-old battleship that had cost the British taxpayer exactly £1,046,992 (£75 million in today's money). Eventually Young was given free reign to salvage her 12in guns without any naval interference. Wilson's hundreds of naval personnel were replaced by a handful of well-trained salvage men. Each gun was 40ft long and weighed 50 tons. They were broken out and lifted, using 100-ton blocks suspended over 60ft sheerlegs, an A-framed heavy-lift crane made from 20in timbers. The first two guns were removed within two weeks and all four were lowered into a lighter within twenty-four hours. The guns were eventually re-used in other battleships.

13

The loss of a Duncan Class battleship in 1906 was equivalent to a Type 42 Destroyer today (which very nearly happened in 2002 when HMS *Nottingham* ran aground off the coast of Australia) with all the ramifications of public cost, blame and humiliation for the Royal Navy. The embarrassment was amplified due to the *Montagu*'s position in a major shipping lane, and within easy access of hundreds of tourists who flocked to see her. Now she is a popular dive site where all that remains among the rocks and kelp are a few piles of armour plating – a reminder of what can happen when senior naval officers, with a poor understanding of salvage dynamics, are allowed to take control. Throughout the next hundred years, this familiar pattern would unfold all too regularly as the Salvage Section and the rigid naval command structure at times clashed over how best to save ships.

Two years after the *Montagu* debacle, the Admiralty allowed Young to command the successful righting of the 5,750-ton cruiser HMS *Gladiator*, which had collided with the 11,000-ton American liner *St Paul* off the Isle of Wight during a blizzard on 25 April 1908. The *St Paul* hit the *Gladiator* so hard on her starboard side that 50ft of her hull plating and internal structure were torn out. Although the *Gladiator* was saved, she was eventually scrapped for less than the salvage costs, but the Admiralty now understood that Young was a gifted and energetic salvage officer, who could be of great use in saving their vessels.

While the various naval bases were returning their salvage plant census details, Admiralty representative William Graham Greene wrote to the Liverpool Salvage Association's General Manager Frank Lowe stating that the Admiralty had, for some time, been planning a special provision for the recovery of warships. Greene said, 'As a first step My Lords would be glad to learn whether your Association would be willing to lend Captain Young's services to the Admiralty during the war, to act as an advisor on salvage matters, at a fixed rate, payable by the Admiralty to the Association.' The Admiralty also enquired if the Association's crack salvage vessel, *Ranger*, would be available for the duration of the war and if so, at what price? Greene, who was also the uncle of British author Graham Greene, later went on to help form the Admiralty's Naval Intelligence Department.

Lowe agreed to the request and Young was formally employed at public expense for a fixed rate of 5 guineas per day. The hire of the salvage vessel was suggested, but the Admiralty rejected the offer, claiming to have no need of the vessel. One of the first jobs Young was asked to undertake was not a salvage operation, but to conduct a thorough battle-readiness survey of all the Admiralty salvage plant now accounted for. Throughout October and November 1914 he visited every naval base to inspect all the pumps, tugs, lighters and cutting equipment available.

On 29 November he submitted his four-page report to Third Sea Lord, Rear Admiral Sir Frederick Charles Tudor. Young wrote: 'I examined the existing appliances as to their adequacy for general salvage work and found they were generally inadequate for salvage work on anything approaching an extensive scale.' His scathing report went on to criticize the shoddy condition of the Navy's salvage plant through lack of basic maintenance. He doubted that some of it even qualified as salvage equipment. 'I feel it my duty to inform you,' Young continued, 'that the efficiency of these could have been materially increased if they had been procured under the specifications made up by a salvage expert. The oil pumps supplied are quite unknown in the salvage world and I think I may go so far as to say they have never been actually tested in salvage work.' Young concluded that the available equipment was nothing more than 'first aid appliances' and offered to list what essential plant should be purchased for use in naval bases for the types of casualties they were likely to encounter.

Young's next concern was the lack of qualified staff to operate the equipment. A training scheme had been put forward before the war to prepare men for just such an eventuality but, much to Young's disgust, the Admiralty had rejected the proposition, a fact that he pointed out clearly in his report. Young also criticized the Admiralty when he wrote: 'It is probably needless to say salvage work cannot be learned in a short time and successful results depend primarily on experience and training, even to the smallest details, the handling and placing of pumps, connecting suctions etc., etc.' Perhaps Young was thinking of Admiral A.K. Wilson when he wrote: 'Some of the heaviest losses sustained by ship owners and underwriters have been caused through the work of the amateur salvor and it is an extraordinary fact that nearly everyone connected with the sea considers themselves quite competent to undertake cases without any experience.'

Young's wake-up call jolted the Admiralty into instant reaction. Equipment was overhauled and new items purchased. A rapid programme to refit some craft as salvage vessels was also carried out. Two new lighters were ordered and two paddle tugs were found, the

Advice and the *Escort*, which, although they had 800 tons and 550 tons per hour pumping capacity respectively, were no match for the *Ranger*'s salvage status and vastly superior 5,450 tons per hour pumping capacity through her many different units. A list of naval personnel who had even the slightest salvage experience was compiled. Altogether forty-nine men, including able seamen, gunners, divers' attendants and stokers who had been divers were all identified for conscription into the Admiralty's new salvage organization. It was not enough, but better than none at all.

The Admiralty reconsidered their previous rejection order to charter the *Ranger*, also adding the Liverpool Salvage Association's smaller vessel, *Linnet*. To give some idea of the *Ranger*'s size and capability as a salvage vessel, forty-eight men were needed to crew her. She was originally built as a gunboat, 157ft long with a black-painted teak hull 6in thick. With an oversized yellow funnel, slightly too wide at the beam, she looked something of a comic character, but she survived two world wars and more than fifty years as a competent salvage vessel. The Admiralty also hired the three ex-gunboats, *Racer*, *Ringdove* and *Thrush*, the latter two needing to be fully refitted as salvage vessels.

Having started from nothing the department was growing well, but was still nowhere near battle ready. Although refits were quickly ordered, they were time-consuming and transferring salvage personnel from other military branches led to a bureaucratic quagmire. Merchant shipping losses were now increasing with every passing month, many of which could have been saved. The first British casualty of the First World War was nowhere near the Western Front. On 3 August 1914, the 6,458-ton British cargo vessel *San Wilfrido* was mined and sunk off Cuxhaven – the day before war was declared. Germany only had about twenty operational U-boats to patrol the North Sea, Irish Sea, English Channel and North Atlantic in 1914 so the Allies considered the *Unterseeboot* an oddity rather than a threat. On 20 October 1914 the cruiser rules entered a new phase when the *U-17* was the first German submarine to capture a British merchant ship. The 866-ton British cargo vessel *Glitra* was steaming about 14 miles off the Norwegian coast. The *U-17*, under the command of Kapitänleutnant Johannes Feldkirchner, surfaced to stop and search her. After her papers were found to be in order the crew was allowed to collect personal effects and take to the lifeboats before Feldkirchner ordered her to be scuttled. But maritime losses were about to increase – rapidly.

One of the main causes was the irretrievable breakdown of maritime law and order through both sides' different interpretations of the London Declaration's careful wording, or their wish not to sign at all. Britain had already breached the Declaration early in the war. Article 56 stated: 'The transfer of an enemy vessel to a neutral flag effected after the outbreak of hostilities is void unless it is proved such a transfer was not made in order to evade the consequences to which an enemy vessel, as such, is exposed.' And Article 57 stated: 'The neutral or enemy character of a vessel is determined by the flag she is entitled to fly.' As early as November 1914, long before the Declaration became a mockery of international diplomacy, First Lord of the Admiralty Winston Churchill initiated a new secret weapon known as the Q ship. The 'Q' was said to stand for 'query', as their true identity was never really known, that is, until it was too late. Many Q ships were used, and were made up of trawlers, colliers, coasters, tugs and at least one salvage vessel. They would normally fly, illegally, the flag of a neutral country such as the United States and were always rusty, unkempt-looking vessels, which gave the impression of a sloppy crew and ship.

But beneath the facade were normally housed a 4in gun, perhaps a couple of 12-pounders and howitzers with depth charges, and even deck-mounted torpedoes as later additions. Once in range, the Q ship lowered her neutral flag and showed her true 'enemy character' by raising the White Ensign at the last minute. Meanwhile the false panelling fell away and a team of Royal Navy gunners opened up with deadly accuracy on their startled prey. Quite understandably U-boat crews became less inclined to surface and board a merchant vessel under international law – not knowing if the merchantman was playing the same game or, more frequently, not.

With starvation threatening at home, and lack of raw materials which were no longer reaching her ports, the German government was coming under intense pressure to act, even if this meant openly breaching international law. The British blockade also ensured that most of Germany's Imperial High Seas Fleet was trapped in the North Sea, but as bigger and better armed U-boats came off the production line, the urge to wage unrestricted U-boat warfare was increasing. With every new starving mouth at home and every U-boat lost at sea, Germany sat back helplessly as food and war material poured into

Britain aboard hundreds of merchant ships every month. Eventually, in February 1915, the German government voted for unrestricted U-boat warfare and declared a 200-mile war zone around the United Kingdom from Norway down to Spain, including Ireland. Fulfilling the legal requirement of 'fair notice', U-boats attacked at will any tanker, cargo or passenger ship within the designated area.

The three merchant ships lost to U-boat action in 1914 jumped to 396 by the end of the following year, many of which were now being sunk without warning. The need to salvage as many merchant vessels as possible instead of just warships was clearly becoming a matter of top priority. With the sheer volume of stranded vessels growing daily, it became necessary to codify exactly what types of ships the fledgling salvage department should attempt to recover. On 4 October 1915, Director of Naval Transport Alexander Kemball-Cook wrote:

> Two kinds of accidents are possible. Marine Risk in such a case owners are liable and would normally arrange salvage either themselves or through underwriters. War Risk in this case expense falls on the Government. It seems better from the point of view of speed and economy that War Risk salvage should be arranged by the Admiralty, either by its own appliances, whether in dockyard or requisitions, or by contract with one of the salvage companies.

With the Admiralty's basic salvage aim now established, the next stage was to appoint special officers to oversee and develop the department. On 22 October this final hurdle was overcome with an official Admiralty memorandum stating: 'It has been decided to establish, for the duration of the war, a special section to be known as the Salvage Section (short title SV) under the Director of Naval Equipment and assistant to the Third Sea Lord to deal with all questions in regard to salvage operations and arrangements.' The Admiralty Salvage Section was now an official Royal Navy resource. Commander J.H. Dathan was given overall control of the department under Third Sea Lord, Rear Admiral Sir Frederick Charles Tudor, while Captain Frederick Young was given the title of 'Naval Salvage Advisor'. His duties included surveying government-chartered war-risk wrecks and reporting back to his superior on the viability of recovery. He was also required for on-the-spot superintendence during salvage operations.

Within days a Fleet Order was issued outlining how to notify the Salvage Section that a ship needed attention. Copies of a special form called 'S 1317' were issued to all naval bases, harbours and port authorities, listing ten simple questions to be answered from which Captain Young or one of his subordinates could make a quick decision on whether salvage was feasible. Speed was essential in despatching an official to the casualty to determine if recovery was viable. Information like the ship's name, location, state of the seabed, position of the head on a magnetic bearing as well as known damage were to be listed. The slightest change in weather conditions or wreck stability also had to be reported at once to avoid a vital salvage operation possibly becoming a lost cause. Finally, the sender had to recommend what might be needed for a possible salvage.

All requests for assistance had to be sent by telegram to the Director of Naval Equipment (or DNE), Clement Greatorex, at the Admiralty in London, marked for the attention of the 'SV Section'. Captain Young then made a report to Greatorex based on the returned questionnaire. Greatorex insisted, 'As a rule it will be desirable to await his [Young's] report before dispatch of a salvage ship but Captain Young should be acquainted with what orders are given, and his advice should not be departed from without very good reason.' Greatorex also knew at any time the location of every salvage vessel. Scattered around the British coast, like taxis in a city, the nearest one to the request for assistance got the job.

Although the Royal Navy was suffering losses from U-boat action, many Admiralty personnel still believed that through sheer volume of tonnage, merchant shipping had little to fear. By Armistice Day 1918 thousands of British and Allied ships had been lost – many due to U-boat attacks. Needless to say, the U-boat menace eventually wreaked havoc on trade supplies, but also inflicted massive losses among the largely defenceless merchant crewmen, who inevitably drowned, burned or froze to death without ever having the chance to retaliate. Almost immediately, Captain Young and the rest of the SV Section were stretched to the limit trying to save stranded vessels in home waters. At times civilian salvage firms had to be contracted to help share the load – sometimes with disastrous consequences beyond the salvor's control.

Chapter 3

'No Cure – No Pay'

Two other factors greatly contributed to merchant shipping losses through enemy attack, many of which could have been prevented. In time of war, as far back as the Roman Empire, warships have protected merchant vessels in convoy formations to secure the safe delivery of food, weapons or troops. Although intrinsic to basic Royal Naval strategy since at least the Napoleonic Wars, the convoy system was not readily accepted by the Admiralty until late in the First World War. Those in favour advocated steaming zigzag patterns in mass formations, which would obviously make it harder for a U-boat to strike and escape. A U-boat also had to be submerged and in position to attack, and if the chance was missed, many hours or days were spent trying get back into position. A concentrated presence of warships as protectors would add to the deterrent.

Those against the convoy system claimed that a cluster of tightly packed vessels made up a considerable target-rich U-boat killing environment. They also argued that a convoy's overall speed was compromised because all ships had to steam at the same rate as the slowest vessel. Even if the enemy did not sink a ship, there was always a risk of collision in such a tight formation. Many ships arriving simultaneously at a port might put too much strain on authorities to allocate enough berths. Finally the Royal Navy really considered itself an *offensive* rather than a *defensive* weapon. Babysitting merchant ships instead of attacking the enemy head on was not well received. This outlook left British and Allied merchant ships plying the high seas without any protection whatsoever, hoping that their individual speed and basic zigzag courses (if they chose to steam them) would save the day.

Another contributing factor was a lack of individual protection commonly found on warships. To avoid damage to Royal Navy vessels from possible torpedo strikes, the Admiralty had used anti-torpedo nets that were in use since the late nineteenth century. The nets were suspended about 30ft in front of the hull from booms 30ft apart, sloping downwards from the ship's side. But they were only effective when a ship was stationary, or going slowly, thus becoming an easier target.

In 1916, Admiral Lionel Halsey wrote:

> At present and in the future, the submarine torpedo menace is more serious than that of the gun and this will continue until ships have been designed and constructed to meet it. I understand that in certain circumstances it is the policy of the Grand Fleet to 'accept the torpedo menace', and presumably the possible damage to our fleet by this 'acceptance' policy has been carefully calculated by the War Staff since we know the accuracy obtained with our own torpedoes and the effect on the structure of our ships by the hits from one or more torpedoes, German torpedoes being certainly not less accurate or less powerful.

For many years, designers had been putting forward ideas for the viability of incorporating 'bulges' around a warship's hull below to just above the water line, but plans were hastened after the sudden and dramatic loss of HMS *Aboukir*, *Hogue* and *Cressy* on 22 September 1914. These old warships formed Cruiser Force C, or more commonly known in the Service as the 'live bait squadron' due to their slow speed and antiquated design. All three warships were among the first Royal Navy casualties from U-boat attack when, within an hour, they were all sunk with the loss of 2,000 men, mostly Reservists and naval cadets.

The bulge was designed to make a torpedo penetrate a false bulkhead and explode away from the ship's side, and was usually located along the amidships area roughly in line with the vessel's most vulnerable compartments. The bulges looked from the outside very much like a submarine's main ballast tanks. To help deaden the blast the hollow curved bulge was often filled with oil or water. They were first fitted to Edgar Class cruisers in 1915, then monitors and eventually battleships such as HMS *Renown*, *Repulse*, *Courageous* and *Royal Oak*. The bulge protection made the warship a much steadier firing platform as it increased her width by as much as 50 per cent. Bulge protection was very successful in both world wars and was eventually adopted by other navies around the world, but was not a panacea as the sinking of the *Royal Oak* in 1939 demonstrated. So if bulge technology was so successful, why not use the same U-boat defence method on merchant ships, and thus cut the alarming losses of both vessels and highly skilled crews?

To counter opposition towards the convoy system the Admiralty was keen for the government to fit anti-submarine bulges to merchant ships. As early as February 1916 Admiralty Director of Naval Construction, Sir Phillip Watts, proposed a viable plan, but after considerable discussions with shipowners, the Board of Trade and Lloyd's, the plan was not pursued, although Admiral Halsey still wrote: 'The consensus of opinion at the Admiralty was favourable. The advantages were pointed out to the Board of Trade, etc., but their objections were based on the commercial considerations involved. But the situation as regards steel supply was such that it was considered better to build as many new unprotected ships as possible.' In 1917 and 1918 the advisability of providing merchant ships with bulge protection was again urged, and Watts even designed a large wheat carrier with bulges, but by then it was too late.

With saving merchant ships and their crews reduced to a cost-cutting exercise, another objection was the time required to build torpedo-proof merchant ships. The benefits would not be obvious for another two years and dozens of ships were being attacked each week. The Admiralty even suggested adding bulges to existing ships, but again time was money. First Sea Lord Admiral Sir Rosslyn Wemyss delayed further discussion on bulge protection for merchant ships until September 1918 – in effect until after the war. By the end of 1916 merchant shipping losses for the year were 1,157. Of these losses thirty-two went to surface craft, 161 to mines and a staggering 964 to U-boat action. The Admiralty Salvage Section's few vessels were already stretched beyond their means as the wrecks kept on piling up around the British coast.

In line with Kemball-Cook's directive that war-risk vessels could be recovered under contract with one of the salvage companies, the need did arise. On 20 February 1916, the 6,387-ton cargo ship SS *Harmatris* left St John, New Brunswick with an extensive cargo of animal feed and empty shell cases. Her next port was Boulogne where she was due to arrive twelve days later. Boulogne was one of the three base ports most extensively used by the British Army on the Western Front throughout the First World War. It was also one of the main AOC (Army Ordnance Corps) base stations along the French coast supplying the vast amounts of weapons and shells needed to feed the artillery guns along the Allied trenches. Liverpool-based Harrison

Line's *Harmatris* was a fine vessel. She was only four years old and one of the biggest merchant ships plying the Atlantic route under Admiralty charter. On 7 March 1916 she eventually reached the Boulogne breakwater at around mid-afternoon, having crossed 3,000 miles of unprotected ocean without any mishap.

Captain T.H. Soanes proceeded to anchor under the breakwater by direction of the port's Examination Vessel. The pilot boarded at 7.00 pm and said that the ship was in an unsafe berth; he remained on board and shifted the ship at 11.00 pm when she anchored, this time, a short distance clear of the breakwater. The *Harmatris* was now about a quarter of a mile off the breakwater and even at anchor a bridge, deck and engine room watch were still maintained. At midnight the ship's watches changed for the next four-hour shift. In the engine room three Spanish firemen – Zambrano, Otega and Lascuran – were attending to their duties while a Greek sailor, George Theotheris, was also on deck watch. The first hour of the watch passed peacefully. The sea was calm and the only visible lights were those in Boulogne and along the French coast, the furthest ones appearing to flicker across the open distance between land and sea. The only noises came from the ship's generators humming and vibrating up through her steel plates.

No one aboard the *Harmatris* saw the trail of bubbles from a torpedo as it propelled its 400lb warhead at 45 knots directly into the *Harmatris*'s engine room. The blast wave compressed within the enclosed steel space, ripping a gash through the bulkhead into the neighbouring boiler-room compartment, instantly killing Zambrano, Otega and Theotheris. Lascuran was left severely injured. The blast was so intense that the twisted metal forced inwards by the inbound torpedo was blown back out like a jagged steel rose. Captain Soanes felt the impact and, as the seawater poured in through the open wound, he wasted no time giving the 'Abandon ship' order. The remaining crew members, half dazed through shock and fear, manned the lifeboats in the early morning blackness and left the *Harmatris* as fast as possible, heading for the safety of Boulogne. Later that morning Lascuran died of his wounds.

Her cargo consisted of more than 2,000 tons of oats and 1,408 tons of hay for transport up to the front line to feed the many thousands of horses in use at that time. She was also carrying a mixed cargo of more than 1,600 tons of Canadian-made empty shell cases and shrapnel. The word 'shrapnel' is often confused with shell fragments that burst from a piece of exploding ordnance. However, the definition of shrapnel is an artillery projectile provided with a bursting charge, and filled with lead balls, exploded in flight by a time fuse. This shell was considered the most effective method for attacking hundreds of troops in the open – fired from up to 4,000yds they could spray as many as 800 lead balls of more than a ½in diameter, shredding anything within the blast area. The shrapnel projectile was named after its nineteenth-century British Army inventor, General Henry Shrapnel.

Divisional Naval Transport Officer (DNTO) in Boulogne, Captain D.M. Hamilton, was absolutely sure that both the *Harmatris* and her cargo could be saved. She was insured under war risk and so qualified for Admiralty salvage. A standard S 1317 form was telegrammed to the Admiralty in London answering their ten basic questions on salvage viability. The *Harmatris* had settled in only 28ft of water and the Admiralty agreed that both the ship and the cargo were considered worthy of recovery. But with all salvage vessels already stretched beyond their limits, the *Harmatris* was offered to a French salvage firm on the standard 'No Cure – No Pay' basis. 'No Cure – No Pay', which dates back hundreds of years, means exactly what it says. If a salvor is contracted to recover a ship, her cargo, or both, he is entitled to a large percentage of the resale value. But should he fail then he receives no payment from the shipowner, or in this case the Admiralty. Within a matter of days the French salvor pulled out of the agreement. Unable to allocate the required naval resources the Admiralty sent a telegram to London's Salvage Association saying, 'If immediate aid is brought then *Harmatris* can probably be saved. British Government has insured war risks and cargo composed partly of shells is very valuable, but Admiralty has no salvage vessel to come to their help. The question is urgent.' Due to her shallow depth the Admiralty favoured the cofferdam method used at Port Arthur in Russia as the best method of building a partition down to the seabed to pump out the water and patch the torpedo damage. Commander Rowand of the Salvage Association was tasked with making all necessary arrangements.

The day after the French salvage firm pulled out he was in Boulogne surveying the full extent of the damage. Under a new 'No Cure – No Pay' agreement he obtained the salvage steamer *Lady of the Isles* from the Western Marine Salvage Company of Penzance in Cornwall. She was already heavily involved in another salvage operation and, having to leave all her pumps on the stranded vessel, had to wait until the Navy supplied others before being deployed to the *Harmatris*. Almost immediately Rowand arranged for the hay and oats to be offloaded onto two Royal Navy lighters and the grabs to take out the empty cases and shrapnel-loaded shells. Barges with cargo grabs, belonging to the Admiralty, were found in London to unload the *Harmatris*'s precious freight and more than 100 French seamen were employed to undertake the manual work.

Draft marks were drawn on the vessel's hull, bow and stern, and the whole area was sounded daily to see how fast she was settling in the sand. As the tide dropped, so did the water in the holds. Rowand decided the best way to refloat the *Harmatris* was, indeed, to build a cofferdam and then secure a wooden patch over the hole, which flexed with the curve of the ship. Once secured and towed ashore, a stronger patch could be fitted before she was towed back to England for permanent repairs. Thus another merchant ship would be saved for the war effort. Commander Rowand said, 'Arrangements were therefore made at once by Captain Berris to have this completed in four days time when it was anticipated that on about April 2nd the ship would have been pumped out, floated, and safely beached inside the breakwater.' Meanwhile divers blasted off the jagged petal-like shards around the hole.

Like many other stranded ships all around the British coast, the *Harmatris* was rapidly becoming another routine salvage operation and looked as if she would very shortly be back in service. Commander Rowand continued:

> But on Tuesday, 28 March, the weather increased to a heavy gale, the sea prevailing swept the upper deck of funnel, bridge and a large part of the deck structure causing an undertow and scour at each end of the vessel. She then settled at bow and stern, and finally broke nearly in two, across, on the fore part of the boiler room, rendering the question of salvaging the ship hopeless.

So close to the shore and so near to recovery, the *Harmatris* salvage operation had ended in disaster.

Although she was now lost, her fixtures, fittings and cargo were still of great value. Everything that could be salvaged, from a gangway davit to Manila ropes, wires, wooden hatch covers, pillowcases and iron-sprung bedsteads filled the extensive inventory of items scrounged out of her wreckage for other ships. Many fragments of the torpedo were also recovered. The last No Cure – No Pay contract signed on the *Harmatris* was to the French salvage firm Galtier, Renoux and Brizard to recover the shells as quickly as possible. On 23 July the agreement was signed with the firm getting 45 per cent of the cargo's net value salved and landed at Boulogne, and 25 per cent of the hull value. Under their salvage contract the true worth of the ship and cargo were to be decided by both an Admiralty representative and a French expert on behalf of the salvors, just in case one side or the other felt unjustly treated. Of course the Admiralty agreement depended on Galtier, Renoux and Brizard recovering at least 80 per cent of the armament or the Admiralty had the right 'To terminate this agreement at any time if their representative considers that the contractors are not using their best endeavours'.

The loss of the *Harmatris* went beyond being another war-risk casualty. Eight days after she was torpedoed an official Admiralty memo stated that the French pilot was to blame; the Master is always in overall command and was also blamed for moving his ship. Captain Soanes also failed to show his Transport Number on arrival as laid down in Admiralty Regulations. The Examination Service and the Port Authorities were criticized for failing to notify the DNTO, Captain Hamilton. He complained to the Admiralty saying:

> I have repeatedly requested to be immediately informed of the arrival of transports in the roads, but find the greatest difficulty in obtaining this information. On this occasion I had no idea that the *Harmatris* had arrived, or I should have urged upon the Port Authorities the necessity of berthing her at the earliest moment, though, as the pilots have the greatest reluctance to bringing large ships in at night and generally refuse to do so at the last moment there is always uncertainty.

The complete breakdown in communication led to the loss of four lives and a valuable ship. As a result of this incident, until the end of the war, all merchant ships eastbound to Boulogne had to wait at Cherbourg until a berth was definitely allocated. Those ships en route from the British coast were also no longer allowed to even sail until a berth was known to be ready for their arrival. The plan no doubt ensured many more merchant ships did not meet the same fate. The *Harmatris* was the 46th vessel to be sunk that year, the 311th since the war had begun.

In 1916, Germany launched a new U-boat type called the UA Class. These were the ultimate in undersea warfare, being 230ft long, weighing 1,500 tons and with a range of more than 12,000 miles.

Most disturbingly of all for British and Allied merchant crews, they carried nineteen torpedoes and twin deck-mounted 5.9in guns with 1,000 rounds each. In the first week of April 1916, fourteen merchant ships were sunk, like the 4,000-ton *Yonne*, which was torpedoed without warning near Algeria. The 3,000-ton *Chic* joined the casualty list when she was sunk near Fastnet the following week with nine of her crew killed, including her captain. All too often the casualty list was still measured in tonnage, cargo or ships lost to enemy action, but the unimaginable suffering of their crews was comparable to, if not worse than, the average soldier on the Western Front. Often suffering from severe burns or blast injuries, merchant seaman were cast adrift in an open lifeboat without the medical care a soldier could expect as quickly as possible in a field hospital.

Adolph von Spiegel was the commander of *U-202*, one of many U-boats picking off merchant ships during the spring of 1916. He was lucky enough to survive the war and, a year after the Armistice, von Spiegel included in his memoirs the death of a merchant ship lost that year.

The steamer appeared to be close to us and looked colossal. I saw the captain walking on his bridge, a small whistle in his mouth. I saw the crew cleaning the deck forward, and I saw, with surprise and a slight shudder, long rows of wooden partitions right along all decks, from which gleamed the shining black and brown backs of horses.

Oh heavens, horses! What a pity, those lovely beasts! But it cannot be helped, I went on thinking. War is war, and every horse the fewer on the Western Front is a reduction of England's fighting power. I must acknowledge, however, that the thought of what must come was a most unpleasant one, and I will describe what happened as briefly as possible.

'Stand by for firing a torpedo!' I called down to the control room.

'FIRE!'

A slight tremor went through the boat – the torpedo had gone. The death-bringing shot was a true one, and the torpedo ran towards the doomed ship at high speed. I could follow its course exactly by the light streak of bubbles, which was left in its wake. I saw that the bubble-track of the torpedo had been discovered on the bridge of the steamer, as frightened arms pointed towards the water and the captain put his hands in front of his eyes and waited resignedly. Then a frightful explosion followed, and we were all thrown against one another by the concussion, and then, like Vulcan, huge and majestic, a column of water two hundred metres high and fifty metres broad, terrible in its beauty and power, shot up to the heavens. 'Hit abaft the second funnel,' I shouted down to the control room.

All her decks were visible to me. From all the hatchways a storming, despairing mass of men were fighting their way on deck, grimy stokers, officers, soldiers, grooms, cooks. They all rushed, ran, screamed for boats, tore and thrust one another from the ladders leading down to them, fought for the lifebelts and jostled one another on the sloping deck. All amongst them, rearing, slipping horses are wedged. The starboard boats could not be lowered on account of the list; everyone therefore ran across to the port boats, which in the hurry and panic, had been lowered with great stupidity either half full or overcrowded. The men left behind were wringing their hands in despair and running to and fro along the decks; finally they threw themselves into the water so as to swim to the boats.

Then a second explosion followed by the escape of white hissing steam from all hatchways and scuttles. The white steam drove the horses mad. I saw a beautiful long-tailed dapple-grey horse take a mighty leap over the berthing rails and land into a fully laden boat. At that point I could not bear the sight any longer, and I lowered the periscope and dived deep.

Such destruction, fear and chaos were repeated in a larger or lesser degree thousands of times throughout the First World War.

Merchant ships beyond British waters had very little chance of salvage recovery, but within Germany's imposed war zone the survival chances increased as more vessels were converted to salvage use. Extra tugs, lighters, purpose-built ships as well as more trained personnel swelled the Salvage Section's ranks. Cargo vessels such as the SS *Batavia*, *Violet*, *San Tirso*, *Araby* and *Falmouth*, were snatched back from total loss. However, as 1916 came to a close Germany was already two years into Britain's starvation blockade. Food rationing was increased and the average German civilian was only allowed five slices of bread, half a cutlet, half a tumbler of milk, a little fat, sugar and potatoes to get through a winter's day. One German newspaper wrote: 'If we were to starve like rats in a trap then surely it was our sacred right to cut off the enemy's supplies as well.' In desperation Germany threatened another unrestricted submarine campaign against Britain – even the knowledge that this move might drag the United States into the war was still a better option. In its defence, Germany wrote to the United States, outlining why such drastic measures were necessary, stating: 'England is using her naval power for a criminal attempt to force Germany into submission by starvation.' The note also warned that Germany would have to use all the weapons at her disposal to break Britain's trade supply. The United States agreed that Britain's refusal to allow food into Germany was severe, but according to Article 24 of the now tattered London Declaration, Britain had every right to stop food from entering Germany, if they saw it as being a conditional contraband of war.

Germany's threats became a reality when she launched her most devastating unrestricted U-boat campaign against Allied shipping. With more ships than ever needing salvage assistance, the job fell neatly into two different recovery methods: either finding, securing and towing a sinking vessel to the safety of the nearest port, or re-floating one that has already struck the bottom in shallow waters around the coast. If refloating a wrecked cargo ship was an extremely hazardous and dangerous operation, salvaging a hospital ship presented many more problems. Most if not all of these vessels were converted ocean liners and their design, albeit fine for passenger comfort, was a salvage officer's nightmare. Their internal venting system ran through the hull and superstructure like a maze of small steel thoroughfares, capable of carrying hundreds of tons of fast-moving water throughout the ship. Then there were dozens, sometimes hundreds of open portholes, as well as increased piping for sanitary and refrigeration requirements.

Having a passenger capacity of nearly 3,000 the transatlantic ocean liner, SS *Asturias*, was well suited for conversion into a troop carrier from Canada across to the United Kingdom, but the ten-year-old Royal Mail steamer became one of the first and largest victims in Germany's new U-boat war. Her transverse bulkheads, or dividing walls between each hold, could not go all the way up to her main deck level as they did on a cargo ship, due to the passenger and crew accommodation layout. This unique design meant water could flow freely between holds, making them 'common' above a certain height, depending on the particular ship. Add to all these design differences the standard salvage complications, such as wind, tide, hull breaches, unique characteristics and degree of damage, and such a salvage operation became a test of skill, nerve and determination.

The Salvage Section's attempt to raise the *Asturias* is a fine example of just how fraught a patch-and-pump operation could become. Her unique salvage taught the Section several important lessons that were applied to many other stranded vessels, not least the importance of pumps and how and where they should be used. Young always believed that: 'Salvage teaches, amongst other things, patience, philosophy and the necessity for unremitting energy, coupled with absolute attention to detail. There is no place for the laggard or the weakling and its followers must be men of resource, ready at all times to accept a temporary defeat and cheerfully to begin again after the work of weeks has been broken up by a storm.' His philosophy was about to be tested to the limit when Greatorex decided that despite all the wrecks needing attention, around the British coast, saving the *Asturias* was to be Young's first and only priority.

Chapter 4

Asturias

A little after 5.00 pm on 1 February 1915, His Majesty's Hospital Ship *Asturias* was en route from France to England when, about 15 miles north-west of Le Havre Lightship, several of her officers and crew spotted a smooth patch of water about 500yds off the ship's starboard quarter. Moments later a thin, white trail of bubbles was seen about 150ft away and rapidly closing on to her stern. Captain Charles Laws took immediate action, ordering his helmsman to steer the 12,015-ton liner sharply to starboard while the engine room increased speed. Like all large ocean-going ships, with the wheel hard over and the engine room telemeter acknowledged, there still came the agonizing hour-like seconds before the slow, lumbering vibration throughout the ship gave way to a gradual and smooth glide onto her new compass bearing.

As everyone braced themselves for the inevitable thud and catastrophic explosion, the torpedo passed right under the stern and disappeared into the open sea. Although the submarine never fired again her periscope was seen clearly for about thirty minutes afterwards, within the *Asturias*'s wake, before sharply turning to starboard and disappearing into the foam. Such an attack on a hospital ship caused outrage in the United Kingdom. The German press claimed the *Asturias* was showing ordinary lights and was mistaken for a troopship. In actual fact it was broad daylight and the French coast was visible 21 miles away. There was no need to show lights let alone a pattern identifying the *Asturias* as something she was not.

At midnight on 21 March 1917, the *Asturias* had just disembarked her wounded at Avonmouth. Then, while steaming 6 miles south of Prawle Point near Salcombe, Devon, another torpedo was fired at her, just clipping her stern in exactly the same area in which she had been missed nearly two years earlier. This time the starboard propeller was immediately blown off before spinning silently down to the seabed. The blast then split her stern tube and shattered the surrounding shell plating right into her Number Five Hold right aft. Her port propeller was out of action and the rudder gone. Although the crew managed to abandon ship, thirty-five were killed and thirty-four injured, including three nurses. The *Asturias* drifted helplessly around the Channel for ten hours before grounding on Bolt Head a few miles west of her original position.

Later that same day, she was clearly visible from the shore. After a brief survey, Admiralty Superintendent at Devonport, A.J. Henneker-Hughan, made first contact with Whitehall regarding her current state. He reported that she was listing to port and, not only was every hold but one flooded, he concluded that saving the *Asturias* looked very doubtful indeed. Admiralty Salvage Officer Captain Pomeroy was despatched from Portland, Dorset, for the short trip around to Bolt Head the following day to make a more informed and detailed survey.

Her condition was not good. The *Asturias* had finally settled on the rocks broadside to the land with a 15° port list, fully sheltered from due west right around the compass card to due east, but entirely exposed to any southerly weather. The explosion had also twisted her bulkheads, making it impossible to close many of the now badly warped doors that no longer sat neatly into their watertight fittings. Although the torpedo inflicted a great deal of damage to her stern, her grounding had made matters much worse – not only were four of her five holds flooded, but also her engine and boiler rooms. The tide ebbed and flowed within many of the compartments, meaning significant damage had occurred. Even so, Pomeroy was confident that she could be saved if her amidships section could be sealed and pumped dry – provided no adverse southerly winds developed. In March such gales could blow up at any time, smashing her steel hull against the rocks like a child's toy boat.

Pomeroy sent his standard S 1317 to Clement Greatorex with all the necessary information to begin her salvage. Greatorex then set in motion the *Asturias* salvage operation by firstly ordering Captain Young to proceed to Salcombe and oversee all operations. Then he instructed the salvage steamer, *Ranger*, to attend; she was then in Greenock, Scotland, about to undergo a major overhaul as her electric wiring had become faulty and many of her pumps needed urgent attention. But Greatorex was adamant she must be used. Finally he ordered Young's Chief Salvage Officer, Lieutenant Kay, to act as his assistant.

Kay had joined the Liverpool Salvage Association from the Cunard Line in 1912 and was a gifted salvage officer. During the war he became a tug captain before being commissioned as a Royal Naval Reserve officer aboard minesweepers. While at Scapa Flow, where the Grand Fleet was then based, he met Young after the *Ranger* moored near his ship. The two men got on immediately and with an acute shortage of competent staff, Kay was soon working for the Admiralty Salvage Section. At the time the *Asturias* was attacked Kay was on leave in his home town of Birkenhead, where he received a telegram from Greatorex apologizing for cutting his leave short, but insisting that he help Young try to save the ship.

Two days after the *Asturias* went aground Young arrived on the scene, his first job being to devise a sound plan to refloat her success-fully before a bout of bad weather made any salvage attempt futile. He started by arranging for two 12in and two 6in pumps to test the after end's integrity for a lift. Once the *Ranger* arrived, her divers would make a more informed investigation of the ship's bottom. Young knew that saving the *Asturias* depended on how, where and how many pumps were to be placed, especially aboard an ocean liner. But even utilizing all his knowledge and experience the situation could still degenerate into less trial and more error.

The *Ranger* arrived finally from Greenock with more pumps as well as experienced salvage divers to make the full hull survey. Their first job was then to plug all the scuppers and close the portholes to prevent as much water as possible from re-entering the ship. One of the *Ranger*'s pumps was lowered down through the engine room skylight while the two 12in pumps were placed in Numbers Four and Five Holds respectively. All standard procedure before any lift would be attempted. On 25 March the weather was still holding and work was progressing well, but the pumps in the two holds were making little impression. Another three 12in and two 6in pumps were added. Each of the two new smaller pumps was put on either side of Number Four Hold, in her wing tanks, to steady her ascent. But, with all available holes sealed, and all the pumps working to full capacity, she still leaked.

Both Young and Kay agreed that there must be some unknown opening in the engine room or a breach right under her hull. Young explained: 'There is no doubt that a very large amount of the leakage to this vessel [is] caused through the water coming up through the scuppers, sanitary pipes and open side ports on the lee side.' To get

33

deeper into the flooded stokehold, welders burned a 4ft^2 hole through the galley deck directly above the compartment and lowered another 12in pump into the space. This eventually began to reduce the water. Nine pumps were now sucking water out of the flooded holds and, although they were not enough, Young was happy with the progress, especially after the ship's saloon deck had been cleared of water, thus making her more stable to lift. Then on the next high tide the saloon deck flooded again. The reason for the leak was not found until some time after rectifying the problem was considered necessary.

On 29 March, the wind freshened slightly from the south-west, but was still not a threat. Inside the *Asturias*, men dashed about her many internal decks checking pumps and hoses. The combined noise level of electric and steam pumps throbbing away deep in the ship must have been intolerable for those having to work so close to them. Now there were seven 1in, five 6in and four other assorted steam and submersible pumps hard at work. Young was confident that the *Asturias* would be under control by the following night. He was finally winning her back – but his belief that patience and unremitting energy were enough was about to be tested again when a serious leak developed in the engine room, so that the pumps could only gain slightly on the rising tide. It was thought to be in the brine room, which supplied the cooling for the *Asturias*'s refrigeration system and was a very complicated location for divers to reach. Extra pumping power could only be positioned through the engine room skylight once again, then lowered down to the deck plating. The following day further leakage into the engine room and after holds was traced to the ship's complex ventilation system. Various shafts were sealed when yet another leak was found between the engine room and the stokehold.

She was now leaking like a sieve and while fighting the internal battle to save the liner, the weather was beginning to turn. Young said: 'Owing to increasing swell today it was necessary to stop pumping and keep her quiet. If she became too light, and the conditions worsened, her hull would split as the much lighter ship grated backwards and forwards on the sharp rocks.'

Four days later the wind swung round to the west, blowing snow squalls at gale force across the *Asturias*, making the normally soft, white flakes sting like frozen glass shards. Conditions were so bad that Young's men had to abandon ship until the sea state improved. When they returned the most important job was to seal her shattered stern section before another storm rendered the job impossible. Sealing the remnants of this area required wooden planks, oakum and cement, which were forced into and across the jagged steel. Oakum was made from old rope fibres, often soaked in tar and used to seal the gaps between planks on a wooden hull. Its very nature made the black, sticky strands perfect for the job. A steel cover was made aboard the *Ranger* to cover the shattered tunnel escape. Once this work was completed the three 12in pumps in this section held and 16ft were gained on the rising tide. Young was confident that 'If weather continues fine the ship will be ready for an attempt to float tomorrow, Sunday, the 8th instant if five or six tugs and escorts are available by noon. The vessel should, if possible, keep close to the land in order that she may be beached in the event of the leakage increasing.'

The many pumps had been working well for nearly a week, and although some water still leaked into her hull, she left the seabed. As she rose higher, so did the sea swell as the wind barrelled in from the west this time. The *Asturias* continued to develop a dangerously unstable attitude due to loose water swilling around inside her and worsening weather conditions, which meant that the tugs would not be able to hold her for long enough. Having left the bottom the tugs had already towed her a short distance astern. Had she been let down in her new position there was no telling how much more damage could have been done leading to a great deal more time and expense for a full recovery – or her complete loss.

The tugs struggled to get the *Asturias* back into position as another weather front moved in. After a day that began so promisingly, she was let down on to the rocks again without further damage but with a 17° list and with water pouring in from some still unknown hull breach. On 11 April another storm developed, first from west-north-west, before shifting to the south-west, causing a very heavy swell. The *Ranger* and HMT (His Majesty's Tug) *Assurance*, which were alongside feeding steam power to several of the pumps, bumped alongside so hard they both ceased pumping and returned to Devonport.

Two days passed before the pumps were tested and found to be working the same as they were before the last gale. True to his unremitting energy and constant optimism, Young confidently reported, with a little caution this time: 'Prospects of floating still remain favourable dependent always on the weather not becoming bad from the south or southeast.' It really was a stormy season. Less than twenty-four hours later a strong south-westerly caused yet another failure and was dangerously close to swinging *Asturias* slightly too much and

35

smashing her against the rocks. The four pumps with which Young began operations had now grown to fifteen. Every compartment had at least two, the shattered Number Five Hold right aft had three 12in, while her Number Four Hold right next to it had water being pumped out through two 12in and two 6in machines. With so many pumps already in use there were precious few left, since others were already working on other distressed ships around the coast. Getting the extra ones had been hard enough, but if Young and Kay could only get the water low enough to exploit the *Asturias*'s own pumping system they would have a much better chance. Plugging more holes would slow down the inrush to some extent. Once this was achieved the water could be lowered sufficiently, and on a test run this did indeed help. Now all they needed was a calm sea for a good chance to get her off the rocks once and for all.

Attempt after attempt still failed because of the bad weather, with the wind constantly veering from the north, west or south-west, but never quite from the dreaded south-east. Water still seeped into the already vented compartments, but through sheer determination Young's men were progressing. Finally a test lift was made and divers were able to plug a great many more rivet holes. The next lift was scheduled for 2.00 am on 16 April, which coincided with a slight breeze from the south-west and a calm sea. After five hours pumping, the *Asturias* began to float as the breeze increased to a moderate gale during the morning and the sea state rapidly deteriorated. The ship was well under control thanks to the pumps, but the wind pressure on the hull, coupled with the loose water in the engine, boiler room and holds caused her to list dangerously. The list reached 22° before she had to be let down again and another attempt had failed.

Finding the boiler-room leak was now essential. Several more pumps were placed in the stokehold and the *Asturias* was raised again, this time to allow divers to crawl underneath her massive hull to find and repair the fracture. They crawled carefully along, groping and grubbing around the rocks and sand – always aware that more than 12,000 tons of steel were balancing precariously above their heads. After many hours searching, all they could report was severe indentations of the hull plates and some leaking rivets, which were quickly and easily made good.

Now two options were available: she could be lifted with finesse or brute force. Finesse required finding the leak and making a more controlled recovery. It was safer, more professional and presented a much wider error margin should a pump fail or one of many other things go wrong. Brute force required using as many pumps as possible to beat the rapid inflow as fast as it entered the hull, by pumping it straight back over the side. It was crude, more dangerous and prone to many more errors, but time was running out and the chances of a gale shifting slightly and wrecking the *Asturias* might now be only hours away. Without knowing exactly where the leak was, and being well aware of their ever-shrinking time frame, Young and Kay opted for brute force in the hope that the sea state would hold long enough for them to save the ship.

Now sixteen high-pressure torrents, varying in diameter from 4in to 1ft, sounded more like distant thunder as they forced the water back into the open sea. Conditions were fine and all the pumps worked well with their combined pumping power of more than 7,000 tons every hour. The vessel gradually eased up from her rocky bed while the port list gradually lessened. The critical balancing act between inrushing and outflowing water was holding. On 20 April, at 7.31 am, Young sent a telegram to Greatorex, saying: '*London* afloat proceeding all well'. He refused to use the ship's real name should the enemy intercept the message. Although she still had a 10° list the gamble had paid off – the *Asturias* was back on the surface.

She arrived in Plymouth Sound some 17 miles west of Bolt Head the next day, although she was still in a very unstable condition and would have listed rapidly if the pumps were stopped. After a gruelling month, Young's philosophy that salvage men must be ready at all times to accept a temporary defeat and cheerfully begin again, had been stretched significantly. Then, just when she was saved, simple naval administration threatened the *Asturias*'s survival.

There was no dry dock available for another nine days as the recently launched, high-speed submarine *J-7* occupied the only dock that could take her. Young was getting more than a little nervous. Another salvage operation would have to be organized if she sank in Plymouth, rendering all their hard work useless. He informed Greatorex: 'It will be a great relief when she is safe in dry dock where a small amount of work could be done which would make the vessel safe under [her] own pumps.' As long as the buckled and twisted watertight doors held out against the intense pressure forcing against them, she should last, but the *Ranger* was now in urgent need of her overhaul and the pumps were much needed elsewhere to salvage other stranded ships.

The *Ranger* had been in continuous use for many months, her boilers needed to be cleaned out without delay and all her pumps were caked in filthy, gritty oil. The *Ranger*'s faulty wiring eventually led to an electrical fire which, although soon extinguished, could well destroy her wooden hull next time. So with fresh pumps needed to relieve the tired salvage vessel, some were scrounged from Devonport to allow the *Ranger* to be relieved. Once the critical changeover from one set to another was successfully completed, like a life-support machine, the *Asturias* was kept alive artificially until the *J-7* could vacate the dock. On 30 April the dry dock was flooded and the *J-7* gently eased out into the North Basin. Just before 9.00 am the *Asturias* was towed into the dock and secured before the water could be drained down. She was saved.

Salvaging such a large ocean liner, often hampered by appalling weather conditions, was an incredible risk and made this a groundbreaking operation in many ways. Young remembered:

> This was the first time that such a large number of pumps have been used on one ship during the war and experience gained by the men from the different dockyards will no doubt be of considerable service. All the pumps worked well and particularly the submersibles, which are undoubtedly the salvage pumps of the future. Their portability and changeability of parts give them many advantages over the others either as lift or force pumps.

Controlling her unstable condition due to so much loose water was another learning curve. Her shallow draft and the amount of superstructure above the main deck, compared to a cargo ship, was the main cause – more water had to be removed than normal for this size of ship. The main leakage was eventually traced back to an open escape hatch next to the shattered bulkhead towards her stern that took the full force of the torpedo blast. With eighteen months left before the war ended and hundreds of ships yet to be attacked, such lessons learned would become vital. But all of the Salvage Section's work on the *Asturias* proved to be of no use to the war effort – she remained in dry dock for two years before being refitted as the cruise liner *Arcadian*; she was finally broken up in 1933.

Apart from being known as one of the twelve hospital ships to have been attacked during the First World War the *Asturias* left one other mark on history. Four months before being torpedoed she was on a routine voyage carrying hundreds of injured men from Le Havre to

Southampton. One of them was an unknown Second Lieutenant called John Ronald Reuel Tolkien of the Lancashire Fusiliers, who was being repatriated for 'trench fever', a particularly unpleasant disease caused by lice that affected more than a million soldiers. He never returned to the Front. While convalescing he started to write *The Fall of Gondolin* on the back of some old army music sheets, which eventually led to a whole new meaning of 'Middle Earth'.

By the time the *Asturias* was safely laid up in Plymouth, Britain was halfway through the worst month for shipping losses since the war had begun. Germany's new, and by far the most destructive, unrestricted U-boat action was really threatening Britain's ability to stay in the war. A complete reorganization of the overstretched and undermanned Salvage Section was desperately needed if the Admiralty was to ensure the vital flow of food and war material from across the Atlantic.

Chapter 5

'An Ever-increasing Menace'

While the killing fields of Arras, Passchendaele and Cambrai were slaughtering thousands of men on both sides in a costly attempt to gain a little more ground, the real outcome of the First World War was being decided on the high seas. If the generals did not know this, the admirals certainly did. 'Our armies might advance a mile a day and slay the Hun in thousands,' said Grand Fleet Commander Admiral David Beatty in January 1917, 'but the real crux lies in whether we blockade the enemy to his knees or whether he does the same to us.' Basically, regardless of almost genocidal loss of life along the 400-mile Western Front, the final victory came down to who would starve first, England or Germany.

Britain's blockade of Germany was already having a serious effect on her civilian population. Despite the strict rationing enforced earlier in the year, by the spring of 1917 Germany's entire cattle population had fallen to only 72 per cent of peacetime numbers and the pig population had dropped to nearly a third. This combined loss resulted in meat rationing being slashed from slightly more than a kilo a week per person to only 135 grams. With the milk ration halved and many other essential foodstuffs having been unavailable for years, Britain feared that imported food would end up in the mouths of German front-line troops. Meanwhile, the health effects on the civilian population were catastrophic – tuberculosis, rickets, influenza, dysentery, scurvy, eye ulceration and malnutrition were common. Half of all children under five died from one illness or another. Female mortality was up by 51 per cent and the national birthrate was down by half.

With Germany on the verge of losing the war on the Home as well as the Western Front, Chief of Admiralty Staff, Admiral Henning von Holtzendorff, knew Germany had the power to act swiftly and effectively to swing the war in the Fatherland's favour. In a memo to Kaiser Wilhelm II, he wrote: 'England will be forced to sue for peace within

40

five months as the result of [Germany] launching an un-restricted U-boat war.' Von Holztendorff's plan was based on sinking about 600,000 tons of merchant shipping each month, which he estimated would be enough to cripple Britain's economy.

Admiral Jellicoe's prophecy the previous year of the ever-increasing menace of the enemy's submarine attacks was no longer a pressing question, but cold, hard reality. From 1 February 1917 Germany's sea-borne blitzkrieg was launched against British and Allied shipping with devastating effect. By the end of the first month, more than double the gross tonnage of merchant shipping had been sunk than for any month since war was declared. Still the government had no firm strategy apart from relying on fortuitous gunfire or the hope that a U-boat would run into one of the many mines strung around the English Channel and North Sea. Airborne attack methods involved kite balloons similar to those used for observation along the Western Front. On land and sea the effect of sighting the enemy from aloft was the same, but at sea up to six destroyers were often involved at a time, each with a kite balloon, to flush out a U-boat. Spotting one was fine, but deploying enough firepower to sink the submarine before it dived was a little more difficult.

Hydrophones were another answer, but during the First World War this primitive form of sonar was very basic and prone to interference from many sources, including the host vessel itself. Depth charges were new and not as yet the sophisticated deterrent they eventually became. More crude attempts were often employed such as outright ramming. The ancient method of protecting merchant vessels in convoys was still not considered viable owing to the shortage of warships and the still entrenched belief that closely packed merchant ships would be easy pickings for a hungry U-boat crew.

With each passing month, the gross tonnage sunk was startlingly close to Holztendorff's plan. As the days drew out so did the kill rates – during March half a million tons were sunk, nearly double the February losses and quadruple any previous month since hostilities had commenced in August 1914. But in April, while the Allied land forces were fighting the Second Battle of Arras, the figure reached a staggering 850,000 tons of shipping lost to enemy action. With May's shipping casualties well in excess of those Holztendorff predicted, Germany was well on target to starve England into submission.

Many volumes have been written about this dark time in British history and all that was achieved with the limited resources available to fend off the U-boat menace until the balance could be tipped. What has not been widely covered, if at all, is the importance of the Admiralty Salvage Section during this crucial time. In fact not one official or unofficial account of the First World War published until now mentions this vital Admiralty department or its defining role in the Allies winning the war.

The Admiralty Salvage Section's organization had changed little during its first nineteen months of operation. An S 1317 form was still completed, answering the ten basic questions needed to record a vessel in need of salvage assistance. The form was then sent directly to Clement Greatorex. But the rising numbers of ships in distress, and ever-limited resources to meet the demand, meant that although the Salvage Section was by now an experienced naval arm, drastic changes were needed if supply was to keep pace with demand.

Ironically the first problem to be addressed was not the effect of increased enemy action, but the very shipping companies which ultimately owned the vessels on Admiralty charter. All too often, in their haste for immediate action, shipping companies would communicate directly with the Department of Trade or Department of Shipping before the Admiralty received official and detailed information. The result was a quagmire of confusion and delay that frequently added vital time, costs and wasted resources to what might well have been a straightforward salvage operation. In early 1916 an informal conference was planned to address five key issues. The first two reaffirmed the Section's salvage role, but points three, four and five addressed far more important areas for concern such as loss of time due to the transfer of papers from one department to another, and the loss of time due to the War Registry and decoding.

As early as spring 1916, plans were being made to rectify the situation. At noon on 10 April the first informal conference took place to establish a system which would utilize the full, expert knowledge and experience of the Salvage Section and enable their plant to be employed to the best possible advantage. Present at the meeting were Clement Greatorex, his soon-to-be-permanent salvage assistant, Captain Christopher Metcalf, and representatives of the Admiralty's Trade and Transport Divisions, Naval Stores and War Registry. Throughout the afternoon each issue was debated and a more simplified approach to how a stranded vessel would be dealt with was drafted.

Instead of the Admiralty being swamped with salvage requests and confused intelligence, all details were to be routed through a local

42

Senior Naval Officer (or SNO), who would be the first point of contact to render all possible first-aid salvage assistance for vessels in collisions, groundings, submarine attacks or damage from enemy mines. Consequently, if the SNO did not then contact the Admiralty, the Salvage Section would not be consulted. Each Admiralty department became responsible in the early stages for its own ships, such as the Transport Department for colliers and oilers, the Yacht Patrol for trawlers, yachts and drifters, and the Trade Division for other types of British merchant ships. The new system worked well and soon helped to alleviate the pressure on the Salvage Section.

Once their internal organization had been tweaked another matter arose that needed urgent attention. Under the Merchant Shipping Act 1894, when Admiralty vessels rendered assistance they were not entitled to claim awards like a private company conducting a similar salvage operation. So major vessel recoveries, costing large sums of taxpayers' money, and often involving considerable danger to the salving crews, were free of charge.

In certain situations Section 557 of the Merchant Shipping Act allowed the Admiralty to grant awards to officers and crews who could claim for and at times recover large sums for their services. These were, however, subject to the Admiralty accepting that the efforts of their personnel were 'arduous' and 'hazardous'. But Section 557 firmly prohibited HM Ships (and thus the Admiralty) from making claims to fill their own coffers, 'For any loss, damage or risk caused by the ship or her stores, tackle or furniture, or for the use of any stores or other articles belonging to His Majesty supplied in order to effect those services or for any other expenses or loss sustained by His Majesty by reason of that service.'

An Admiralty minute dated 3 April 1916 crystallized their argument for commercial salvage award. 'It is one thing for His Majesty's ships, when on their ordinary avocation, to render such assistance as lies in their power to merchant ships in distress, and another for specially-fitted salvage vessels being employed by the Crown, with the effect of deliberately saving the underwriters' pockets.' The Admiralty sought opinions from the Board of Trade, Lloyd's and the Law Officers to determine exactly what the position was regarding their right to profit from salvaging ships. The Board of Trade was of the opinion that Section 557 did not bar the Crown from raising a claim for salvage. The only bar, they felt, was a claim for out-of-pocket expenses or loss of equipment.

Some ideas were put forward such as inviting the underwriters to contribute towards a vessel's recovery. Lloyd's Chairman, Sir Raymond Beck, informed the Admiralty that salvage services were rendered to the cargo as well as the vessel, and in the event of a ship with general cargo being assisted, the amount of the award would be treated as a general average and divided between both ship and cargo. He said that it was not viable in such a case to obtain the consent of all the shippers of cargo, and until this could be given it would be impossible for an adjuster to include such a charge in his general average statement. But Admiralty Director of Navigation, P. Nelson Ward, saw the matter from another perspective when he said somewhat acidly, 'It is not seen how we can enforce salvage claims in respect of HM Ships. The conditions under consideration are entirely novel, and only legislation or patriotic self-denial by owners or underwriters can adapt our present position to them.'

On 9 June 1916, the Admiralty received the Law Officers' formal written opinion. The memorandum explained how Section 557 debarred any claim for salvage services rendered by any of His Majesty's ships, including any salvage steamer or tug belonging to, or temporarily in possession of the Admiralty under charter party, even if it only operated under demise of the Admiralty. Having said that, they were adamant that the 1894 Act was inadequate to deal with the present situation regarding salvage and recommended that the matter be brought before Parliament to change the law in favour of the Admiralty. 'The law as it stands,' continued the memo, 'is not in accordance with the interests of the public or of shipowners or underwriters and ought not to apply in the abnormal circumstances during the present war.' Off the record the Law Officers were confident that there would be little difficulty in getting the Bill through both Houses.

Instead of revoking Section 557 the Salvage Bill wanted to add to the Merchant Shipping Act:

Where salvage services are rendered by any ship belonging to His Majesty and that ship is a ship specially equipped with salvage plant, or is a tug, the Admiralty shall, notwithstanding anything contained in Section 557 of the Merchant Shipping Act, 1894, be entitled to claim salvage on behalf of His Majesty for such services, and shall have the same rights and remedies as if the ships rendering such services did not belong to His Majesty.

44

The Bill received its second reading in the House of Commons on 10 August and was passed without a vote. Six days later it went to the House of Lords and was passed with virtually no debate and again with no vote, becoming statute law on 23 August.

Within months the demands on the Admiralty Salvage Section far outstripped the need to recover just HM vessels because, for the first time since Henry VIII formed the Royal Navy, around 1510, Great Britain's thin lifeline of cargo ships became – albeit briefly – more important than all the combined firepower of Britain's naval defence. Changes to its internal organization were established just in time to meet the increasing demand early the following year. But if April 1917 was the worst month for tonnage sunk during the whole war, then the 17th was one of the worst days the British Merchant Navy would have to endure throughout the whole four-year campaign. Eleven ships were sunk, steaming to or from British ports during this one 24-hour period.

At about 9.30 pm the tide was ebbing in the English Channel the 3,820-ton general cargo ship *Clan Southerland* proceeded en route from Bombay to Glasgow via London, carrying 1,000 tons of manganese ore and 3,000 tons of general cargo. She would soon become one of the ships for which the Admiralty could now claim salvage, but her recovery and award gained a great deal of press notoriety throughout 1917 and 1918.

As she passed about 12 miles east-south-east of Start Point, Devon, the *Clan Southerland* was one of the last ships to be hit that dreadful day. A torpedo struck her starboard side, blowing away part of the bridge and forward starboard lifeboats, while exploding inside her Number Two Hold. The shock wave jerked up through the ship, blowing the captain out of his cabin, smashing crockery and splintering wood as many loose items were blown around her accommodation block as if affected by rapid decompression. The engines stopped immediately, with the whole compartment suddenly becoming a fog of scalding hot steam as high-pressure pipes burst under the strain.

Her 62-man crew, who were mostly foreign personnel, scrambled for the remaining port lifeboats. The sea around the *Clan Southerland* soon became a confusion of men, lifeboats and cargo spewing out of the gaping starboard hull breach. Although her steering gear was jammed over 15° to port, and she was in danger of breaking in two, her recovery was short and sweet. The torpedo-boat destroyer HMS *Bittern* happened to be nearby at the time and assisted the Admiralty tugs *Woonda*, *Fortitude* and *Flintshire*, along with the armed trawler,

Lois, to tow the *Clan Southerland* into Devonport, 25 miles north-west of Start Point. Her commander, Lieutenant E.K. Irving, oversaw the entire salvage operation. He put the *Woonda* ahead on the port bow and *Fortitude* on the starboard bow with *Lois* aft; the *Flintshire* was ordered to circle round to watch for any further enemy attack.

Apart from the *Fortitude* swinging stern first to the *Clan Souther-land* because her towline was too long, and having to be released, Irving's biggest problem happened 9 miles from Start Point when the *Clan Southerland* started breaking up. He later stated: 'The decks were giving gradually, and the cargo was forcing up Number Two Hatches and beams. She would never have got to Devonport, as the upper deck over the injured hold was rapidly giving way.' With Irving's small convoy only making 4 knots and the sea getting up to Force 7, his only chance was to run her ashore in the mud at Dartmouth about 8 miles north-east of Start Point. About 3 miles off Dartmouth HMS *Bittern* had to close up on the *Clan Southerland*'s port side. The *Fortitude* now closed on her starboard side while the *Woonda* and *Lois* shortened their towlines to maximize control over the disintegrating ship. Through an incredible piece of seamanship, Irving managed to run her ashore less than eighteen hours after the torpedo first struck.

The next day, the *Clan Southerland*'s master, Captain William Calderwood returned to his ship, or tried to, for the Admiralty refused him permission to go back on board for another two days. When Calderwood did gain access he found that every cabin, pantry and bonded locker had been looted. All the crew passageways and public areas were full of stripped beds, overturned furniture and anything fragile was smashed to pieces among the debris. He was dismayed to find everything from personal underclothes to pyjamas and safety pins, right up to bonded stores such as rum and tobacco, had been taken. A number of weapons and ammunition were also gone. The only possessions the 2nd Engineer had left were an old boiler suit and two shirts.

With the revised Section 557 so recently enacted, the Admiralty, along with the tug crews and some shore-side personnel, all put in their claims. However, due to such a serious theft the situation became unclear whether a salvage award or custodial sentence would be due. Altogether nine vessels were involved in recovering the *Clan Southerland* by the time she reached the mud. But several never put personnel aboard her, or if they did, they were only there for a matter of minutes. The only vessel that had a number of men on board throughout was HMS *Bittern*. In fact, when the salvage operation began, there were twenty personnel transferred from HMS *Bittern* and, as the operation intensified, that figure doubled.

Fifteen months passed before the *Clan Southerland* case was settled. On 31 July 1918, Mr Justice Hill awarded eight prizes and the breakdown gives a good idea of what the Admiralty as salvors could now expect: the Admiralty was given £6,000 (£180,000 today) for the use of their vessels. The crew of the *Woonda* and *Lois* were awarded £360 each (or about £11,000); the crew of the *Fortitude* received £330 (or £10,000). Another tug involved called the *Boarhound* was given £500 (or £15,000) and Captain Edwards of the *Lois* personally received £200 (or £6,000). Lieutenant Irving was given £300 for his eighteen hours work (or a little under £9,000) and the rest of HMS *Bittern*'s officers and crew were able to share £900 (or nearly £30,000) among her 72-man complement. If divided equally that equates to more than £400 each today. The ship and her cargo were valued at £8.4m. in today's currency. The total salvage award would now equal £258,000, or 10 per cent of the combined value. Taking into consideration the one-off outlay, and upkeep, of the salvage plant, the Admiralty was by far the winner.

After awarding the salvage prizes, Mr Justice Hill stated:

For some reason, which it is very difficult to understand, permission to return onboard his ship [Captain Calderwood] was not granted him by the Admiralty authorities until the morning of the 20th. I can see no justification for that delay. This was especially so, as the Admiralty was only claiming salvage, and had no more right to keep Calderwood from his ship than any other civilian salvors would have had.

I am forced, most unwillingly, to the conclusion that it was done by some of the salvors. There is, in addition, some evidence directly implicating some of the crew of HMS *Bittern*. The pilot saw three of HMS *Bittern*'s crew, who looked like stokers, each passing a bundle to men on HMS *Bittern*, while others were standing around on the ship. I have hesitated long to find men from HMS *Bittern* guilty, the more so because they have since lost their lives in the service of their country.

During heavy fog in the early hours of 4 April 1918 HMS *Bittern* collided with the cargo ship SS *Kenilworth* and sank rapidly, taking her entire complement of sixty men with her.

Justice Hill continued:

> But, in any judgment, there is no other alternative. I find that the defendants have established beyond all reasonable doubt that there was thieving on a large scale from the *Clan Southerland* by men belonging to the crew of HMS *Bittern*, and I find further that it was on such a scale that it must have been known, either at the time or afterwards, to the rest of the crew. It can only have escaped the knowledge of Lieutenant Irving and his officers because they did not exercise reasonable diligence to prevent it, and to detect it. With proper supervision Irving should have known about the thefts and been able to stop them, or find the goods.

Irving's defence that he posted two sentries at each side of the accommodation block was considered not enough of an effort.

Mr Justice Hill did attempt to give some mitigating circumstances to HMS *Bittern*'s crew:

> I have little doubt that everyone supposed the *Clan Southerland* was sinking, and was little likely to be salved. And, but for that, I cannot think the property would have been removed. As to the persons actually engaged in or privy to the theft, there can be no doubt at all that the result is forfeiture of salvage. The law which rewards salvors, not on the basis of a *quantum meruit* [reasonable value for services], but with a liberal compensation to encourage the saving of property at sea, requires of them the strictest honesty in regard to the property, while in their possession.

Mr Justice Hill posthumously punished HMS *Bittern*'s crew by forfeiting their entire salvage reward regardless of who among their number was guilty, mainly because although not all were involved in the looting, many must have had information vital to the trial. Lieutenant Irving was exonerated of any part in the thefts, but was largely blamed for not exercising enough control over his crew. His punishment was to have his £300 prize slashed by two thirds, a not inconsiderable sum in those days. Many relatives of the dead seamen wrote to the Admiralty to explain how their sons, fathers, brothers or husbands were not involved in the looting and that they should get the salvage prize as the next of kin. But the law was explicit and not one relative received payment, however persuasive their argument or genuine need.

The whole case was a great embarrassment to the Admiralty who had fought so hard for the right to claim salvage, and now their own Royal Navy crews were guilty of embezzling from ships in distress. But the *Clan Southerland* incident soon faded away amid the chaos and carnage being fought under von Holztendorff's new submarine offensive. Although fully revised to meet the increasing shipping casualties, the risks posed to Admiralty Salvage personnel also rose in proportion.

Chapter 6

Casualties of War

As the First World War fanned out across the Mediterranean, new conflicts opened up in Turkey, Salonika, the Balkans, North Africa and well into the Middle East, quite often with as much mindless zeal as similar campaigns along the Western Front. All these theatres needed constant supplies of fresh men, food and weapons of war to keep the fight going, requiring many merchant ships to carry the replacements. Germany wanted to offer what protection it could to its new allies, which meant deploying a handful of U-boats to disrupt the Allied supply lines whenever and wherever possible. As the war progressed, so did the number of German and Austro-Hungarian U-boats prowling the Mediterranean, Adriatic and Aegean Seas.

By 1918 the Admiralty had commandeered nearly all the British merchant shipping available to supply the many battlefronts. The Leyland Shipping Line of Liverpool was one of the many companies to suffer heavy losses, especially during the new U-boat offensive of 1917. Several of their ships were sunk in the Mediterranean, including the 5,088-ton *Georgian*, which was torpedoed off Crete, and the 5,861-ton *Cameronian*, which was torpedoed 50 miles north-west of Alexandria with the loss of sixty-three lives. But the most notorious Leyland vessel, the SS *Californian*, was the first to be lost to enemy action when she was torpedoed 61 miles south-west of Cape Matapan, Greece, on 9 November 1915. Three years earlier, on the night of 14/15 April 1912, the *Californian* was en route from Liverpool to Boston when she stopped engines about 375 miles south-east of Newfoundland due to large ice fields in the area. During the night some of her crew members reported seeing a brightly lit ocean liner on the horizon which launched several white rockets. After reports to the captain, Stanley Lord, went unheeded they paid no more attention – until the next morning when Lord and his crew realized how they could have greatly lessened the full horror of the *Titanic*'s loss.

Six years later, 29-year-old U-boat ace Oberleutnant Heino von Heimburg, aboard *UB-68*, was on patrol off Sardinia when he sighted the *Californian*'s sister ship, the SS *Kingstonian*, carrying troops and equipment from Alexandria to Marseilles. Heimburg was an outstanding officer who, the previous year, had become one of only thirty U-boat commanders to be awarded the prestigious Blue Max. The *Orden Pour le Mérite*, to give it its correct name, after its inception in the French-speaking Prussian Court, was Germany's highest decoration for valour and was never again awarded after the 1918 Armistice.

Heimburg sighted the *Kingstonian* through his attack periscope and fired a single torpedo at his target. Although the missile caused some damage, he had missed her vital engine-room compartment and the *Kingstonian*'s master managed to run her aground in Carloforte roadstead, between the small island of San Pietro and Sardinia's south-west coast. His Majesty's Salvage Vessel *Dalkeith* was one of several of the new purpose-built craft now working in the Mediterranean. She had been moored alongside the 5,259-ton cargo ship SS *Upada* which was anchored about a mile away from the *Kingstonian* when she was ordered to moor alongside the stricken cargo vessel to pump her out. The *Kingstonian*'s salvage was a routine exercise, which required her deep freshwater tanks to be pumped out to raise her higher in the water for repairs to proceed. About two hours later the *Dalkeith* secured alongside the *Kingstonian*'s starboard side while the tug, *Moose*, made fast to the *Dalkeith* to give assistance.

Engineer Lieutenant Commander Smith was in charge of salvage operations along with assistant salvage officer Lieutenant J. Wilson-Alexander and their Chief Officer, Lieutenant E.J. Bull. Although the *Dalkeith*'s officers were all British, her crew were mainly Greek nationals. Smith set up an 8in pump, rigged with 1½in pipes in the *Kingstonian*'s Number Two Tween Deck to reach into her deep freshwater tanks. Once she was lightened enough the *Kingstonian* would be towed 152 miles round to Porto Torres in Sardinia's capital, Cagliari, for permanent repairs and another merchant ship would have been saved.

The Italian authorities provided an armed trawler to cover the southern approach and the French tug, *Somme 12*, which was to guard the towing operation to Cagliari, also helped cover the approach. Extensive shoals around the northern entrance ensured no protection was necessary there. At lunchtime Smith gave the order to commence pumping, which continued non-stop until 10.00 pm when work ceased

51

until the next morning. All hoses were disconnected from the *Kingstonian* at the end of the working night, but left in place for Monday morning to continue the salvage operation. Although the day's work was finished, it was the custom to stay alongside the vessel the salvage men were working on at the time.

Engineer Richard Furlong and Telegraphist Norman Rennard were among the *Dalkeith*'s thirty or so complement. Nightwatchman, Greek sailor Triandaphilus Georgarakis, was to walk the decks at regular intervals until daybreak and alert the *Dalkeith*'s captain, Lieutenant Arthur Atkins, of any possible danger. Able Seaman Denis Bennett was keeping the gun watch until Lance Corporal William Tyler was due to relieve him the following morning. The night was very still with a slight westerly breeze and almost no moon. All three ships were lying with their bows facing the small town of Carloforte about 2 miles off. The only noises came from the water slapping against the fenders between the three ships and some auxiliary machinery running deep inside the *Dalkeith*.

By the early hours of Monday morning the *Dalkeith*'s personnel had been asleep for several hours. Georgarakis was carrying out regular deck walks with nothing to report and the trawlers were sweeping the southern channel. Tyler was manning his gun with nothing to see, except blackness to starboard and the flickering lights of Carloforte some way off to port.

Sometime between sunset and 5.40 am Oberleutnant Wolfgang Steinbauer, commanding the *UB-48*, entered the Carloforte roadstead looking for prey. Through his periscope Steinbauer had more than one choice to attack. The *Upada* was a good couple of miles to his starboard side, several sailing schooners lay about 700yds off his bow, and the *Kingstonian* lay 1,000yds dead ahead with her two salvage vessels moored alongside. The *Kingstonian* was, without a doubt, an unlucky ship. Not only did two U-boats choose to attack her in as many weeks, but Steinbauer, like von Heimburg, was also a U-boat ace and another of the thirty commanders to be awarded the coveted Blue Max.

All four ships in the roadstead were blacked out according to regulations, but Steinbauer was still able to see his prey. He was also able to calculate exactly where to aim his torpedo for maximum devastation, especially as the *Kingstonian* was now a stationary target. Steinbauer ordered his torpedo crew to prepare one to launch. When the reply came back to the control room that the tube was ready, he gave the single-word order to fire.

Unlike Heimburg's earlier attack, Steinbauer's single torpedo passed right under the *Moose* and *Dalkeith* and punched a hole directly in the forward end of the *Kingstonian*'s boiler room. This time the effect was catastrophic. The blast ripped the 6,564-ton cargo ship in half at her bridge section – the stern sank immediately while her fore end listed to port, but bobbed precariously on the surface. As the blast radiated out, it tore off much of the *Dalkeith*'s bottom, peeling it back like a can opener, causing the open sea to pour in.

A bulkhead between the forward hold and her bunker also collapsed, instantly flooding the engine room. The water inrush was rapid because a watertight door had been left open between the after stokehold and the engine room. While most of the *Dalkeith*'s crew slept, she sank in less than ninety seconds and what began as a routine salvage operation now became one of survival.

Telegraphist Norman Rennard was in his cabin on the upper deck and when the explosion occurred he bolted for his cabin door, but the explosion had jammed it hard into its wooden frame; he was trapped. Just after launching the torpedo, Steinbauer surfaced the *UB-48* to assess the damage to the three ships. The *Dalkeith*'s crew, many suffering from severe burns and blast injuries, tried to reach the tugboat, *Moose*, and safety when he decided to wreak even more havoc on his enemies.

Aboard the *Moose*, Able Seaman Denis Bennet was one of two men manning the ship's defensive gun, which was mounted on the *Moose*'s foredeck. As he looked out to sea, two bright yellow muzzle flashes came from the *UB-48*'s deck gun about a minute after the torpedo had exploded. 'I tried to get the gun to bear on the submarine, but by that time she was away abaft the beam and the gun would not bear.' It was as if Steinbauer knew this and made sure his submarine was not within firing range.

Seconds later 4in shrapnel shells exploded around the injured and dying men shredding anything or anybody in their way. The shell fragments or shrapnel pellets seriously injured several crew members as they clawed, scrambled or rolled their mangled bodies into the water. The *Dalkeith*'s captain, Lieutenant Arthur Atkins, was sound asleep a few minutes before Steinbauer surfaced. He later wrote:

I woke very slowly and was stunned. I got out of my room and found the ship was sinking quickly. Very soon I had to go into the water during the time the submarine was firing. She started

53

shelling immediately after the torpedo had struck. She [the *Dalkeith*] went too quickly. It was just a scramble out of the ship to get away. Some got away and some did not.

Steinbauer kept the *UB-48* moving forward in a southerly direction past the sinking ships, constantly firing as he went. Fortunately a shell blast managed to free Telegraphist Norman Rennard's cabin door from its frame and he dashed for the nearest exit. He recalled: 'I was unable to get out until [the door] was either broken down by a shell or burst open by an explosion. As soon as I was out I went into the water. I came to the surface and the submarine was shelling the three ships alongside one another. I then swam to the *Moose* and got on board.'

Engineer Richard Furlong was also very lucky to escape. He was in his cabin asleep when the torpedo struck and his first thought was that the *Dalkeith* was blowing steam, so he got up to investigate. 'When I stepped out of [my] room I was in the water and I barely had time to get to the ship's side when the *Dalkeith* sank.' He jumped into the water between the *Kingstonian* and the *Dalkeith* and swam as hard as he could for the *Moose*, struggling for at least ten minutes to reach her. Cold, exhausted but alive he was hauled aboard.

The *Moose* escaped damage from Steinbauer's torpedo, but the *UB-48* then showered her with shrapnel shells, one of which penetrated her boiler room, causing steam to escape under very high pressure. Another shell punched into her steering gear and a third one exploded into her mast, sending the *Moose*'s funnel crashing down onto a wooden tender on her main deck. With her gun useless and the *Dalkeith* dragging her down, her captain, Lieutenant William Summers, gave the order to let go her mooring lines until she could get up steam and escape. But with the *Dalkeith* sinking so quickly, some mooring lines parted before they could be saved. Due to her internal damage, the *Moose* could not get up steam and was drifting helplessly out of control.

A defensive gun was fitted aboard the *Kingstonian*'s still floating bow section. She opened fire immediately her gun crew sighted the *UB-48*'s muzzle flashes, but as soon as they did so, the bow section began listing to port, rendering the gun useless as it could now only shoot into the sky. As the *Kingstonian* sank deeper she settled upright and her gun crew tried once again to attack the *UB-48*, but by now smoke and steam escaping from the *Moose* had formed a screen between the *Kingstonian* and Steinbauer's U-boat. Still the *Kingstonian* managed to fire five shots in the general direction of the muzzle flashes, but it was never known if these caused any damage.

In the sea around the attack area the screaming of escaping steam and dying men merged as the blood, burning oil and assorted blast debris covered the surface of the water. As the *Dalkeith*'s surviving personnel fought for their lives, Summers thought he had two boats aboard the *Moose* to launch but the ship's funnel had crushed his port boat and a shell burst had shattered his starboard one. He could only watch and listen to the dying men. Within twenty minutes of Steinbauer's barrage, all three guns aboard the stricken vessels, and their searchlights, were useless. They could neither attack the submarine nor defend themselves against Steinbauer's deadly hour-long onslaught.

The *Dalkeith*'s Chief Officer, Lieutenant E.J. Bull, was injured while still in his cabin when the torpedo struck. He instinctively made for the ship's bridge as the highest point and, although injured, he managed to jump across to the *Moose* before his ship sank. Seeing men were in the water needing help, and that the *Moose*'s boats were useless, he disregarded his own safety and began a single-handed rescue operation. Cold, wet and bleeding from his wounds, Bull got down into the *Dalkeith*'s motorboat, which had been tied up alongside the *Kingstonian*, cast her adrift and pushed her aft, picking as many men out of the water as he could. 'He got me out of the water,' said Atkins. 'His presence at the time in the boat was very encouraging and I think his action, in the condition he was, was quite a worthy one.' He later recommended Bull for his actions.

Atkins felt that Steinbauer only ceased shelling because the early dawn was quickly turning to full daylight. After vanishing back into the Mediterranean the *UB-48* left behind two sunken ships and one disabled. Ten men were dead or dying, two were severely injured and fifteen were slightly hurt. Of those killed, the bodies of Assistant Salvage Officer Wilson-Alexander, Lance Corporal William Tyler, and a stoker, William Smith, were never recovered.

The bodies of five drowned Greek sailors, most of them engine-room personnel, were later found, including nightwatchman Triandaphilus Georgarakis. The men were buried ashore in Carloforte. With no hospital facilities to help the other injured men, a small schoolhouse was converted into a makeshift medical centre. Of the two severely injured men, another Greek sailor, Constantine Rousso, died of his wounds later that day. Aboard the *Kingstonian*, flying shrapnel had killed one man and her Fourth Officer was slightly injured. The *Moose* was towed inshore for repairs. On 1 May, salvage personnel started removing pumps and other equipment from the *Kingstonian*'s holds and plant from the *Dalkeith*. Four days later, all attempts to save more equipment from the *Dalkeith* failed when her upper housing was torn off in a gale and other wreckage was washed away.

Casualties among the Salvage Section were not always directly due to enemy action, but through simple administrative decisions being made at Admiralty headquarters in London. Around lunchtime on 18 December 1917, the 2,805-ton cargo ship SS *Riversdale* was steaming from the Tyne down to Falmouth to join a Mediterranean-bound convoy, when about 1½ miles off Prawle Point, Devon, a torpedo detonated in her fore end, causing a fire that gutted the crew accommodation. After all but six of the crew had abandoned ship, her master managed to run the *Riversdale* ashore under her own steam in nearby Ellender Cove. Although now aground, her position was still somewhat precarious. She was touching the bottom along her entire length and the rising swell was beating both her bow and stern violently against the sharp rocks, threatening more severe damage. She was only 6ft away from a large rock, at a perfect right angle, ready to punch a hole straight through the stern plating.

Her recovery was given to the Devonport Salvage Corps. The 'Salvage Party', as it was more commonly known, was only formed by the Admiralty in March 1916 and had already gained a reputation as a crack salvage unit which had never lost a ship. Its personnel were made up entirely of volunteers from within the Dockyard and were placed directly under the Salvage Officer, Commander William Colegrave. He was also a brilliant leader, inspiring almost godlike loyalty from his men. Admiralty Superintendent A.J. Henneker-Hughan said of Devonport's Dockyard Corps, 'The Salvage Party of this dockyard has been organized with much care and trouble; the men know Commander Colegrave well and work for him with all their might.'

Seven hours after the *Riversdale* was hit, Colegrave, his assistant, Lieutenant Lanyon and Dockyard Fitter Hindmarsh were among the team who were out searching around the *Riversdale*'s last known position. By now it was dark with a heavy, confused swell rolling across the sea with no fixed pattern. In such bleak conditions the search was called off until daylight when he hoped to have better luck. By mid morning on the 19th, Colegrave had found her. The *Riversdale*'s Number One and Number Two Holds were flooded and there was a leak into the boiler room. Number Two Hold took eight hours to reach sea level and neither space ebbed and flowed with the tide, meaning there was no severe damage. Apart from that, all her vital areas were watertight.

Colegrave guided his men through a standard salvage operation between 19 December and Christmas Eve. He wanted to tow her round to Plymouth on Boxing Day. The bulkhead between Number Two Hold and the engine room was shorn up with planks as it bulged under the pressure of coal and water pressing against it. The damage to the fore end was also covered over and made watertight with patches, and about 300 tons of coal were either dumped over the side or loaded into another ship. Additional pumps were needed to control some minor damage from the constant beating against the rocks. On 24 December the *Riversdale* was ready for a trial lift when, from a warm office in London, a routine order set in motion a tragic chain of events.

Without any reason being given, Clement Greatorex decided to relieve Colegrave from the salvage operation and put Commander G.J. Wheeler in his place for the final, but crucial, salvage phase. On Christmas Day, Wheeler ordered the tugboat, *Rover*, to start towing the *Riversdale* from astern. The steamer swung around, but failed to come off the rocks with the tide. On Boxing Day *Rover* tried again, assisted by the *Woonda*. A pump failure ensured that the attempt did not succeed and more pumps were needed to stem other leaks if she was going to be saved. Time and tide were running against Wheeler, who later remarked, 'There was every possibility of the ship breaking up in a few hours.' If the situation had not deteriorated enough, an enemy submarine was reported to be 'definitely' in the area and the *Woonda* had to head back to Plymouth until the alert was over, adding precious hours to the job. A well-prepared and simple lift was now spiralling into chaos.

Two days later conditions changed in Wheeler's favour. The recently unsettled weather moderated and the pumps worked well. At 4.40 am the *Rover* and the *Woonda* were ready with their towlines bar taut as they eased the *Riversdale* off the rocks. Exactly one hour and five minutes later she was afloat and under tow in the lee of the land, should Wheeler need to run her aground quickly. He decided to stay on board the *Riversdale* along with Dockyard Fitter Hindmarsh,

Lieutenant Lanyon and a small group of essential salvage workers. 'Every thing appeared satisfactory,' Wheeler continued, 'wind NE, Force 3, sea calm, no swell. Towing commenced stern first at 3kts towards Salcombe and at this point it was remarked by Hindmarsh that the vessel appeared good enough to take round to Cardiff if weather conditions remained unchanged.'

Within minutes the sea state changed as another confused swell rippled across the water, spilling in different directions as the peaks and troughs piled into each other. By 6.15 pm, only ninety minutes after getting underway, the colliding waves were crashing hard against the *Riversdale*'s hull. Wheeler, Lanyon, Hindmarsh and the other men aboard could see that she was going down by the head, as thousands of tons of water pummelled against their salvage patches. Exactly seven minutes later, the *Riversdale* was gone. The salvage team was in the freezing water, trying to keep breathing and fighting the paralysing cold.

The drifter *Rennew* had accompanied the two tugs. She picked up many survivors, but not everyone made it. Wheeler later testified that only the salvage party deemed absolutely necessary was on board and they had all been supplied with lifebelts. The majority of the men were quickly taken on board the *Rennew*, which had remained alongside as long as possible. Lanyon was reported to have been on the drifter but later no trace of this officer could be found. The ship's donkeyman was picked up by the tug *Rover*, but he later succumbed to exposure. Wheeler said, 'I am unable to give any definite personal knowledge of happenings after the vessel sank, as going down with the ship and being hit by wreckage, I have very little recollection of being picked up by the drifter half an hour later.'

There is now no telling whether or not Colegrave's men resented Wheeler's sudden presence, or if he lost their respect during the last few days of the salvage operation. Whatever the reason strong lessons were learned that reverberated all the way up to the Admiralty in Whitehall. Captain of Dockyard for Devonport, Rear Admiral John Nicholas, reported to the Admiralty, saying, 'I would respectfully suggest that future Salvage operations in this area may be conducted by Devonport Dockyard and supervised by its own officers, unless their services are required elsewhere.'

Two months later an Admiralty order was issued to resolve the matter. In reply to Nicholas's submission, the order stated:

Whilst the Dockyard Salvage Corps should continue to render immediate First Aid to all vessels in distress, it is imperative that, if available, an expert Salvage Officer should take charge of operations as soon as possible. The present salvage policy necessitates close co-operation between the Admiralty and the leading Salvage Association and Underwriters and the retention of their confidence and it is certain that its success would be imperiled if the most experienced Salvage Officers available were not sent to take charge of operations.

Throughout the rest of 1918, Colegrave and his team continued to excel at ship recovery. One incident, later in the year, was a classic example of how far Admiralty salvage had come in such a short time, and just how slick ship and cargo recovery could be under the control of experts.

Chapter 7

Third Time Lucky

On the same day that Oberleutnant Heino von Heimburg fired his torpedo into the *Kingstonian*, Captain Albert Benjamin Donald was making final preparations for the 4,538-ton armed merchant cruiser, SS *Tanfield*, to set sail from London Docks. She was one of five ships in Mercantile Convoy OR 1, carrying a valuable cargo including armoured cars, motor cars, ammunition wagons, aircraft parts and general cargo bound for India. The *Tanfield*'s value, including her goods, was more than £1 million (or £37 million today).

The *Tanfield* arrived safely at her rendezvous point near the Isle of Wight on 13 April. Convoy OR 1 was in a typical formation to maximize on all the ships' safety, not only from the enemy but also from the distinct possibility that two or more vessels might well collide. Each vessel had to steam 400yds apart at 10 knots in three separate columns. Each column was placed 800yds apart – not a great deal of space for five very large cargo ships, as they also had to steer a synchronized zigzag course without losing their positions.

In the centre column and leading the convoy was the SS *Merkara* with the Commodore of the Convoy, Captain F.G. Brown, aboard. His job was to oversee the entire formation, make any changes necessary en route and communicate any essential information to the other ships by way of an encoded convoy cipher. Behind the *Merkara* was the SS *Tantilus*, completing the middle column. To their right was the SS *Mahanda* with the convoy's deputy commodore aboard, should the *Merkara* be lost, and behind her steamed the SS *Media*. The *Tanfield* was the only ship forming the left column.

The small armada steamed its perfectly synchronized, almost graceful, zigzag course towards Eddystone Lighthouse off the Cornish coast. Then they would head south to Gibraltar, through the Mediterranean, transit the Suez Canal and onwards to Bombay and Karachi. OR 1 had the added security of six armed trawlers to protect the five ships, each equipped with hydrophone systems. Two were on each beam, one ahead and the other astern. The trawlers enveloped the five ships in a tightly meshed sub-oceanic field that could detect an enemy submarine anywhere in the area. Still, with all this protection, the *Tanfield* kept a constant watch, not only with the standard crow's nest deck rating keeping a sharp lookout, but another on her forecastle, two on her bridge and two men on her 3in gun platform. Altogether six pairs of eyes were constantly watching the surrounding sea, while the trawlers scanned below.

Most major incidents are never the result of a single act, but a seemingly random series of events that suddenly merge. After three quiet days steaming in harmony several such minor events were about to conspire against Convoy OR 1. Firstly, Captain Donald was not a well man. He had been in command of one merchant ship or another for the whole duration of the war. Not only was he exhausted but also, since 1914, two of his ships had been torpedoed and sunk under his command and another had unfortunately collided with an iceberg. He had an Indian crew and his British officers were unaccustomed to working with them. Lastly as a result of a minor collision between two of the other convoy ships in broad daylight during poor visibility, Captain Brown ordered all the ships to slow down, cease zigzagging and steam a straight course as night fell.

The night was very dark and hazy. Visibility was patchy as heavy banks of cool mist floated over the Channel. By 9.00 pm all eleven ships were steaming steadily at 8 knots, but the weather was not getting any better. Captain Donald and his senior officers were on the *Tanfield*'s bridge constantly checking their position in relation to the rest of the convoy to avoid another collision. At 9.15 pm, when the convoy was 35 miles west of Eddystone Light, the other vessels surrounding the *Tanfield* saw a bright orange burst of light leap upwards through the mist roughly where she was supposed to be. A loud explosion and a large column of white water closely followed the light, now diffusing through the foggy haze. Then five minutes later they picked up the *Tanfield*'s SOS, quickly followed by a series of red distress rockets fired from her bridge. Captain Brown despatched three of his escort trawlers to the *Tanfield*, this time reverting back to a standard zigzag course, just in case the U-boat was still in the area.

Mass panic broke out among the sinking ship's Indian crew. Only one officer, Chief Engineer Ernest Fleuriot, could speak Hindustani, but his authority as a senior officer, and fluency in their own language, meant nothing. His shouts in their native tongue for order and to remain calm were barely even heard above the men desperately trying to leave the ship. As the *Tanfield* took on a heavy port list, men ran, pushed, shoved and screamed wildly as the panic rapidly degenerated into anarchy.

Without Donald's order to abandon ship the crew were already on their way. He later described how 'The native crew at once ran to the boats and panic ensued, it was then a case of "every man for himself", boats, rafts all being utilized.' Donald had lost control of the crew, but when some of the officers realized all the boats would soon be gone they, too, deserted their posts – among them Chief Officer J.H. Williams – and an emotionally shattered Donald.

With the captain, chief officer and crew now gone, the *Tanfield*'s four engineers, wireless operator and her two gunners made the first gallant effort to salvage their ship. Without any idea of how bad the damage was, they still decided to stay on board and try to get a towline to one of the advancing trawlers. About forty-five minutes later one of the escort trawlers reached her to rescue the men. Meanwhile the remaining crew members attempted to pass a towline from her forward bollards down to the trawler *John Abbot*. Shortly afterwards a second trawler came alongside and Captain Donald pleaded with the remaining crew members to abandon ship, as she could now go down very fast at any time. The men had risked their lives to stay on board and secure a towline, but now they had to leave – all their efforts had been in vain. Shortly after they were safely away their towline parted and the trawlers lost sight of the *Tanfield* as she slipped into the misty darkness. More by luck than judgement, just after daybreak a steamer was sighted that proved to be the *Tanfield*.

Captain Donald, his chief officer and several engineers reboarded the sinking vessel to make a second salvage attempt by securing a much stronger steel towline to the *John Abbot*. Should she stay afloat long enough, and the weather conditions hold, there was every chance she could be towed back to Plymouth. The trawler *Aurea* then came alongside. Donald continued, '[She] took master, officers and engineers off, as we did not think it advisable to remain on board seeing that all the boats and rafts were gone and we could not render any further assistance.' The *John Abbot* now had a secure line on board – just as the weather turned and the *Tanfield* settled lower in the water.

Before too long the *John Abbot* looked as if she was dragging rather than towing the fully laden ship towards the shore, a situation made somewhat worse by the water pouring into her through the hull breach, and the weather deteriorating with every passing minute. To help her reach Plymouth two salvage tugs, the 400-ton *Assurance* and the much larger 700-ton paddle tug *Industrious*, were despatched in the early hours of the morning, escorted by a torpedo boat and an armed trawler to meet the *John Abbot*. At about 9.30 am the sky was heavily overcast and the sea state had worsened with rain squalling across the waves. Acting Master J. Mitchell aboard the *Assurance* spotted the *John Abbot*, straining under her dead load with a Force 4 headwind piling against her bows. She was now making no headway at all.

When Captain Mitchell was close enough to assess the situation fully he could see that the *Tanfield* was listing further to port and speed was now essential to try to rescue both ship and cargo. To save precious minutes the *John Abbot* attempted to pass her towing hawser across to the *Assurance*, but somehow the line parted and the abandoned *Tanfield* was now helpless and at the mercy of the sea. With the ship deserted and the only line connecting her to forward motion now gone, Fred Hill, the First Mate, had to place some of his own crewmen on board to make fast the *Assurance*'s much bigger – and stronger – towline. Hill immediately volunteered to lead the boarding party, along with two able seamen. Captain Mitchell lowered the *Assurance*'s starboard boat into a very heavy swell with his chief officer and the two able seamen aboard. With great difficulty they rowed across the churning open sea between the two vessels and managed to board the listing steamer. Once safely at her steeply sloping bows, crewmen aboard both the *Assurance* and *Industrious* threw heaving lines attached to the much stronger towlines to the soaked and freezing men aboard the *Tanfield*, who made them fast and were then to remain on board until she reached Plymouth – or sank on the way.

During all this time the *Assurance* and *Tanfield* were liable to submarine attack and in danger from mines. The *Tanfield* was badly holed and had her after bulkhead collapsed she would have sunk immediately. Then more than 5,000 tons of ship and cargo would have been lost, barely giving the tug crews time to slip their towlines and escape before being dragged down with her. Once both lines were secured the *John Abbot* was able to head back to Plymouth under her own steam and the two bigger tugs took up an ever-greater strain against both the seawater outside, and, increasingly, inside the stricken ship. To speed

63

the *Tanfield*'s journey, Hill tried to get her hand-steering gear to work, but it was jammed, making her much more difficult to control. Captain Mitchell was becoming concerned, with good reason, as the head wind drove the rising sea into the tugs and their charge. 'My men remained aboard the *Tanfield*, but were apparently unable to steer her although she followed moderately well, she was gradually settling down aft.' An attempt to put aboard an engineer and fireman to restart the engines also had to be abandoned. By now the *Tanfield*'s engine room was mostly under water.

The *Assurance* and *Industrious* gradually eased their engines forward and the slack was taken up on the two towing lines. They went rapidly from floating loosely on the ocean to creaking and groaning as their seawater was squeezed out and quickly vaporized in the high wind. The *Tanfield* initially refused to move. Then, ever so slowly, she began to creep towards Plymouth. Now the third and most pivotal salvage attempt was being planned. Devonport Salvage Corps Commander William Colegrave was tasked with meeting her in the open sea and taking over full command of the salvage operation. At 10.45 pm on 16 April, Colegrave, along with Devonport Yard Foreman Charles Owen and one assistant, left Devonport Dockyard to meet the *Tanfield*, *Assurance* and *Industrious* near Penlee Point, Cornwall. Colegrave soon met the two tugs – not aboard a purpose-built salvage vessel, but the only available craft, the 65ft harbour steam launch, *D.2*. She was normally used for ferrying officers, men and materials around Plymouth Sound, but now she was well into the open sea.

Colegrave's most immediate task was to obtain a full damage report and put into effect whatever was necessary to keep the vessel afloat long enough to reach Plymouth. He ordered Owen to get the facts. Owen's report was more than a little shocking: on making a survey of the ship, he reported back to Colegrave that the vessel was open to the sea in all her machinery spaces, and in her Number Four Hold. Owen knew that if by any means water penetrated the *Tanfield*'s Number Five Hold to the level of seawater outside the ship, she would go down. A similar effect sank the *Titanic*; she could have stayed afloat with four compartments flooded, but not with five.

Owen needed to know if Number Five Hold was leaking. He, along with his assistant, opened the *Tanfield*'s carpenter's store to get the necessary blocks and mallets to knock out the hatch wedges from the top of Number Five Hold on her open deck; they could then remove the hatch covers and quickly gain access to the hold. Knocking out the wedges was not an easy task. They were and still are always hammered in with the widest end facing the ship's bow so the weather will drive them in harder rather than force them out. Removing them in the safety of a port can be hard, but on a listing, rolling and sinking ship, facing into bad weather, trying to strike a heavy mallet onto the end of a rain-swollen wedge was a very difficult and hazardous operation.

Once Owen and his assistant were inside they saw seawater streaming in through the rivet holes in the bulkhead between Numbers Four and Five Holds. He knew that if the inrush was allowed to continue the ship would founder as there was already about 15ft of water in the compartment. Owen and his assistant then took immediate steps to stop all the leaks they could by plugging them with whatever was available. Soundings were taken at intervals, but the water was still rising at about 3ft every hour until more holes were located and plugged.

Owen decided that the inflow, although much lessened, still threatened the ship's survival. He suggested to Colegrave that the *Industrious* should come alongside and use her powerful pumps to expel the many tons of water now slopping around the bottom of Number Five Hold. While Owen and his assistant did their best to remove the water, Colegrave ordered the *Assurance* to steam as fast as possible towards Plymouth Sound and to a position where the *Tanfield* could be grounded if necessary. However, the rising water was not only a danger to the ship.

'I directed the tug *Industrious* to make fast on the port quarter,' Colegrave later explained, 'and do her utmost to keep the vessel afloat by pumping the water out of Number Five Hold.' The *Industrious* rigged one of her 4in salvage pumps to reduce the water volume, just in time to save the cargo. 'This was very necessary as the water was rising to the vicinity of the motor cars, which had been placed on top of the general cargo in the hold, and the water was already up to some of the axles of some of the cars.'

The *Assurance* and *Industrious* struggled against the weather for another twelve hours to complete the last 80 miles or so from Penlee Point to the safety of Plymouth Sound, but the *Tanfield* was still far from being saved. Just before midnight on 16/17 April Colegrave took on a pilot for the last leg and was finally able to relieve the two tugs that had worked nearly non-stop for three days to cover 56 miles of open water. Entering Plymouth Sound at night in a stable ship under her own steam would be difficult enough, especially with the break-water and many large and small vessels bobbing at anchor or moored to buoys. About a ½ mile before Colegrave got the *Tanfield* in to the Sound, Pilot James Crowther arrived aboard the Harbour Master's Special Service Tug, *Boarhound*, to assist Colegrave in getting the sinking vessel through the maze of small ships in the area.

Immediately Crowther was aboard he ordered the *Boarhound* to steam aft of the *Tanfield* and act as her rudder. Then the *Assurance* was moved from ahead to the *Tanfield*'s starboard side to further steady her progress. These precautions became critical because, although Colegrave had saved the *Tanfield* from being lost in the open sea, these new events threatened to cause her almost certain loss a second time. The *Tanfield* then proceeded into the Sound on a strong ebb tide with every possibility that, in her disabled condition, the steamer would slam into the breakwater, let alone hit one of the many anchored craft.

Eventually, after picking a way through the anchored vessels, missing the breakwater and constantly running a pump in her Number Five Hold, the *Tanfield* was brought to a halt in shallow water where she could be quickly beached if necessary. The *Industrious* ceased pumping for the night, but all tugs remained in the vicinity in case they should be needed. There were still 5 miles to go for the *Tanfield* to be safely dry-docked and repaired. At daybreak several more hours of pumping were needed before enough water could be removed for the five-hour tow to Plymouth harbour's North Lock.

The anchors were fully run out and ditched as she had no steam for the windlass and were buoyed for later recovery. The *Tanfield* arrived at the North Lock of Number Five Basin at 2.15 pm, whereupon a 6in salvage pump was immediately placed on board to deal with the water leaking into Number Five Hold. Colegrave recommended that all the general cargo and motor cars should be removed at once so as to lighten the ship and give much better access to her blast damage. She was soon dry-docked, permanently repaired, back in service under government charter and was not attacked again for the remaining few months of the war. Another vessel – and her precious cargo – could be rotated back into the war effort.

Chief Engineer Ernest Fleuriot and Radio Operator Adam Redpath both received awards for their actions in trying to save their ship. Both Chief Officer Williams and Captain Donald were subjected to an official inquiry held by the Marine Engineers' Association to ascertain why they had deserted their posts at such a crucial time. Donald was asked how much time elapsed between the explosion and when the ship was abandoned. He replied that about four minutes passed, which somewhat riled the Marine Engineers' Association investigators who pointed out that four minutes was nowhere near long enough to survey the torpedo damage and make an informed decision to abandon – or save – his ship.

Donald also failed to produce the *Tanfield*'s confidential books when he arrived at Plymouth. His actions were made worse after he firstly stated that the books were left locked up on board, then changed his story saying that he always kept them on his person. Either way he did not produce them when required to do so. The inquiry was convinced that it was extremely doubtful that he even had the books with him when he abandoned the *Tanfield*, and that his actions were carried out with the utmost haste. After all the evidence was taken the inquiry decided that Donald was not in a fit state to take command of any vessel on government service or insured under the War Risks Scheme. They recommended that the Board of Trade, owners and the War Risks Association be informed to this effect. The conduct of Chief Officer Williams was considered highly unsatisfactory, but ultimately he *was* under Donald's orders and managed to keep his job.

Donald was mentally and emotionally shattered after four years under the intense pressure of the possibility of being sunk at any moment, which he had now survived three times. But Donald and Williams did return to their ship in a gallant, but vain attempt to save it the following morning. These facts were given to the inquiry, but the Marine Engineers' Committee chairman, D. Bramah, concluded, 'My Committee believe this is a case in which responsible officers have deserted their posts, thus jeopardizing the lives of those remaining. It is stated that in order to minimize the gallantry displayed, these facts will not be made known.' In the official report on the incident, listing dozens of questions in a standard seven-page printed booklet, Question 39(b) asked how the crew behaved. The two-word reply gives nothing of the true events away by stating, 'Very well.' Ironically, by the time the Marine Engineer's Association Committee had passed judgement on Donald, he had already resigned his commission with no intention of ever going back to sea.

Although all three attempts to save the *Tanfield* took skill and courage to put into effect, two of them played a key role in her eventual recovery. Or, to put it in Colegrave's own words:

The promptitude of the services rendered by the tugs in bringing the vessel into a position of safety and later in the *Industrious* pumping and thereby keeping the vessel afloat she was saved from almost certain total loss. Even when she had been brought into harbour energetic measures had to be taken under my directions which resulted in keeping the vessel afloat and saving her very valuable general cargo.

Commander Colegrave's expertise and courage, as well as those of the men of the *Assurance* and *Industrious*, saved a very valuable ship and her cargo that could so easily have been lost. The *Tanfield* went on to operate throughout the Second World War without incident and carried on as a successful cargo carrier until 1950.

Chapter 8

Future Plans?

The Salvage Section had grown significantly since the *Ranger* had started recovering stranded vessels for the Admiralty. Fifteen salvage ships were now stationed around the United Kingdom and the Mediterranean, with the *Ranger*, the *Linnet* and the *Ringdove* forming the Section's nucleus, along with the much larger 1,000-ton *Reindeer*, *Melita* and *Mariner*. The fully redesigned *Racer* with her eight submersible electric, steam and compressed air pumps, capable of expelling 3,000 tons of water per hour, was an added bonus for the fleet. Six hopper barges had also been converted into lifting craft. The *Alligator*, *Buffalo*, *Crocodile*, *Dromedary*, *Hippopotamus* and *Rhinoceros* were each about 700 tons displacement, all with a lifting capacity of 1,000 tons.

The manpower had also grown. Under Captain Young there were now six naval and twenty salvage officers, increasing to thirty in 1918; there were also literally hundreds of crew members needed to man the ships as well as divers and shore-side staff. Innovative salvage techniques were being developed to meet the demand. Young's own invention, called the 'Standard Patch', became an integral part of the Section's many successful operations. Torpedo and mine damage often blew out several hundred square feet of hull plating, often well below the waterline. Such a jagged, open, steel hole often made a speedy repair very difficult to accomplish. Young's ready-made patch was made with 6in thick lengths of pitch-pine planking, linked together with eyebolts that were driven through the ship's side. Steel wires ran through the bolts and once they were pulled taut the patch moulded perfectly to the shape of the hull. It was quick, effective, and made the salvage of many vessels possible. The Admiralty Salvage Section was now the largest and best-equipped operation of its kind in the world.

Admiral Edward Phillpotts succeeded Director of Naval Equipment Clement Greatorex in January 1918. Two months later he said that, owing to the critical losses of British and Allied merchant ships and the increasing need to protect what was left wherever possible, it had become 'Urgently necessary in the national interests for the Admiralty to take over the direction of all salvage operations, and to render assistance to British and Allied vessels and to neutral ships in all ports of the world. And with increased plant and appliances.' For the first time since the war began the Section was tasked with salvaging marine as well as war risk vessels. A two-page form, called the Admiralty Standard Form of Salvage Agreement, or D 46 for short, replaced the old S 1317 and was issued to all salvage craft (owned or hired) and tugboats. The D 46 consisted of thirteen points covering every salvage eventuality and was very similar to the Lloyd's No Cure – No Pay agreement.

Becoming self-supporting was not as easy as Phillpotts had envisaged. Although the technical process of saving ships and their cargoes was well established, the Salvage Section never had a clerical department. At first glance this paperwork might appear trivial because of such an outstanding success rate when it came to saving ships, but then, as today, competent administrative support can have a significant impact on the success of any enterprise. Phillpotts was adamant that clerical staff should be employed, or the new Section would not be able to cope with its latest role – in spite of all its experience and courage on the high seas. Not just any clerical staff would do. A sound understanding of complicated issues such as shipping finance and a thorough knowledge of marine insurance law were essential. This was especially important if the new Salvage Section was going to gain the confidence of shipowners and underwriters.

Phillpotts was adamant that the organization as it stood was entirely unable to cope with its own administration, owing principally to the lack of professionally trained and experienced personnel:

> with the result that the clerical work is greatly in abeyance and underwriters and owners are complaining of the difficulty in obtaining accounts for the services rendered by the Section. Very large sums of money are owing to the Admiralty for past work, which there is difficulty in collecting, due to the want of staff, and to so many departments being concerned.

Representatives from the Liverpool Association for the Protection of Commercial Interests in Respect to Wrecked and Damaged Property reported back to the Admiralty on the true state of the Salvage Section's accounts. In a repeat of Captain Young's damning report on the state of Admiralty salvage facilities back in 1914, there was no care or control of incoming and outgoing earnings and expenses – their accounts were a shambles. The Association's manager, Harold Sumner, made a full enquiry into the present methods of dealing with accounts and found that the only records in connection with work carried out were contained in dockets, collected from telegrams and correspondence passing through the Department. He wrote with grave concern that this was a very insecure method of recording their work and any claims based on such scant records were liable to serious errors and omissions.

For all the recent legislation granted to the Section for salvage award, and the power now vested in the Admiralty to control all salvage operations, the Section simply did not have the resources to keep up with the ever-growing paperwork mountain. Sumner reported that the Salvage Section was therefore, 'as matters stand, not in a position to institute a system of book-keeping and, for the purpose of formulating claims against shipowners and other interested parties, for recovery of the expenses and services would be under the necessity of applying to the various departments concerned for the particulars and vouchers required to substantiate its claim'.

The Association recommended that all accounts in connection with the business of salvage should pass through the Salvage Section so that proper records could be maintained and provide evidence of the costs of any given salvage operation and financial profit or loss. Details of vessels involved were also to be recorded. These included the length of time that a vessel was engaged at a job plus the quantity of coal used and the amount of provisions consumed. All stores and material issued to salvage ships, including galley utensils, beds and bedding destroyed, had to be accounted for.

The list went on to include all details of pumps, tools and material used, lost or broken during a salvage operation as well as any damage to ships and to their equipment. An accounts officer, his assistant, four clerks and two typists were needed to catch up with, and then control, the paperwork. Having already lent Young to the Admiralty, the Liverpool Salvage Association offered the necessary clerical staff to keep the Salvage Section operative, which was accepted. On 1 April 1918 the new Section was in full operation as an association in its own right, this time with Captain Young's status as Naval Salvage Advisor changed to 'Head of the Salvage Section'. He was now the Section's first active Chief Salvage Officer. The following month Germany launched another fifty-five U-boats, the most of any month during the whole war, but over the same period, sixteen were destroyed, breaking another record.

The full potential of the convoy system was also coming into force and proving extremely successful, but there were still huge losses. In April 1918, seventy-two merchant ships were lost, followed by sixty in May and fifty-one in June. These were much less than for the same time in the previous year, but many more needed salvaging, like the 5,167-ton troopship *Comrie Castle*. She was torpedoed in the English Channel on 14 March 1918 with the loss of nine lives before being run aground for a standard patch-and-pump operation. Other operations were concluded with a little more daring and imagination, and show just how far a salvage officer would go to save a ship.

In the early hours of 17 May 1918 a troopship convoy was returning to New York from Britain after delivering fresh men for the Western Front. The convoy encountered heavy fog shortly after sailing while rounding the coast of Antrim in Northern Ireland. Unfortunately the convoy's commodore misjudged the distance from the land and drove the convoy's whole port wing, including the liners *Manora*, *Aeneas* and *Oriana*, as well as two escort destroyers, up on to the rock. The *Manora* and two destroyers were refloated with no trouble, but the *Aeneas* was stuck fast, supported for about 100ft of her amidships section with each end being fully waterborne at all times due to the small tide in the area. The Rescue Tugs *Sonia* and *Milewater* were sent to her assistance and after several unsuccessful attempts she was finally pulled clear of the rocks two days later.

However, the *Oriana* had hit the jagged coastline at 11 knots, driving her bow well clear of the high-water mark. On 18 May, Lieutenant Kay arrived to take over salvage operations. She was holed forward and required pumping out after divers patched her in her Number One and Number Two Holds, but the attempt to raise her failed, mainly because the sea was too calm. Wave motion was needed to give her lift before she could be pulled clear. Without it, Kay would have to create it and he boldly requested a Royal Navy vessel – in time of war – for the task. The Moon Class destroyer HMS *Millbrook* was selected. The *Oriana*'s official salvage report states rather prosaically: 'Commander Kay reports HMS *Millbrook* engaged to pass close to raise swell.' Kay's imaginative plan was a little more colourful, and illustrates how anything could be done once a salvage officer was committed to success.

The *Millbrook*'s mission was to run at full speed toward the stricken liner and turn sharply at the last possible moment, to create a bow wave powerful enough, it was hoped, to dislodge the *Oriana*. Gliding across the glass-like blue sea faster than a hydrofoil, the *Millbrook* made her first run straight at the liner. Having turned at the last moment a substantial white-crested wave churned the still water into a large swell, which ploughed into the stricken ship. She barely moved. Four more runs were attempted by which time an unusual localized sea state had developed. On the sixth run the *Oriana* rolled with the constant wave motion and gradually slipped free of the rocks with an 18° list. A few days later she arrived safely in Princes Dock, Glasgow. Kay's technique certainly did not become an isolated case – once proved as a useful salvage tool, similar motion effects were later achieved using explosives to generate waves.

As the German army retreated back across France and Belgium to the fatherland, Captain Young and the crew of the *Ranger* were faced with the biggest and most arduous salvage operation of the entire First World War. By then the *U-Bootflottile Flandern* operated many submarines from between Zeebrugge, Ostend and the port of Bruges, about 8 miles inland, with two canals linking all three. To reduce the merchant shipping losses even further, Admiral Jellicoe came up with the idea of 'putting a cork' in the two canal entrances, thus sealing all three bases.

Dover Patrol Commander, Vice Admiral Sir Richard Keyes, was tasked with devising a sound plan for five aging Apollo Class cruisers to be scuttled across each entrance. Two of them, the 3,400-ton cruisers HMS *Brilliant* and *Sirius*, were to go to Ostend and their sister ships *Intrepid*, *Thetis* and *Iphigenia* to Zeebrugge. On 22 April 1918 the slightly bigger 5,750-ton Arrogant Class cruiser, HMS *Vindictive*, led the five cruisers together with more than seventy support vessels for the attack. Several hours after entering the North Sea, *Brilliant* and *Sirius*, along with their support craft, turned south towards Ostend, while the remainder of the attack fleet pressed on to Zeebrugge. Just after midnight on St George's Day the *Vindictive*, along with two Mersey ferries, landed at the mole, a stone and concrete pier jutting 1½ miles out from Zeebrugge into the North Sea. An assault team of

200 volunteers emerged from below decks, their mission to put the seaward-facing guns out of action and distract the German defences from the raid's true objective.

HMS *Thetis*, *Intrepid* and *Iphigenia* had been loaded with explosive charges at key points and 1,500 tons of concrete were poured below each waterline before leaving Britain. With the sky now alive with hot metal exploding all around, and raining down on the cruisers, *Iphigenia* and *Intrepid* made it into the canal's mouth, their charges were blown and the ships sank like stones. The *Thetis* ran on to a sandbank slightly to the north-west of the entrance before she, too, detonated and sank.

During a raid that took barely two hours, 500 casualties were incurred with 200 men killed. Eight Victoria Crosses were awarded among more than 200 medals won that night – or one medal for about every thirty seconds the attack was in progress. Unfortunately none of the ships were scuttled in the right areas – at Ostend both the *Brilliant* and the *Sirius* were also off target – and within days it was business as usual for the U-boat offensive.

A few weeks later the *Vindictive* sailed, as a blockship this time, bound for Ostend. Her mission was to close the canal entrance where the *Brilliant* and *Sirius* had failed. She was only partially successful, and again the canal was in limited use within days. As 1918 progressed, Zeebrugge and Ostend came under Allied control as the German Army retreated back across Europe and the port blockages had to be removed.

Frederick Young was tasked with clearing the old warships. Before starting he needed facts about how the ships were scuttled. The Admiralty informed him that when arranging the alterations required to convert them into blockships, special attention had been paid to ensure every possible obstruction against their salvage by the enemy. Besides the four large charges that were blown in the bottom, smaller charges were detonated in certain areas to breach key watertight bulkheads. 'Nothing is known in this Department,' continued the report, 'as to what arrangements were actually carried out, nor how the ships are placed, nor what steps have hitherto been taken by the enemy towards removing them. Even if, however, they could have originally been salved, it is considered that the enemy, when withdrawing from the coast, will leave them in such a condition.' The retreating German Army did more than just leave the ships where they had sunk.

74

In Ostend the steamer *La Flandre* was jammed in line with the *Vindictive*, sealing off the space she had failed to cover and a large armed trawler was rammed into the *La Flandre* for good measure. Further inside the harbour a bucket dredger was sunk and another one capsized on top of it. In the middle of the channel a third large dredger was capsized and many smaller craft were sunk across the inner harbour. All the lock gates leading through the canal entrance were blown up and another dredger was rammed across the main entrance. The cranes on the quays had all been blown up and left in the harbour where they fell. All bridges connecting the various parts of the port had been destroyed. Finally, the twisted steel debris was booby-trapped with mines. Zeebrugge had undergone the same fate where, among all the toppled cranes, scuttled ships and strategically placed mines, the channels dredged around the *Iphigenia* and *Intrepid* to allow the U-boats to enter and leave were now firmly blocked.

Wherever a ship had been sunk nature made the job even worse. The ships had settled into 10ft of the mud and a further 18ft of solid clay. Young first tried the conventional method of passing wires under a wreck prior to lifting. The usual way to get a wire underneath was to 'sweep' it, meaning that a wire was strung between two tugs then literally dragged underneath and into position for lifting. Six weeks later, and after many different attempts had been made, the Salvage Section was no nearer to clearing their first ship, let alone the harbour.

The mud and clay had to be removed or the ships would only settle deeper into the seabed. Young knew that there was a firefighting tug-boat on the Belgian coast. Was it possible, he thought, to adapt the high-pressure water cannon on her stern to wash mud and clay away instead of flames? Her water cannon was disconnected and bolted onto a heavily weighted stage, which was then lowered down to the seabed, with water being supplied through a flexible 6in copper hose-pipe. A diver went down, pointed the cannon's nozzle at the mud, opened the water valve and came up. The water was then turned on and a jet hit the mud with a force of 90lb/in^2.

After about fifteen minutes the diver went down and reported that the mud had been blasted away to such an extent that the stage was already 2ft down into the clay. Steadily the stage was lowered until it came below the turn of the ship's bilge. The divers then drove a passage right under the ship to the point where they could stand upright within the clay tunnels and pass 9in wires underneath in pairs. After three weeks thirty-two wires, each with a breaking strain of 250 tons, were in position for a lift. Meanwhile the cement had to be removed and the only way was to chip it out.

Although most of the Salvage Section had been disbanded and scattered among private buyers nearly two years earlier, the *Vindictive* was the last ship the Section lifted. Her hull was also full of cement, but her position was much worse than any of the other sunken ships. Being in the harbour mouth meant she had taken the full brunt of the North Sea weather, her back was broken and her stern had fallen away 7ft from the line of the deck, causing silt and mud to pour in. Both sections had to be bolted back together with huge girders to give some support and she was successfully raised on the second attempt.

In 1919 the question of saving merchant ship casualties was under consideration. With the Shipping Controller anxious to restore merchant salvage to private hands as soon as possible, the Admiralty issued a circular to all underwriters and shipowners, saying that from 5 May 1919 the Salvage Section would relinquish all its responsibilities and would remain in being only as long as operations on the Belgian Coast continued. There also remained several hundred motor, steam and electrical submersible pumps, several hundred diving sets, hundreds of miles of wire and rope, and a mass of other gear. Faced with the costs of protection from weather, maintenance and obsolescence the Admiralty-owned plant was sold for what it would fetch. Pumps, which had cost £1,900, were sold for as little as £90 and £150, and the salvage vessels were practically given away. Contemporary feeling was that there was no chance of another world war of such magnitude, so no long-term plans were ever put in place to retain a salvage arm. Two decades later this decision would have disastrous consequences.

Although Young had been made a commodore, and although he was eventually knighted for his salvage work, he was still disappointed. His son Desmond remembered, 'My father received, for his services to merchant vessels, neither thanks nor recognition from Lloyd's, the Ministry of Shipping, or any of the owners or underwriters concerned.' All three of these had profited from the £50 million-worth of ships and cargoes salved between 1915 and 1919 (or £2 billion today). 'The only complaint I ever heard him make was that [now] Commander Kay and his other officers had not even a medal to show for four years incessant work, which, though little was known of it at the time or afterwards, was a not inconsiderable contribution towards winning the war.'

The end of Admiralty salvage operations had one twist in store for Captain Young. His original contract had not been altered since the start of the war when the Section was only tasked with recovering naval vessels. This oversight meant that he had a legal right to claim a salvage award on every merchant ship and its cargo under his direction. Shipping solicitor Mr North Lewis was a family friend who offered to represent him, informing Desmond, 'The case would have to be settled out of court. But the values involved are so enormous that I feel confident I could get him at least £250,000 [or £7.6 million today], perhaps more, without difficulty.'

Desmond explained, 'I hastened to report this conversation to my father, supposing that he would be as pleased and excited as I was.'

Young replied, 'Will you kindly tell our friend Mr North Lewis that I have no wish to make money out of my country's misfortunes – and have no intention of trying to do so.'

'I could not quite see why the underwriters should be identified with the country,' said Desmond, 'though it was true that it was the taxpayer who carried the risk in wartime. He was not prepared to argue the point with me. At least it could not be said of him that he was one of those hard-faced men who look as though they had done well out of the war.'

But, as Young always maintained until his death three days before his seventieth birthday in 1927, 'Honours and awards, like prize money, have a tendency to go aft.' That is, towards more senior military officers.

Due to the sheer number of ships needing salvage during the war, a triage system was necessary to save only those vessels that stood a good chance of surviving the rigours of lifting and towing. When the Salvage Section ceased operations there were more than 400 ships still wrecked around the British and Irish coasts. Similar to the Internet bubbles of the early 1990s, dozens of salvage start-up companies offered convincing prospectuses showing how the millions of pounds of shipping and cargoes lying around the coast could be salvaged with ease.

It is unlikely that these dubious firms mentioned in their glossy brochures that many of the ships had suffered greatly from the weather and tide, let alone enemy attack, or that a good many were still imprisoned within the minefields that had sunk them in the first place. Young had no illusions about the sudden surge in get-rich-quick salvage firms. He said, 'Most of them are in a position where it is not possible to lift them and the only barges that can lift the others are the Admiralty lifting craft, which will be wanted on the Belgian coast for the next year at least – by which time the price of ships will probably have fallen.' Like many Internet bubble companies, civilian salvage vessels, plant and thus shares were bought at a market peak. And, without warning, they plummeted overnight. One salvage company vessel was bought and fitted out for £45,000 – after the 1921 slump she eventually fetched only £1,500.

A list of all 416 wrecks abandoned around the British and Irish coasts was issued to reputable salvage firms both at home and abroad, but the Admiralty insisted that, in dealing with individual cases, it would only advise on the danger of raising these ships and would have no further responsibility. Some wrecks were cleared, but the majority of firms found the work much more costly, just as Young had predicted two years earlier, when the 1921 slump caused the price of scrap metal to fall. Before too long many bubble firms sank with less trace than the ships they promised to save. Others, though, such as the scrap dealer Ernest Cox of Cox & Danks, bought a large amount of ex-Admiralty salvage plant and against all odds he managed to recover many of the scuttled German warships in Scapa Flow, Orkney.

From 1914 to 1918 about 5,000 British and Allied merchant ships were sunk through enemy action. Among the very few known records about the actual salvage figures, the number of ships recovered is given as 500, or 10 per cent of all those attacked. However, recently discovered records in the United Kingdom's National Archives puts the figure at more than 800. Of these, 90 were Royal Navy vessels, including 10 submarines; 20 foreign vessels were also saved, including 11 U-boats and 2 Zeppelins. The total number of merchant ships salvaged was 730, or more than 15 per cent of all those attacked.

Throughout the war the Admiralty published weekly shipping movements to and from the United Kingdom; these averaged in excess of 2,500 voyages each way. Based on this figure, clawing back about 700 merchant vessels alone in four years may not seem very much, but all coasters and short-sea traders as small as 300 tons, which repeatedly entered and left British ports, were purposely added to artificially inflate the figures and discourage the enemy. According to the Ministry of Shipping the actual number of ocean traders keeping the supply lines open was only about 130 arrivals and departures per week.

Based on this statistic alone, further research must now be undertaken to assess the full impact of Admiralty salvage, both to acknowledge, finally, the debt owed to the men of the Admiralty Salvage Section and their long-term effect on keeping supply lines open during the first Battle of the Atlantic. And without the availability of so much salvaged merchant shipping, just how much shorter Britain's six-week deadline could have been – in which case, Jellicoe's fear of an enforced peace with Germany might have meant a completely different outcome to the First World War.

Chapter 9

Going for Gold!

In June 1917, Captain Young was dealing with eight casualties simultaneously in the Scillies alone. Four of them were the *Great City*, *Kathlamba*, *Eastgate* and *York Castle*, each with a combined cargo/vessel value of £300,000 (more than £10 million today); all eight had been torpedoed. Although the Section was under great strain to keep up with demand in both home waters and the Mediterranean, a small salvage party was held back from normal duties and deployed off the Irish coast where the cargo – rather than the ship – was the objective. When this job was finally completed more salvage men would be decorated than for any other operation during the First World War.

The 17,000-ton White Star liner, RMS *Laurentic*, was requisitioned as a troopship for the Canadian Expeditionary Force in 1914. The following year her military career changed when she was converted into an armed merchant cruiser, a role she carried out for the rest of her working life. Under cover of darkness on 24 January 1917, Captain Reginald Norton took her out of Liverpool heading first to Lough Swilly, a narrow inlet on Ireland's north-west coast, and then on to Halifax, Nova Scotia, the following day. This was no ordinary crossing for her second-class baggage room held forty-three tons of gold bullion destined for the United States as part-payment for food and war materials.

Forward of this precious cargo were three crew members being held as prisoners in the ship's cell. Their names and crimes are irrelevant, but two were firemen and their offences were deemed serious enough to separate them from the other 467 men on board. On 25 January, Captain Norton ordered Action Stations, darkened his ship and closed her watertight doors. With no moon and a rising gale she steamed out of Lough Swilly one hour later, into a black North Atlantic swell.

Warrant Telegraphist Arthur Bower was just finishing transmitting routine traffic to the coastal station at Malin Head on Ireland's northernmost tip. 'I was awaiting the signal of receipt from the above-named station when an explosion took place which shook me severely.' The *Laurentic* had run at full speed onto a mine that detonated just ahead of her foremast on the port side. Bower continued, 'I then attempted gathering the codebooks together, but was knocked down by another explosion, slightly more violent than the first. This time all lights were extinguished.' Meanwhile Captain Norton and the rest of the bridge watch were flung around like rag dolls as all the glass windows blew inwards on the driving gale. As the bitterly cold Atlantic swell gushed in through the shattered hull plating, all eight engine-room officers and ratings on watch were killed instantly.

Among the throngs of desperate men scrambling through the darkness to the lifeboats was Shipwright W.M. Herrington. He ran for the boat deck, fumbling in the dark through the pitch-black passageways and stairwells, to see if the lifeboats were being lowered. Upon his arrival Herrington later recalled, 'I was informed by an RNR seaman that three prisoners were in the cells. I made my way down to the cells, but found I could not release them, as I hadn't the keys.'

The *Laurentic* was now listing 10° and clearly was not going to last long. Telegraphist Bower knew it. He tried desperately to find matches to burn transmission messages to light his attempt at connecting up her emergency radio. While the paper quickly flared up, casting flickering shadows around the sloping deck, he connected it just as Captain Norton arrived. Norton asked Bower if an SOS had been sent. On hearing not, he ordered the distress signal to be transmitted at once. Bower complied, but the message never arrived. He tried again; still his transmission set failed. Bower continued:

> Chief PO Buller had used all his matches and the wind had blown out the paper he was burning. I felt for my fuses in the dark, and found them to be all in order. By degrees I traced my circuit throughout by sense of touch, at last, going to my accumulators. I found I was standing in acid and my accumulators had all, apparently, been canted or completely upset by the first or second explosion.

Bower tried to right the leaking batteries as the acid splashed over his hands, but they were too heavy.

The *Laurentic*'s 10° port list had levelled out, but she was now going down much faster. Norton had already ordered the release of the prisoners, but something troubled him. 'Fearing, though the sentry had the key, and was ordered to release them, he might not have done so, I went down there and found them still confined, and no sign of the sentry.' The three men were trapped behind thick, wooden doors in total darkness, fully aware the ship was sinking – and that the 'abandon ship' order had been given. After no doubt trying to reassure the men, Norton returned to the bridge and ordered his navigating officer, Lieutenant Walker to find a carpenter. On the boat deck he saw Shipwright Arthur Harrington who, along with three other men, returned to the carpenter's store where in desperation Harrington just grabbed a fire axe. They ran forward to where the prisoners were now screaming for their lives, kicking and punching the solid wooden doors. Harrington lifted the axe above his head and hacked into the thick door as hard as he could. One! Two! Three! blows rained down as the wood split open. The prisoners bolted out. They, along with the other officers and crew ran upwards towards the boat deck, where only one boat remained alongside. All the men piled in, Captain Norton being the last to leave. Less than ten minutes later the *Laurentic* – with her precious cargo – struck the bottom of the Atlantic 132ft down.

Commander Guybon Chesney Castell Damant RN was, apart from being a highly competent Admiralty salvage officer, an expert diver. In 1906 he had set the deepest diving record for the time at 210ft. That same year the Admiralty approached the eminent Scottish physiologist, John Scott Haldane, asking him to carry out the first serious research into decompression sickness, or as it is better known, the 'bends'. Both men worked together for two years (often using live goats as test subjects) before publishing their joint paper 'The Prevention of Compressed-Air Illness' in 1908. The paper published for the first time the correct tables for staged decompression timings. Both the Royal Navy and United States Navy adopted their tables, saving many divers from being crippled, blinded or even killed by the effects of too rapid an ascent.

Being more than 100ft down was not the only obstacle. The *Laurentic* was also exposed to the full run of Atlantic weather from the north and the west. The second-class baggage room was on the starboard side, about 40ft from the stern. The easiest way to get to it was from an entry port, or shell door. These are heavy sets of doors built into a ship's hull for easy entry and exit. In Damant's favour, because of the *Laurentic*'s size, her starboard shell door was only 62ft down rather than the full 132ft to the seabed. Even so, Lough Swilly's surface swell created horizontal surges as the peaks and troughs passed over any given spot, meaning the salvage vessel had to be moored at all four corners while in position above the wreck – a technique that is still being used today.

The initial survey located another problem. After the *Laurentic* had hit the seabed all the lifeboat wires were still hanging down the full 60ft from their davits. These were mainly three-fold purchases, meaning the wires were threaded three times through one heavy block on the davit and another with a large iron hook on its end at the point where the lifeboat was released. The design allowed for much greater pulling power. But on the seabed during bad surface weather the scend, or upward movement of the heavy sea, lashed these long wires to and fro like giant slow-motion steel whips. On more than one occasion a diver had to get out of the way of a flailing block and wire to avoid being killed or seriously injured. Once the twin shell doors were located, they were blasted open with guncotton charges, blowing them about 2ft into the ship. The heavy steel slabs were then slung and hoisted up to the surface, but the entry point was still far from being easily accessible. Tons of smashed wooden furniture and waterlogged stores clogged up the passage to such an extent that it was completely impassable for some time.

Another heavy iron gate then had to be blasted before salvage diver E.C. 'Dusty' Miller could get to the baggage room's steel door. Miller broke through it with a sledgehammer and chisel. When the door gave way he literally fell into the room, sliding down the stores that revealed the intact bullion boxes. They were only 1ft^2 by 5in deep, but each one weighed 140lb. By the following morning Miller had removed four of the heavy boxes, dragging them 40ft along a sloping narrow passageway past newly disturbed debris and over two watertight door coamings. This was quite an achievement while wearing a cumbersome diving suit 62ft below the surface. All things considered, with more men deployed, salvaging the remaining gold was relatively easy and Damant confidently felt that the whole operation would only take a couple of weeks.

Shortly afterwards, however, the capricious nature of marine salvage once again changed everything. Damant later noted:

In quiet weather all the operations up to this, might have been done in a couple of days; but we were struggling against a succession of mid-winter gales with snow squalls, and could only hang on to the moorings for short intervals, so a fortnight had elapsed. Yet the back of the job seemed to be broken, and with ordinary luck a few weeks more should have seen the end of it; as a matter of fact it was going to last seven years.

Before the storm abated there were already signs that something was wrong. Smashed chairs, tables, wooden panelling and everything else that could float were drifting towards the nearby Irish coastline. For Damant and his salvage team this was not a good sign.

All the wreckage was coming from inside the *Laurentic*, meaning a massive hull breach must have occurred. Once the storm subsided the divers descended to the starboard shell door, but it was no longer there. The storm had ripped the liner in half, her decks collapsing into one another all along the fracture line. It was like being on a different ship. The shell door, which had been at 62ft before the gale, was now on the seabed. Getting in through the entry port the men could only penetrate a few feet along the passage as the deckhead, or roof, had closed down to within 18in of the deck, the narrow space between being jammed solid with crumpled steel, bulkheads and wreckage. This was a severe setback. But Damant knew that a passage had to be forced through, somehow. The only way to reach the baggage room was to carefully blast a path as they went, shoring up the collapsing corridor like a mineshaft. Although time-consuming the baggage room was eventually reached, but when the door was opened there was nothing but a gaping hole where the room used to be. The forty or so tons of gold had scattered like seeds in the wind as they filtered throughout the twisted and crumpled wreckage.

All Damant could do was to cut down vertically through the *Laurentic*'s remains, roughly at the place where the gold was reckoned to be. This was a slow job, removing the wreckage 'plate by plate and beam by beam till the gold was exposed'. Quite often jagged pieces of metal weighing five tons or more had to be hoisted up 120ft by the salvage ship's derricks, often swaying violently because either the ship was rolling or the wave action while in ascent played against the solid mass being lifted. Altogether more than 2,000 tons of steel had to be removed by the time salvage operations ceased. The danger did not only come from the wreck.

Having helped to lay down the guiding rules on decompression, Damant, more than any other diver worldwide, knew how far he could push the boundaries. This would be unthinkable under today's strict health and safety culture, but in 1917 recovering the gold was a government, and so a Salvage Section, priority. He insisted early on in the operation:

> Safety had to be subordinated to speed, and the official decompression periods were deliberately shortened till the minor symptoms of compressed air illness began to appear among the men. With experience we learned to expect symptoms in cases where a man got foul and had to struggle to clear himself, or was doing exceptionally well in digging out gold, or was experiencing trivial mishaps under water (such as dropping a tool and being unable to find it) which might prevent him from carrying out his allotted task and so injure his proper pride.

Damant knew that the length of time a man was on the bottom was almost equal to the amount of time he had to stage decompress, meaning coming back up his shot rope to set depths for set times until all the nitrogen was out of his blood. With speed ever the main concern, he decided that shorter dives would mean quicker decompression times and thus his men would be back in the water faster. According to Damant, a diver at 115ft for ninety minutes had to work more slowly and required a decompression time of eighty-seven minutes with some being cut to as low as forty. But if a thirty-minute dive was adopted, the decompression times could be substantially reduced, thus allowing the diver to return to the job much quicker and work 'at top speed, as if they were boxing, or running a race'.

Although a dive now took only thirty minutes a great deal had to be achieved before the diver came back to the surface. Four minutes before a duty diver was ordered back up, his relief dropped down the shot line, taking about a minute to reach the bottom. His first job was to haul down about 30ft of air pipe so he could move around freely. He then lashed the pipe and, by telephone in his helmet, ordered the pipe to be pulled taut so it would not get caught on any jagged wreckage. A large hopper was placed near the shot rope to pile in the debris and a bucket nearby to place the gold ingots. The relief diver helped his partner to manhandle a large sack of sand and other small debris he had dug out up into the hopper before beginning his own work. He blasted away most of the compacted seabed with a high-pressure water hose that ended with a 2ft metal pipe for burrowing deep into the sand. A pressure of only $70in^2$ could be used because rocks and sharp pieces of debris would get caught in the vortex and pummelled into the divers' bare hands, or sound like an echoing jack-hammer as pieces chinked off their helmets.

The pressure hose was stopped and the diver bagged the loose debris while feeling for the gold about ten minutes after he began. This became quite an art, sometimes taking as long as six months to perfect, whereby a diver could tell gold from steel, copper or any other smooth-faced debris by touch alone. Groping through the sharp sand took its toll. Damant recalled:

> The fingernails used to get worn down to a strip barely ¼in wide, and the outer layers of skin on the extremity of each finger would be rubbed away so as to leave a raw surface about an 1in across on each finger. The pain of this condition was specially bad at night after a day's work was over, and the less injured skin, which had been soaked in salt water all day began to dry and shrink.

One can barely imagine the pain of going back down the following day and forcing bare, blood-raw fingers back into the freezing, razor-sharp sand until another day's work was done.

Thirteen minutes after the hose was stopped the diver had five minutes to place any gold bars into a bucket, untie his air pipe and prepare the sack of debris for his relief to help tip into the hopper. Once his relief arrived the duty diver started his staged decompression being five minutes at 30ft below the surface, ten minutes at 20ft and finally fifteen minutes at 10ft from the top. Quite often the diver did vigorous exercises to help dissipate the nitrogen from his blood. Out of 5,000 dives, or 'dips' as they were more commonly called, there were only thirty minor cases of the bends reported.

Damant ceased salvage operations as the weather deteriorated towards the end of 1917. Altogether his team had raised 542 gold ingots, weighing a little more than five metric tons. Although plans were made to continue work during the spring and summer of 1918, Young cancelled all further efforts, as the divers and salvage plant were needed for vital and highly confidential work in the Dover Straits. The Admiralty wanted to know as much about the different U-boat types as possible – their armament, operational distances and structural design – so any chance to get inside one was not be missed. The *Laurentic* divers, having already gained U-boat salvage experience, were ideally placed for this very dangerous work. Young was also becoming concerned about all the salvage plant tied up on the

Laurentic job and was keen to release it for other more pressing ship recoveries.

Detailed information about this side of the Salvage Section's work is still largely unknown. Damant did write a memo to the Director of Naval Intelligence, William Hall, telling the DNI quite plainly what the divers went through in the line of duty.

> Under circumstances which are known to you, these men were diving almost daily in the active minefields between Dover and Gris Nez. It was well known to them that the explosion of a mine within a mile of the operations would be fatal to the diver. No steps could be taken to avoid the mines; the men had to dive right amongst them and in fact sighted them under water at a distance of 10ft or less on more than one occasion. They also entered and placed charges within damaged enemy submarines having active mines and torpedoes in the tubes.

On several occasions exploding depth charges severely shook some divers during attacks on enemy submarines a short distance away. On one occasion the shock was so great a hatch slammed shut, trapping a diver who was working inside a sunken U-boat. He had great difficulty forcing the heavy steel hatch back up again and escaping from a very unpleasant death. Often this work was carried out among the corpses of the drowned U-boat crew. Damant insisted to his superior that, 'Nothing but the extreme urgency of the work which was impressed on me by yourself, the last Director of Naval Intelligence and Admiral Keyes at Dover would have justified me in asking men to take such risks. They never hesitated to go down and [never] has a man left the bottom without orders during a depth charge attack.' Five of the divers were decorated for this work, including two who received the DCM.

Once the U-boat work was finished salvage operations on the *Laurentic* were due to continue during the spring and summer of 1919, but Young wanted all operations cancelled permanently. He was adamant that the Salvage Section was now closed, except for work on the Belgian cost, and insisted that any further recovery should be handed over to the owners of the bullion, the Bank of England, who could employ a commercial firm to finish the job. But, like the U-boat operations, the *Laurentic*'s cargo salvage was confidential. In a memo dated 21 June 1919, the government's position was made quite clear: 'The Treasury are anxious that the fact that this gold has been lost should not become public property, at any rate for some time to come.'

87

A few weeks earlier, while Young was clearing Ostend, he showed a complete change of mind and ordered Damant to return to Lough Swilly and continue raising the gold.

Throughout 1919 a respectable 315 ingots were recovered, but finding the gold was becoming harder. Upon returning for the 1920 season the whole year was spent just clearing debris, with only seven ingots recovered. Again the salvage operation came under threat of closure. The seven ingots were worth about £9,000 at 1920 prices, and the cost of running the salvage vessel, *Racer*, with her 58-man crew was more than £12,000 for the whole season. The following year was also largely taken up with clearing debris and only forty-three ingots were found. Large centrifugal pumps and dredging grabs were tried, but these failed because there was simply not enough space for them in which to work. The only way was to remove the seabed by hand, a grim task, often made worse by days of work being undone as the hole was filled up again in a few hours by another storm.

The Salvage Section even considered using an experimental gold detector. Two ideas were put forward: an 'induction balance' method, that might detect gold without actual contact; and another method by which a probe thrust into the debris should give an electric induction on making contact with an ingot. There is no record if they were ever used, or even worked.

Getting rid of the sand was a constant battle that the men were losing, so to boost their enthusiasm Damant set up a competition to see who could move the most in one day. Each diver's load was carefully measured and weighed. Years after operations ceased, Damant remembered fondly how the weights of sand per man steadily increased. 'As brains came to the aid of muscle and new dodges for saving twenty seconds here, and getting an extra 3lb or 4lb there with some queer-shaped scoop made by the blacksmith came into action.' Much more gold was found, sometimes with divers burrowing in underneath the wreckage head first to reach a bar.

In 1922 the Salvage Section raised 895 ingots and the Admiralty was concerned that the Irish Republican Army might steal the gold for their own rearmament. After the Anglo-Irish Treaty was signed on 6 December 1921 the two-year Irish War of Independence was due to come to an official end, but factions within the IRA were divided as to whether the Treaty was right for Ireland. The disagreement soon escalated into a bitter nine-month dispute that split the IRA into pro-Treaty, with about 8,000 fighters, and anti-Treaty, with about 15,000 men, who were not all armed. Meanwhile the *Laurentic*'s gold was stored aboard the *Racer*, waiting to be signed over to an armed escort for the long journey to the Bank of Ireland in Belfast and on to the Bank of England. In May 1922, fearing an armed raid, the Admiralty stated that all gold aboard the *Racer* was to be transferred to the W Class escort destroyer HMS *Warwick* 'as frequently as possible', but adding, 'Gold on board *Racer* is to be so disposed that in event of raid by an armed vessel manned by Irish Republicans or others it can be tipped overboard and recovered later.' No such raid took place and all of the gold recovered was returned safely to the Bank of England.

In 1923 a staggering 1,255 ingots were recovered, tapering off to 129 in 1924. The remaining twenty-five bars were proving very hard to locate and with costs mounting the Admiralty decided that it was becoming uneconomical to find them. Altogether 3,186 out of 3,211 ingots were salvaged at a cost of 3 per cent of their total value – the loss of the remaining twenty-five ingots being a small price to pay for such a successful recovery. The *Racer*'s company were given one eighth of 1 per cent in salvage reward, a little more than £6,000. This sum divided between the crew averaged about £100 each, which in the early 1920s equated to a bonus of a little more than £3,000. In December 1924 King George V approved the awards of nine OBEs to the *Racer*'s crew and divers for 'meritorious services'.

Further attempts were made to salvage the remaining twenty-five ingots in the mid 1980s. The attempt failed and the ¾ ton of gold – valued at more than £2 million today – is still scattered among the *Laurentic*'s rusting remains across the entrance to Lough Swilly.

Chapter 10

More War, More Salvage

Ten years after the last gold ingot left the bed of Lough Swilly, Adolph Hitler's Nazi Party came to power and for the next five years Europe edged slowly towards another major conflict. Although war with Germany looked likely, a need for salvage on a mass scale was not considered until just months before hostilities began. At 10.30 am on Tuesday, 29 July 1938, a meeting was held at the Admiralty in Whitehall. Present were nineteen men, representing all interested parties, including Lloyd's, the Board of Trade, the Ministry of Transport and several Admiralty departments. This time, unlike its predecessor, the new salvage organization's primary function was to recover merchant shipping, not Royal Navy vessels as before.

The first stage was to conduct another salvage plant census, both within the Royal Navy and from commercial enterprise. Seven months later the salvage census was finished and, for the Admiralty at least, the position was much worse than when Captain Young compiled his damning report in 1914. Throughout the whole of the United Kingdom the Admiralty possessed just four salvage pumps as their – once first-rate – salvage capability, and these were kept for use aboard warships, should the need ever arise. However, the situation in the private sector looked much healthier and, although the seven biggest firms were finding commercial survival hard, they did offer the potential of an instant first-rate salvage organization. For the Admiralty's plan to succeed, it was vital that agreement should be reached on how the firms were to be employed. One idea was to license each operator to the Admiralty, but many problems were foreseen.

Some firms, it was thought, might not have the incentive to maintain their plant to a high enough standard, and certainly no desire to build up their stock. The licence method might also work against the salvage firms. If they had to stop work halfway through a job and, at the behest of the Admiralty attend a more urgent case, the salvage firm

90

would suffer financial and professional difficulties by uprooting its entire operation. A secret Whitehall Minute dated only '1939' stated:

> It is essential for the Admiralty to exercise control over all salvage operations in wartime. If private firms are left to themselves, they will naturally select work which is likely to prove more remunerative, and unlucrative work, although it may be of national importance, such as port clearance, would be liable to suffer. To enable the Admiralty to control the operations, i.e. (a) order any particular salvage operation without necessarily having regard to gain, and (b) stop work on a casualty if more important work has to be done, it will be necessary to control the salvage firms and associations and expand the existing resources, all of which are in private hands.

But how could these civilian operators be left to do such vital and little understood work while conforming to care and control from Whitehall? The only option available was to enter into agreements with seven companies and slowly integrate more plant and ships for them to manage, maintain and operate on the Admiralty's behalf. In the first instance the British coast was divided into seven areas. The first, and biggest, area was from Cape Wrath, on Scotland's extreme north-west tip, to Land's End. This was to be covered by the Liverpool & Glasgow Salvage Association. Metal Industries of Scapa Flow operated from Cape Wrath to Troup Head down the east coast. Leith Towage and Salvage covered from Troup Head to Holy Island, while Thomas Round and Sons covered from Holy Island to Flamborough Head. The Port of London Authority (or PLA) and Dover Harbour Board covered the coast around to Beachy Head, from where Risdon Beazley covered the remaining coastline around to Land's End. To strengthen further any particular area, equipment and manpower was to be transferable between each firm as necessary.

The Admiralty in turn would pay a fixed fee for services rendered, and the occasional bonus, the rest of the salvage awards feeding back to the Admiralty to run the new salvage department, and prevent the private firms from war profiteering. In theory it was a sound and simple plan; in practice the Admiralty's instant salvage department idea was fraught with internal and external problems that dogged the new organization for the first three years of the war. While the necessary arrangements to sign up the private firms were still taking place, and with hostilities looking imminent, a working salvage department was rushed into operation only two days before war was declared. The new venture, now called the Admiralty Salvage Department, was formally opened on 23 November 1939 in Room 45, West Block at the Admiralty's head office in Whitehall, with its own telephone extension for all urgent communications. Unlike during the First World War hierarchy, the Department was no longer under the control of the Director of Naval Equipment. Commodore, later Admiral, A.R. Dewar was made Director of Salvage. Below Dewar was Head of Salvage, C.M. Dodwell. Later on Deputy Head of Salvage, John R. Polland, was added to the command structure and would ultimately play a key role in the success of D-Day.

While the Salvage Department pressed ahead, the Admiralty was faced with its first major external problem. The Merchant Shipping (Salvage) Act 1916 only granted the Admiralty awards where salvage services were rendered by any ship belonging to the Admiralty that was purpose-built for salvage work. There was no mention of ships acting for the Admiralty under agreement. So, although the Admiralty were financially supporting and controlling the seven firms at public expense, all salvage awards were claimable both by the persons actually rendering the service, and ultimately by owners of the ships and plant.

The law would again have to be modified as any awards generated at public expense were by definition for public spending and not commercial enterprise. On 7 March 1940 a Bill was published for the Admiralty to gain full salvage rights. The Merchant Shipping (Salvage) Bill stated: 'Any person authorized by His Majesty shall be entitled to claim salvage on His behalf for those services, and shall have the same rights and remedies as if the services had not been rendered on behalf of His Majesty.' Should the new Bill be passed as drafted, the Admiralty would have a total state monopoly on both salvage and awards. But such all-covering power did not sit well with some interested parties.

In 1916, changing the law was a relatively easy step, but in 1939 the process was a little more complex. After the modified Section 557 was ratified, Royal Navy warships still managed to claim salvage awards, although the law strictly forbade such a practice. The Admiralty admitted: 'This disability, however, was by the advice of the Law Officers of the Crown, to a certain extent circumvented by voluntary agreements made with the representatives of the salved property.' Between 1934 and 1938 alone Royal Navy warships salvaged seventeen vessels amounting to more than 50,000 tons. All contracts were signed on the D 46 form and not one purpose-built salvage craft, as described in Section 557, was present.

In 1935 the 9,000-ton tanker, SS *Valverda*, was en route from Curacao to England, carrying petrol. A few days into her voyage an engine-room fire broke out. The heavy cruiser, HMS *Frobisher*, intercepted her SOS and reached the vessel the following day. She put a line aboard and with the help of the cruiser, HMS *Guardian*, the *Valverda* was towed 900 miles to Bermuda and saved. Quite often in critical situations a salvage operation went ahead with the written agreement being signed at a later date. In this case the D 46 was signed in London with her owners and the Royal Navy agreeing to the salvage several days after the *Valverda*'s master had accepted the tow. The Admiralty was eventually awarded £11,000 for their part, which today equates to £5.9 million. Two years later the House of Lords overruled the award and considered it illegal for Royal Navy vessels to work around Section 557 to win a salvage contract. Lord Justice Wright declared that the practice 'was contrary to public policy by permitting voluntary contracting out of the disabilities imposed on the Crown by the 1916 Act'. Had the *Valverda* case not come to light it was possible that the common law practice could have gone on, but with the loophole now closed, more precise legislation had to be passed, although such a move was unpopular outside of the Admiralty.

The Chamber of Shipping, which operated most of the ships then in existence, was also strongly opposed to the new Bill. General Manager H.M. Cleminson wrote a rather long-winded letter to the Admiralty expressing fully the Chamber's strong feelings that the proposed change would not, under any circumstances, be in the public interest. To prove their case, the Chamber went fully into every possible permutation of what might happen as a result of such far-reaching power. This boiled down to fourteen points as to why the Admiralty must never gain full salvage rights. But the Admiralty, at least on paper, countered every argument.

The Chamber was adamant that salvage award was in place to attract commercial organizations and was not the sole domain of one of His Majesty's warships which 'subject to the performance of her military duties she owes a duty to go to the aid of merchant shipping in distress and there is no case for compensating warships for the interruption of commercial operations'. The Admiralty commented that, indeed, the principal of awards to the Crown was agreed in the

Merchant Shipping (Salvage) Act back in 1916. The present proposal, they claimed, rather flippantly, 'merely fills in the gaps'.

More importantly, Cleminson's committee felt that the situation might well arise when a nearby merchant ship was much more able and willing to assist a vessel in distress than a Royal Naval vessel some distance away. And under the proposed new law, only the Royal Navy could give assistance, albeit possibly too late. The Admiralty did not agree. A rather cutting reply stated: 'In war, salvage is a state monopoly, and monopoly makes salvage expensive. [Cleminson's] argument is a contradiction. The best salvage skill in this country is in our service, so shipowners receive benefit, not damage, from this.' With so many ships needing recovery, and no control over the private firms, the Admiralty was justified in seeking awards for vessels conducting salvage work under their order. And more importantly it was 'most desirable that the Department should be able to claim some return on their expenditure, on the same basis as applies, by age-long custom of the sea, to private salvors. In short, the effect of the attached Bill is to remove the statutory disability in full.'

Now the shipowners raised their concerns. One of the reasons Royal Navy vessels had been denied salvage rights under the 1894 Merchant Shipping Act was not out of some patriotic duty to their country's merchant fleet, but because some naval officers had been prone literally to hijacking merchant ships for financial gain at least until the mid nineteenth century. The Parliamentary Council member, Sir John Stainton KBE, stated, 'Sections 558 to 563 were apparently enacted in 1853 in view of complaints by shipowners about the harsh and arbitrary conduct of certain naval officers who had been in the habit of seizing a ship which they alleged they had salved, and refusing to give up possession till they had been paid salvage.'

The Chamber of Shipping felt that a fair deal on salvage awards was not possible as the Admiralty would have 100 per cent control of all salvage from all their vessels, and it could be that salvage services were once again pressed on a merchant vessel against the master's or the company's will. The Admiralty said that claims settled with them were much more favourable than with private commercial firms, adding that of the offers of help which had been refused, in practically every case the subsequent result of legal proceedings had been more favourable to the Admiralty rather than the aggrieved shipowner. The Admiralty was sure that common sense would prevail, as a ship in distress was highly unlikely to refuse help, to save lives as well as the ship. If so, the position in law was quite clear: a salvage award on behalf of the Admiralty could only be sought provided that the Court was satisfied that the master, acting in his right mind, would not have refused such help in the first place.

Throughout all the correspondence and bickering, merchant ships were still being lost around the British coast. An Italian vessel went ashore on the Goodwin Sands, a 10-mile sandbank 6 miles east of Deal, Kent. The Admiralty agreed to undertake her salvage. She was refloated, beached at Deal and pumped out before being towed round to London for repair. The salvage officer ordered two tugs for the tow. Once the Italian ship was delivered, the tugs' owner promptly arrested the ship and demanded bail of £5,000 (more than £200,000 today) on the grounds that towing a damaged ship amounted to salvage services. 'This has put the Admiralty in a difficult position vis-à-vis the Italians,' said Salvage Director Commodore Dewar, 'who say that the Admiralty having undertaken the salvage, they ought only to have them to deal with. It is with a view to strengthening the Admiralty's position in such a case that I have proposed my Defence Regulation.'

The Emergency Powers (Defence) Act 1939 was debated, passed and achieved Royal Assent in less than eight hours, nine days before war was declared. It gave much more latitude in asserting new regulations for the greater good of the country in time of war. A directive put into force under this Act was called a Defence Regulation and, subject to the Privy Council, and thus the approval of King George VI, it could come into force automatically without Parliamentary debate.

Dewar wanted to enforce his Defence Regulation in advance of the new salvage Act coming into effect as the legal process was moving too slowly, and, if more ships were to be saved quickly, he had to act. Dewar stated, 'It is not desired to have these special powers except in the war, when the overriding importance of keeping available as much mercantile tonnage as possible, and of preventing obstruction to ports and harbours justifies the Admiralty in disregarding the wishes of owners and the rights of other volunteer salvors.' In the spring of 1940 Dewar got his way and the Admiralty was granted the power they wanted ahead of any Parliamentary debate on the new law. Regulation 43A said that the Admiralty, or any person authorized by them, could now provide salvage services in respect of any vessels, cargo or property. The Regulation added rather strongly:

Any person acting on behalf of His Majesty may take such steps and use such force as may appear to that person to be reasonably necessary for securing compliance with any direction given under this Regulation or, where an offence against the Regulation has been committed by reason of failure to comply with any such direction, for enabling proceedings in respect of the offence to be effectually taken.

However, overcoming the British legal system still proved to be rather easier than gaining the full co-operation of the commercial salvage companies.

The Admiralty had to alter many of the contracts to suit each company's demands, meaning that some were able to negotiate better deals than others. The Port of London Authority, for instance, refused to agree to no salvage award and managed to cut a deal whereby the firm split awards with the Admiralty. No other salvage firm managed this. Southampton-based Risdon Beazely were paid £20,000 for the services of three salvage officers and two vessels. The Liverpool & Glasgow Salvage Association had also signed the same agreement. Metal Industries were the only firm who flatly refused to sign. Their reluctance became so acute that it finally constituted an 'interference with the war effort'. But this was not without justification.

Each agreement specified that key salvage personnel were to be seconded to the Admiralty and, although being given Royal Naval Reserve commissions, they were formally known as Civil Salvage Officers. They were to be paid between £750 and £1,500 per annum, depending on experience, at a time when the average yearly wage for a shore-based engineer was about £360. The Admiralty wanted three men from Metal Industries to sign the agreement: 50-year-old Thomas McKenzie, 29-year-old Harry Murray Taylor and 37-year-old James Robertson. They had all learnt the salvage business working for Cox & Danks raising the scuttled German fleet in Scapa Flow prior to continuing their work for Metal Industries, and were all highly skilled men.

On 23 December 1941, the Admiralty wrote to McKenzie, Murray Taylor and Robertson informing them that Metal Industries had sanctioned their appointments to the Salvage Department. Through some miscommunication Metal Industries' approval had never been sought, or at least the three men had no knowledge until they opened the official envelopes and fully digested their contents. All three were outraged at their alleged sudden transfer to government control without any discussion, and they made their grievances known, both to their employers and to the Admiralty. After what must have been a very troubled Christmas, McKenzie wrote to the Admiralty saying: 'My directors assure me that they have never at any time suggested to my Lords Commissioners of the Admiralty that the terms offered in your letter would be accepted, and I have on a number of occasions informed the Director of Salvage personally that I would not accept the terms suggested.'

Murray Taylor was even more cutting when he wrote quite bluntly: 'I am surprised to learn that the Lords Commissioners of the Admiralty understand that I will become a Civil Salvage Officer under the terms and conditions laid down in your communications and would be pleased to be informed upon what information this statement is based.' Some of the problems were minor, like there being no provision for work outside the scope of the Salvage Department (such as surveys, preparing and sinking blockships) or a salary advance. But other non-existent provisions cut right to the core of the men's health and financial well-being.

Their once-only pay offer fell well below what they were earning. The figure was supposed to be based on the few years' previous earnings and £1,500 for a Chief Salvage Officer was not enough, at least for McKenzie. Metal Industries had already informed the Admiralty that in 1937, 1938 and 1939 he had earned £6,540, £5,040 and £5,040 respectively. In today's terms his pay for those three years amounted to approximately £500,000. Most of this money comprised bonuses for raising battleships in Scapa Flow after he had decided to take a lower salary and base most of his income on bonuses, which were still legitimate earnings under the Admiralty specification. But the Admiralty flatly refused to pay such a high amount and the problem still had not been solved by the summer of 1942. A conference was held between Metal Industries' personnel and Admiralty staff from the Salvage Department. When pressed to increase the men's salaries, Head of Salvage, C.M. Dodwell, said, 'We understand that the Company [Metal Industries] wanted to pay Mr McKenzie so much, but the Admiralty cannot pay him a Prime Minister's salary.'

A way of getting over the difficulty was to pay Metal Industries a lump sum, the amount agreed being £7,000, or a little more than £200,000 today. Still, it was a great deal less than Risdon Beazley had negotiated for roughly the same service. The £7,000 was to cover all wages and any bonuses the firm wished to pay its officers who were, under the new agreement, still employed by Metal Industries, but only on loan to the Admiralty. Robertson and Murray Taylor received £900 per annum and McKenzie settled for £4,500 – by comparison, Prime Minister Winston Churchill was drawing a fraction of the full £10,000 per annum he was entitled to. The next and last stumbling block was beyond everyone's control, and buried deep in legislation enacted long before civilian salvage officers were ever deemed of vital importance in a new global conflict.

All serving officers and men were entitled to insurance cover while working for the war effort, both for themselves and their dependants. The Treasury had explored a special provision for civilian staff members such as workers engaged in ships' trials and repairs, because they were running the same risk as those in the armed services. But the Treasury was unwilling to agree that such alteration to the law should be made. It was impracticable to legislate for degrees of risk to which the civilian population might be subjected both on land and at sea. Unions representing shipbuilding yard workers had already tried to claim special cover for their members who had to go out into the open sea for trials, but the Employers' Federation refused the request. Similarly the Admiralty refused to allow its contractors special cover, particularly those engaged in salvage work.

The Employers' Federation felt that no special arrangements could be made with Admiralty personnel without raising the whole question of those who, in the course of their duties, were required to go afloat for varying periods of time. McKenzie, Robertson and Murray Taylor refused to give in to Admiralty pressure to sign without such an agreement. Murray Taylor summed up the feelings of all three men when he wrote to the Admiralty in the summer of 1942:

> I would be failing in my duty towards my dependents if I signed an Agreement which did not make adequate provision for them in the event of my death or disablement. I would prefer therefore, that a clause be inserted in the Agreement to the effect that I will be eligible for compensation in respect of death or disablement in the course of my duties at a rate compatible with my responsibilities.

He had every right to be concerned. Two salvage vessels had already been mined and surface aircraft had sunk another. One lighter and a third ship had been lost through accident, and later in the war a salvage ship called the *Boston Salvor* took a direct hit from a V1 rocket in March 1945 while clearing Antwerp harbour.

A Bill would have to go before Parliament to allow Salvage personnel the right to receive full compensation. The Bill was passed in August 1942 and included a payout of £5,000 for death or serious injury. Two months later Metal Industries finally signed the Agreement. After nearly three years the Admiralty Salvage Department had grown in size and was now fully functional in every way. Even Winston Churchill had taken a keen personal interest in salvage – from 1940 onwards he had asked for regular reports on its progress. One report he received in January 1941 showed that, although the Department was in chaos, their results were startling. After reading the report he wrote to the Import Executive:

> I learn that the salvage organization has recently made as great contribution to the maintenance of our shipping capacity as new construction, about 370,000 gross tons having been salved, as against 340,000 tons built, while the number of ships being dealt with by the salvage organization has increased very rapidly, from ten in August to about thirty now.
>
> They are to be congratulated on this, and I feel sure that if anything can be done to assist in the expansion of their equipment and finding of suitable officers, your Executive will see that such measures are taken.

It is doubtful he ever knew that at least one salvage officer was taking home more money each month, raising ships, than he was for leading the country in time of war. Now with all four agreements signed, all the necessary legislation in place and friends in the highest of places, the Admiralty Salvage Department began to play out its now forgotten, yet vital role, in the Allies winning the Second World War.

Chapter 11

'The Happy Time'

Germany's second Battle of the Atlantic began barely twelve hours after the Second World War was declared, when Oberleutnant Fritz-Julius Lemp, aboard *U-30*, torpedoed and sank the 13,500-ton Cunard liner SS *Athenia* bound for Montreal, with 1,103 civilians aboard. More than 110 passengers and crew were killed. Before the end of 1939 another 220 British and Allied merchant ships were sunk. Many of these attacks were made by U-boats operating as single units, often after making the hazardous journey from German submarine bases, such as Wilhelmshaven, Hamburg and Kiel. The following year, three events occurred that rapidly accelerated the *U-bootswaffe*'s kill rates and threatened Britain's ability to stay at war for the second time in twenty-one years.

While Winston Churchill was being summoned to Buckingham Palace to form a new government on 10 May 1940, more than 4,000,000 heavily armed German and Italian troops, split into three groups, were swarming into France along her eastern border. In the centre, under the command of General Wilhelm von Leeb, Major General Erwin Rommel punched the 7th Panzer Division through the Ardennes Forest, skirting the Maginot Line, and onwards into France. Like a single, efficient killing machine, thousands of tanks and men poured through France's first and last real line of defence, reaching Avesnes, about 170km north-west of Paris, five days later. Missing the capital, Rommel's men ran though France faster and further than any army in history, putting his entire division out of radio range in a matter of days.

Pushing on via Abbeville, Rouen and Dieppe he finally reached Cherbourg on France's north-west tip on 19 June. Six days later, on 25 June, Paris and thus most of France fell. Taking France opened up a whole new Atlantic coastline from which to launch Germany's U-boat assaults on British and Allied merchant shipping – from Lorient,

St Nazaire and Brest. These renewed attacks commenced when the *U-30* entered Lorient on 7 July, ten months after sinking the *Athenia*.

It was now that Admiral Dönitz developed the 'wolf pack' attack method. As the name implies, U-boats would stay within range of each other and hunt in groups for the greater good of the pack rather than the individual. He knew through experience during the last few months of 1918 that U-boats attacking en masse could inflict far greater damage than single submarines, especially when faced with large convoys of slow-moving vessels. The technique was simple. U-boats usually steamed on the surface, at the limit of visibility, astern of the convoy at the same speed and course. As night fell the submarine sped past the convoy on the surface to gain an attack advantage. Travelling on the surface was not as dangerous as it might seem. The ASDIC (Anti-submarine Detection Investigation Committee) sonar systems aboard the convoys' escort protection vessels were only designed to detect U-boats while they were submerged. All too often the U-boat crews knew they were being hunted; one U-Boat commander described the ASDIC signal as resembling fingers running over a comb, or peas rattling in a tin as it bounced off his vessel. The sleek U-boat design meant that very little of their bulk was above sea level and thus the submarine was virtually invisible over a relatively short distance while surfaced, an image made all the more deceptive in poor or no light conditions.

With increasing numbers of U-boats entering the Atlantic, there was a much greater chance of one spotting a convoy and reporting its course, speed and size to others in the area. Once alerted they gathered like wolves around their prey and simply waited for the most opportune moment to attack. Although they all acted independently once on site, quite often the effect was instant. Seeing such violent destruction often caused the convoy to scatter like startled deer, the wolves then moved in for the kill and picked off the stragglers at will. This new tactic was very successful and led to a dramatic increase in merchant shipping losses. In 1940 the figure rose to 1,059 merchant ships lost, 1,299 in 1941, peaking at 1,664 the following year. Most of the losses were in the North Atlantic.

Winston Churchill had every reason to be concerned when he said that the U-boat campaign was the only thing that really frightened him. What April 1917 was to the first Battle of the Atlantic, so May 1942 was to the second one. More than 600,000 tons of merchant shipping were lost to U-boat action alone. The German submarines were far superior in number and design than anything Britain could offer – for a while the *U-bootswaffe* owned the Atlantic and quite rightly, at least in the enemy's eyes, this really was *'Die Glückliche Zeit'* or 'The Happy Time'.

The pressure on the Salvage Department to save as many stricken ships as possible, before they succumbed to damage, bad weather or renewed enemy attack, increased as losses grew. Not all attacks were due to U-boat action. Chief Salvage Officer Thomas McKenzie wrote:

> Soon after the outbreak of war, shipping casualties due to enemy action commenced and they continued to increase and multiply. Within a few weeks ships were being torpedoed, bombed and mined in all areas around the coast. Salvage craft, lifting craft, tugs, lighters and other vessels suitable or capable of being adapted for use on salvage work were requisitioned and put into commission with the least possible delay.

The stress on the Salvage Department's ships and plant was equal to that of its personnel. McKenzie continued:

> Shortages of skilled salvage officers was, however, always acute and the more experienced officers had a very strenuous time racing from one major casualty to another by land, sea or air over a very wide area. It was no uncommon thing for a chief salvage officer to have a dozen or more major operations on his hands at one time, or for an agent to have thirty or more casualties on his hands at any one time, and more coming in daily.

McKenzie was so concerned about the lack of equipment that he wrote a candid letter to the Director of Salvage, Admiral Dewar. Metal Industries' situation was made even worse when the powerful 1,164-ton Rescue Tug *Salvage King* became a total loss after she ran aground off Duncansby Head, Scotland on 12 September 1940, further inhibiting their ability to save ships. He told Dewar:

> I do hope you will let us have something to replace *Salvage King* before the next 'Blitz' starts in the early spring. We are badly off for Rescue Tugs here now, so please use your influence in this direction. Their Lordships must realize that if we are to carry out our work successfully we must have the ships and plant to do it with, just the same as the other Services. Salvage ships in wartime

are of prime importance, and those under your command have already saved their cost many times over.

Although limited resources and personnel were still endemic throughout the Salvage Department, between September 1939 and December 1940 Metal Industries alone salvaged more than seventy ships, including both Royal Navy and merchant vessels. It is a testament to the hard work and ingenuity employed by just one of the private salvage firms at a time when they were still undergoing a somewhat tense transformation to Admiralty control.

One of their first operations was not to save a ship or its cargo, but the crew. On 14 October 1939, *U-47* stole into Scapa Flow and sent four torpedoes into the 29,000-ton, ageing, Revenge Class battleship HMS *Royal Oak*. More than 1,000 men were asleep below decks when she capsized and sank in total darkness within fifteen minutes. Once the alarm was raised Metal Industries' own tug, *Imperious*, pulled ninety-three survivors out of the freezing, oily water as well as many bodies. At first the Royal Navy believed that sabotage was the cause, until the following day, when one of McKenzie's salvage divers recovered parts of an electrically driven torpedo.

By the following summer many ships needed assistance. In June 1940, the fully laden 10,517-ton motor tanker, *Danmark*, was at anchor in Inganess Bay, 2 miles east of Kirkwall, Orkney's capital. She was carrying 8,600 tons of refined petrol and 6,000 tons of kerosene, when *U-23* torpedoed her. The explosion was so violent that the *Danmark* broke her back, her shattered amidships section resting on the seabed while her bow and stern remained afloat in a lake of petrol stretching out for half a mile around the wreck. McKenzie's salvage men were aboard four hours later, but the dense fumes, and the possibility of one final massive fireball, drove them away until the following day when most of the leaked petrol had evaporated or dispersed. Salvage divers descended 200ft to assess the damage and not surprisingly they had no good news to report. The ship was a total loss, but her cargo was still of tremendous value to the war effort.

The remaining petrol had nearly all leaked from the breached tanks, but the kerosene tanks were still intact. McKenzie requested a tanker to recover the kerosene, but none were available. As the hours passed the stress on the bow and stern sections was becoming too great and ever so slowly the *Danmark*'s after end, with the remainder of the petrol still aboard, sank while her bow bobbed precariously on

103

the surface. Refusing to give up, McKenzie rigged salvage pumps inside the *Danmark*'s bow section and pumped the kerosene into the Metal Industries' salvage vessel *Bertha* until a tanker could be found. Altogether more than 4,000 tons of kerosene were successfully salvaged before this section also went to the bottom.

The fate of the 11,500-ton cargo ship *Beacon Grange* illustrates the monetary return for salvage. She caught fire after *U-552* torpedoed her in Moray Firth near Inverness. The two vessels, *Salvage King* and the 840-ton Brigand Class Rescue Tug HMS *Brigand*, managed to get the fire partially under control before towing her into Kirkwall. Shortly afterwards the fire broke out once again and burned furiously for two days after she was run ashore away from the main town. The *Bertha* and the *Salvage King* eventually put out the fire. McKenzie wrote: '*Beacon Grange* is only two years old, cost £750,000 to build and had a most valuable general cargo worth about £450,000. The total damage to the ship and cargo will probably not exceed £150,000, representing a saving of over £1m. The vessel would undoubtedly have been completely burned out and become a total loss [but] for the assistance rendered by *Salvage King* and *Bertha*.'

Sometimes a ship was severely mauled from above as well as below the sea, and still a salvage team went to the rescue. On 11 September 1940, the 6,000-ton MV *Alexia* was in Convoy OB 191 when *U-99* torpedoed her in the Moray Firth. With six oil tanks, her engine room and all after compartments flooded, the U-boat surfaced to shell and machine-gun the *Alexia* before giving her up for lost. The *Brigand* managed to tow her to Kirkwall, by which time her stern was nearly under water when the *Bertha* reached her. McKenzie's men started pumping out her flooded compartments and managed to keep the water down for four days while salvage divers patched the bomb damage before the compartments were pumped dry. Then, 'Steering gear, auxiliary pumps, degaussing etc., were put in working order and the ship made ready for towing to repair port.' The *Alexia* was eventually converted into a MAC (Merchant Aircraft Carrier) ship and renamed HMS *Alexia*, serving as a convoy escort ship in the North Atlantic until 1945. After the war she was converted back to a merchant ship, renamed *Ianthina* and eventually scrapped in 1954.

The speed of a recovery was at times startling. On 6 November 1940, the SS *Hanborough* was abandoned while on fire in both her port and starboard bunkers, and her Number Five Hold. Her main water inlets were also leaking badly with 2ft of seawater already flooding the engine room. The bomb damage was located mostly on her starboard side and main deck area. Within three hours the *Bertha* was in attendance, the fires were extinguished, the holes soon patched and another otherwise wrecked merchant ship was saved.

Although the new Salvage Department was created to recover merchant vessels, quite often warships were in need of urgent assistance. One in particular went on to play a decisive role in the history of the Second World War. On 17 April, the 9,750-ton Kent Class heavy cruiser, HMS *Suffolk*, took a severe port list after enemy attack in the North Sea and was going down by the stern with her quarterdeck already under water. She limped into Scapa Flow under tow from the tug *Imperious* and the 241-ton Rescue Tug *Hendon*. McKenzie boarded her immediately and after a preliminary survey he decided to beach her at once, as serious secondary flooding was still taking place throughout the ship.

The main salvage team moved in at once to pump out and patch one main blast hole and more than 100 smaller ones around the area. She was refloated fifteen days later and left Scapa Flow for permanent repair. Thirteen months later HMS *Suffolk* was on patrol near Denmark when her radar operators detected a large group of German warships breaking out into the Atlantic. At daybreak the next day she was involved in what became known at the Battle of the Denmark Strait, which led to the final destruction of the German battleship, *Bismarck*, having engaged her twice and firing several salvoes during the chase.

In July 1941 the Admiralty released a statement saying just how well overall the Salvage Department and Rescue Tug Service had done since September 1939. But for reasons of national security actual numbers of merchant ships, tonnages and any allusion to warships salvaged was still classified. Altogether, the statement claimed that £40 million worth of cargo and shipping had been saved. The spokesman added, 'It is possible to reveal that of the £40,000,000 about £26,000,000 represents merchant ships which had been damaged, or sunk, by bomb, mine or torpedo, but which are now sailing the seas once more.' The remaining £14 million represented cargoes saved, including £8 million of foodstuffs and £6 million of war materials, the latter comprising munitions, tanks, aeroplane parts, oil, nitrates and production machinery. Bearing in mind that these values must be multiplied by about thirty times to gauge their true worth today, the Salvage Department's success was staggering.

The spokesman who, if not Admiral Dewar himself, was certainly speaking with his authority, claimed that the figures represented 'approximately 97 per cent of all ships we have been able to get at, but we shall not be completely satisfied until we have salvaged the remaining 3 per cent'. The spokesman revealed that no matter how badly damaged a ship became, it was made serviceable again if humanly possible. If a ship was too badly damaged to be reclaimed or rebuilt, the scrap metal was cut up into furnace-size pieces and smelted down to make new ships, tanks and other weapons of war. In many cases gigantic jobs of ship surgery were carried out to make the ships fit for service again. If the bows of one ship were too badly damaged, while the stern of a second vessel was still in relatively seaworthy condition, the two good parts were cut away and joined together to form an entirely new ship. On one occasion the undamaged portion of a ship was kept as a 'spare' until a good fit could be found to match.

Sometimes the portion was recovered, only to save its precious cargo. When the 4,996-ton SS *Loch Maddy* fell behind from Convoy HX 19, Captain William James Park ordered his crew to abandon ship after *U-57* put one torpedo into her amidships section. Like many other merchant ships she remained afloat after being abandoned, but in the early hours of the following morning, *U-23* slammed another torpedo into the drifting ship, this time blowing her in half and sending her entire bow section straight to the bottom. But her stern section refused to sink and was found drifting about 20 miles out from the Orkney island of Copinsay. The section was towed into Inganess Bay where the *Bertha* salvage party and naval ratings saved 11,000 tons of timber worth £27,000.

A year after the general public was informed, at least in part, of how well the Admiralty's combined salvage organization had been working, a classified account of ships-saved-versus-costs-involved was compiled, detailing how salvage was truly helping to win the Battle of the Atlantic. Between 3 September 1939 and 31 August 1942 the number of salvage craft rose to twenty, not including Rescue Tugs, and the total working costs were £3,586,200. Nevertheless, during this period, 465 ships were saved at a value of more than £34 million and cargo worth in excess of £19 million, totalling £55m. The amount of salvage awards to all types of vessels involved in salvage work, including rescue tugs, Royal Navy vessels and salvage craft was £530,500 (or in today's currency £17.5 million). In addition to the merchant vessels saved, a further 261 Royal Navy vessels, mostly corvettes, mine-sweepers and trawlers worth in excess of £35 million, were salvaged. Altogether, twenty salvage craft along with rescue tugs saved 726 vessels worth £88 million. Today that would equate to about £2.9 billion.

At the start of the war, all shipyards in Britain were fully solicited and the building of much-needed new salvage vessels was not deemed a priority. To reach the speed necessary to keep up with demand, the Admiralty converted some older vessels to salvage use. But under the new US Lend-Lease Act approved by Congress on 11 March 1941, the floodgates of money and machinery were opened. Altogether under this Act Britain received more than $30 billion in food and raw materials by the end of the war. Part of this was spent on more salvage vessels and plant, bringing the Department up to strength much more quickly.

With staffing problems always an issue, anyone with a seagoing and/or an engineering background was recruited for salvage work. Some officers were found from as far away as Bombay and the Yangtze River and were brought back to the United Kingdom to work for the Admiralty. Before France fell, a number of salvage men and ships escaped to England as well as some from the Dutch salvage firm, Smit, which is today a world leader in marine salvage. However, those already employed could leave at any time, as salvage was still not considered essential despite all it had achieved for the war effort. Some experienced salvage clerical and administration staff were also migrating towards the Army, Navy or Air Force to fight Germany in a more conventional way. In 1942, Admiralty salvage fell under the Essential Work (General Provision) Order 1941, which added building and engineering to those jobs deemed of value to the war effort. The Order was framed to fit established industries. Finally, recognized as an important arm of the fight against Germany, and an established industry in its own right, salvage personnel became exempt from military service and its seagoing personnel came under the same heading as conventional merchant seamen.

By August 1943 the Salvage Department was a very focused organization. Since August the previous year another 195 merchant ships had been saved. The number of Royal Navy vessels needing salvage assistance reached another 202 for the same period. Altogether, for the

107

first four years of the Second World War, 1,123 ships, including Royal Navy vessels, were saved, as well as vital cargo worth £22 million. The total value of shipping and cargo salvaged reached £113 million – more than £3.7 billion today.

There were now thirty salvage vessels available, but only twenty-nine appeared on the Admiralty list. Throughout the summer and autumn of 1939 the Liverpool & Glasgow Salvage Association was engaged in recovering the T Class submarine HMS *Thetis* that had sunk with the loss of ninety-nine lives during her trials on 1 June that year. There was no purpose-built vessel available to lift a 1,200-ton submarine off the seabed, so the 3,350-ton collier SS *Zelo* was converted to do the job. She needed to be reinforced with eight sets of bollards and lifting gear. Once over the *Thetis* wreck, wires were passed down from one side of the *Zelo* at low tide, under the stricken submarine, and back up to the ship to form a steel cradle. The *Thetis* was then strung stern-first beneath the *Zelo*, and carried 8 miles towards Anglesey before her beaching in Moelfre Bay.

Prior to the completion of the *Thetis* salvage operation, the Director of Naval Intelligence, Geoffrey Cooke, wrote an internal Admiralty memo to ensure that if a German submarine was within salvage reach, if at all possible, Naval Intelligence wanted it raised. To save time and money, all the purpose-built salvage plant from the *Thetis* operation was to be kept intact and held in readiness, complete with sufficient crew, to deploy to a U-boat wreck site and begin immediate salvage. Converting another ship similar to the *Zelo* would cost approximately £20,000 and take two weeks to fit out. By the time Cooke's memo filtered through the system, the *Zelo* was already being stripped, but the plan was hastily reversed and she was soon back to full working order.

The early months of 1943 determined which side would win the second Battle of the Atlantic. Germany now had 300 U-boats, of which 100 were on patrol at any one time, more than enough to cripple Britain's trade supplies, but as the year progressed less merchant ships were being lost through enemy action. In fact, by the year's end 597 were sunk compared with about 1,664 for the 'happy time' of 1942. Increased convoy protection played a decisive role with more than 500 escort vessels now available to cover the many convoys leaving Canadian and American ports every week; better radar as well as long-range aircraft cover added to their defence. Convoys also increased in size, releasing more escorts to shepherd more ships to the safety of

British ports. Convoy protection had improved greatly since the First World War and, likewise, the ability to salvage more heavily damaged ships grew. The 3,670-ton SS *Coulmore* epitomized one of the many well-protected and armed merchant ships then crossing the Atlantic. She stood every chance of reaching her destination unscathed, but the result of her being attacked, in one of the most severely mauled convoys of the Second World War, was twofold. Not only was her high loss of life so unnecessary, when the Battle of the Atlantic was so nearly won, but her recovery showed how advanced Admiralty salvage had become when faced with saving a ship against seemingly impossible odds.

Chapter 12

SS *Coulmore*

At noon on 23 February 1943, the 4,665-ton Norwegian cargo ship SS *Bonneville* led the 59-vessel convoy SC 121 from New York, bound for Hull. As well as carrying her cargo of explosives, the *Bonneville* was the convoy's lead ship with Commodore Harry Charles Birnie and his seven-man staff controlling all messages and orders required to make the three-week crossing as safe as possible. The convoy was divided into eleven columns in numerical order from left to right. Column Two had five ships, the fourth being the SS *Coulmore*. She was carrying a general cargo of phosphates, aircraft parts and vaccines with a combined value of more than three times the ship. Among her 47-man crew were five naval and two military DEMS (Defensively Equipped Merchant Ship) ratings, who manned the *Coulmore*'s various weapons systems that made her better prepared to fight than some smaller Royal Naval vessels.

Her ordnance included one 4in gun at her stern for attack and defence against surface craft. At her bow was a 12-pounder, also for use against surface craft. Elsewhere around her decks were four Oerlikon anti-aircraft guns, two twin-Marlin machine guns and two PAC (parachute and cable) anti-aircraft rockets, an early type of wire-guided missile that was largely ineffective. The convoy's overall escort protection included one destroyer, four corvettes and a United States Coastguard cutter. As the procession steamed away from the American coast and into the North Atlantic, the main concern was the severe winter weather, causing the many ships to pitch and roll as they tried to stay in formation. Although the *Coulmore* was only seven years old her seaworthiness was questionable and she was far from a happy ship. The entire sanitation system had been blocked since they had been in New York and a faulty door on the main deck allowed storm-driven seawater to pour into the accommodation block, flooding all the starboard cabins in which, under these appalling conditions, two men still had to eat and live in each room.

Commodore Sir Frederick Young, the Admiralty's first proper Chief Salvage Officer.

(Swaine)

2. HMS *Montagu* after running aground on Shutter Point, Lundy Island, in 1906. Young was appointed as salvage advisor to Admiral Sir Knyvet Wilson who had ultimate control over her recovery. Wilson still had not succeeded after six months and, to Young's disgust, the state-of-the-art battleship was lost needlessly.

(Ministry of Defence, Salvage & Mooring Operation.

3. HMS *Gladiator* in dry dock at Portsmouth Harbour in 1908, the letters A to F referring to areas of damage. Even with such a severe hull breach the *Gladiator* was raised and the Admiralty realized the value of salvage as a legitimate naval arm.

(Stephen Cribb, Southse

4. An early photograph of the salvage vessel, *Ranger*, in her full bunting. She was the first Admiralty salvage vessel, having been chartered from the Liverpool Salvage Association for the duration of the First World War. Although small and built of teak this ex-gunboat was a highly effective salvage vessel and saw action in both world wars during her fifty-year working life. *(Stephen Cribb, Penzance)*

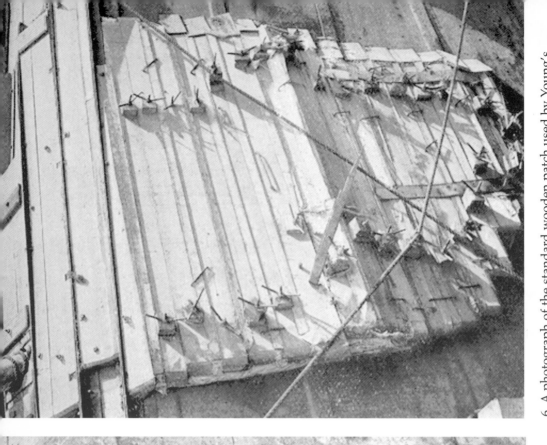

6. A photograph of the standard wooden patch used by Young's

5. A typical hull breach that would normally mean another

The liner *Asturias*, being used as a hospital ship at the time, photographed aground off Salcombe in 1917 after a torpedo attack. Her construction made her salvage very complicated, but Young did succeed in saving her. *(The National Archives, Kew)*

The troopship *Oriana* was one of several vessels comprising a westbound convoy passing Northern Ireland in May 1918. Due to a navigational error the convoy's entire port wing ran onto rocks. Innovative, although drastic, measures were needed to free her. *(Copyright MPL)*

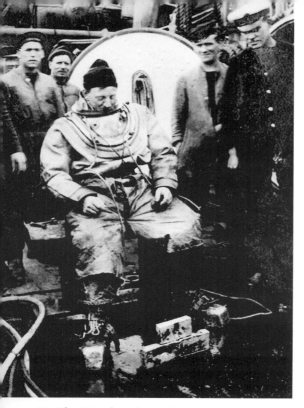

9. A salvage diver looking down at the bars of gold he had found deep within the *Laurentic*'s remains. Much of the gold was found by touch alone. Altogether only twenty-five bars out of 3,211 could not be reached.
(The National Archives, Kew)

10. The North Atlantic in early spring 1943. The SS *Coulmore* was one of thousands of ships attacked during Germany's U-boat offensive. Here she has been abandoned after a torpedo hit her bow. Although more than 400 miles from land, sinking and adrift in this raging sea, a combined salvage effort ensured that she and her cargo were saved.
(Naval History Photograph/NOAA USA)

1. The salvage vessel *Bertha* at Lyness in Scapa Flow, Orkney. She was originally purchased and refitted to recover scuttled German warships in Scapa Flow after salvage firm Cox & Danks sold its interests to Metal Industries. The company went on to work for the Admiralty throughout the Second World War in which the *Bertha* and her salvage personnel achieved a great deal of success during the Battle of the Atlantic and Operation Overlord. *(Orkney Museum & Archive)*

2. Tugs towing a large Phoenix Unit across the Channel on D-Day, 6 June 1944. These units were part of the Mulberry Harbours that made the Allied landings possible and kept the troops supplied with weapons, ammunition and food during the battles that followed. Their delivery to Normandy was only made possible after Deputy Salvage Director John Polland discovered and corrected serious design and construction flaws just in time for the initial assault phase. *(Imperial War Museum, H 39300)*

13. Sword Beach on D-Day littered with stranded and sinking landing craft. Altogether more than twenty inbound craft were mined during the first wave alone. There would be many more across all five beaches during the weeks to come.

(Imperial War Museum, B 5225)

14. A typical purpose-built Admiralty salvage vessel that took part in Operation Overlord. This picture was taken exactly one week after D-Day and shows the vessel preparing to raise a German landing craft scuttled at Port-en-Bessin, the main link-up point for American and British forces. The Admiralty Salvage Department went on to raise or clear more than 1,700 ships, often under shellfire, to keep the supply routes open as the Allies moved north towards Germany. Many salvage men were decorated for their efforts. *(Imperial War Museum, A 24130)*

15. John Polland seen here while salvaging the remains of the de Havilland Comet, Yoke Peter, near Elba, Italy in 1954. He was an outstanding salvage officer who played a key role in recovering much of the crashed airliner. *(ITN Archive/Stills)*

16. Contact George. This grainy image looks like nothing very special, but after being positively identified as part of Yoke Peter's fuselage, the Comet was finally found. *(The National Archives, Kew)*

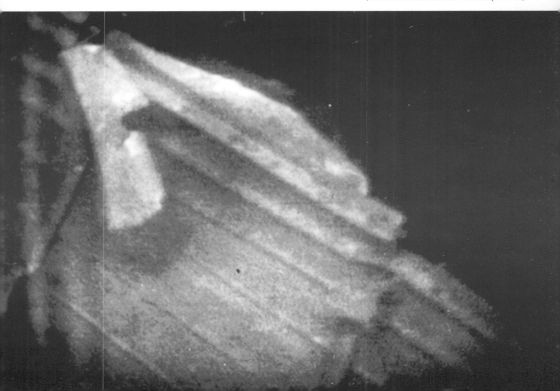

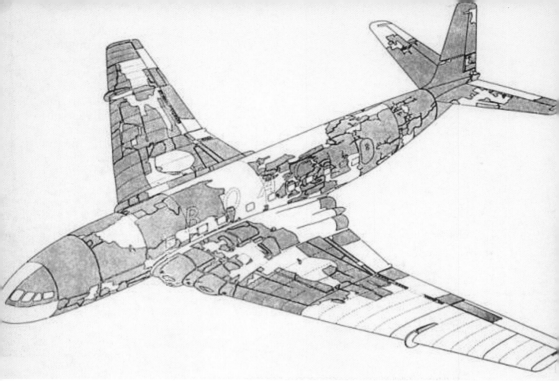

17. A diagram of Yoke Peter, the shaded areas showing the vast amount of wreckage the Salvage Service recovered, mainly using television, a diving bell, grab and five chartered Italian trawlers. *(The National Archives, Kew)*

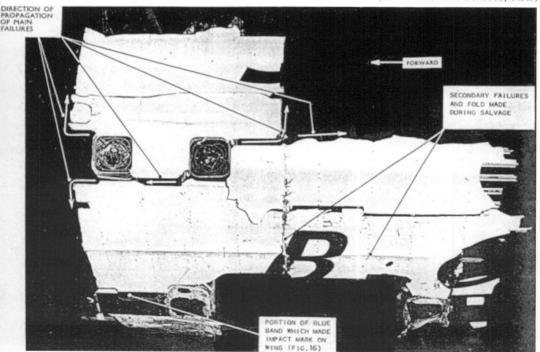

DIRECTION OF PROPAGATION OF MAIN FAILURES

FORWARD

SECONDARY FAILURES AND FOLD MADE DURING SALVAGE

PORTION OF BLUE BAND WHICH MADE IMPACT MARK ON WING (FIG.16)

18. This crucial piece of salvaged Comet wreckage shows the top of the fuselage at the two aerial windows just behind the flight deck. It proved that metal fatigue caused the catastrophic failure of the aircraft. This discovery led to all windows in jet airliners being made smaller and slightly rounded ever since. *(The National Archives, Kew)*

19. Port Said Harbour in 1956 after President Abdel Nasser ordered ships to be scuttled here and along the Suez Canal, ensuring the vital waterway was blocked. Admiralty Salvage personnel cleared thirteen ships from Port Said before Nasser refused to allow them to operate in the main canal. *(ITN Archive/Stills)*

20. One of the first ships the Admiralty raised in 1956, following the Suez Crisis, was this pontoon crane weighing 400 tons. Although not a particularly heavy salvage operation, visibility at the bottom of Port Said Harbour was less than 4ft. This created many problems for the salvage divers on all the wrecks they recovered.

(ITN Archive/Stills)

21. A salvage vessel, believed to be the *Irishman*, approaches the burnt-out hulk of the Cunard container ship *Atlantic Conveyor* which was struck by an Exocet missile on 25 May 1982. She sank before the attempt could be made.

22. The Argentine submarine *Santa Fe* was attacked and sunk at South Georgia on 25 April 1982, going down close to shore while packed with ordnance to resupply the garrison there. First attempts to raise her were made in 1982. The *Salvageman* is seen here, during her last and only successful attempt three years later, when the submarine was towed into deep water and scuttled. *(Ministry of Defence, Salvage & Mooring Operation*

T 12:39:49:17

23. This is one of the images, taken more than 2½ miles down, that ended the long search for the bulk carrier MV *Derbyshire* in 1997, after the Salvage & Mooring Operations put together an expedition to find the wreck and try to discover the reason for her loss.

(Crown Copyright/MoD)

24. With the area resembling an aircraft crash site rather than a sunken ship, the *Derbyshire*'s rapid disintegration was her biggest mystery. Simply through adjusting the light frequency on the cameras it was possible to explore the crystalline structure of the steel and show how she was literally blown to pieces during her journey to the bottom of the Pacific.

(Crown Copyright/MoD)

25. Morgyn Davies OBE the current MoD Chief Salvage and Mooring Officer, who has been largely responsible for the way today's salvage organization operates. *(Ministry of Defence, Salvage & Mooring Operations)*

26. S&MO chartered the Singapore-based *Pacific Commodore* (left) and the Dubai-based *Seabulk Harrier* to undertake salvage operations during Gulf War II. Their main task was to undertake surface operations only, but when two Sea King helicopters collided they were pushed to the limit to recover the wreckage and the dead. *(Ministry of Defence, Salvage & Mooring Operations)*

27. Salvage is not always an underwater operation. This picture shows the hydraulic aircraft deck jammed in the 'down' position aboard RFA *Argus* in 2003, during Gulf War II. S&MO commandeered a cargo ship where her derrick could literally pull the platform up to deck level, where it was welded into position.

(Ministry of Defence, Salvage & Mooring Operations)

28. All that was left of Sea Kings XV650 and XV704 after their mid-air collision on 22 March 2003. Both the *Pacific Commodore* and the *Seabulk Harrier* lacked the ability to lift the helicopters from the seabed. During this combined United States and Royal Navy salvage operation a barge was chartered and a standard road crane welded to its deck, to lift the remains of the two aircraft back to the surface.

(Ministry of Defence, Salvage & Mooring Operations)

29. A modern salvage ship can be a far cry from the *Ranger* a hundred years ago. Today a heavy-lift vessel will flood tanks similar to a submarine, sit neatly underneath the casualty then blow her tanks and the vessel is lifted clear of the water. Here one of three nuclear-fuelled Russian submarines is recovered and taken away for safe disposal aboard the MV *Transshelf*. For scale, note the white figure towards the submarine's stern. *(Ministry of Defence, Salvage & Mooring Operations)*

30. The shape of salvage to come. As more warships and military aircraft are built from lightweight composite materials, so S&MO has to learn new and more demanding salvage techniques. When this Merlin helicopter crashed, parts sank and stayed in place while others drifted for miles, creating an ever-changing debris field. A small aircraft is one thing, but recovering all the wreckage from a composite-built warship is still an unknown quantity. *(Ministry of Defence, Salvage & Mooring Operations)*

Frost had got into the electrical apparatus, making some of the internal and external lights switch on and off at random, plunging the ship's interior into total darkness or lighting her up like a tower block, showing her position for many miles. But more worryingly for the crew, the ship's alarm system often sounded for no reason. Able Seaman Albert Carter said that the alarms had a habit of going off when there was nothing happening, creating mass panic. Many of her crew slept fully clothed with their lifejackets on.

On the fourth day, three tankers broke away from Column One, bound for Halifax, Nova Scotia, and the *Coulmore* was moved into the vacant position, exposing her to the open sea. Two days later, at 10.00 am, the *Coulmore*'s lookout spotted a surfaced submarine off her port side amidships. The crew immediately opened fire with their port Oerlikon gun, but the submarine was so close that the guns could no be brought sufficiently to bear. As the submarine made off the *Coulmore*'s gun crew continued to fire and were sure they had scored at least some hits before the enemy submarine slipped away. From then on wireless messages buzzed around the convoy, confirming more U-boat sightings.

Little did Commodore Birnie and the rest of Convoy SC 121 know that two wolf packs, comprising twenty-six U-boats, had converged beneath them. Late in the evening on 7 March the *Coulmore* received another submarine warning from the *Bonneville* and an hour later the 'all clear' signal. Then the torpedo strikes began. By midnight two ships were lost. The next day six more were gone. To strengthen the convoy escort on 9 March, the United States' cutters *Bibb* and *Ingham*, and the destroyer USS *Babbitt,* arrived with long-range air support to drive off any surfaced U-boats. Aboard the *Coulmore* the tension was mounting. The faulty lighting system had flashed her position too many times and one false alarm after another had sent the petrified men scrambling for the boat deck. Whether through superstition or not, some men were convinced the *Coulmore* was next. Among the submarines prowling around beneath SC 121 was *U-405*, commanded by Rolf-Heinrich Hopmann. At about 10.00 pm he fired a single torpedo at a vessel on the convoy's port wing. The *Coulmore*'s lookout saw a ship explode in that area at 10.09 pm, the same time that the *Bonneville* was reported hit. Twenty-three-year-old Oberleutnant Robert Schetelig, commanding the *U-229*, was already lining up another target in his crosswires. Before the sound of the explosion on the *Bonneville* had died away, the *Coulmore*'s crew felt a dull thud resound throughout their ship.

This time the alarm bells failed to sound, but without knowing the full extent of the damage the crew still ran for the boats. Second Radio Officer Nichols got away in a lifeboat with another thirteen men, including the sixteen-year-old deck boy, Triggs, who was on his first trip to sea. Able Seaman Chalecroft and Able Seaman A. Cooper, along with several catering and engine-room personnel also got into the boat. It was dark, raining hard and the wind speed was around Force 7. Scars of foam streaked down the 13ft-high waves. As the lifeboat pitched and rolled in the darkness a patch repaired badly back in New York began to leak.

The freezing water soon began to fill the boat and there was utter confusion among the cold, wet and frightened men as they shouted into the darkness and tried to man the oars. Able Seaman Cooper, who had been on watch at the time the torpedo struck, noted, 'We had much difficulty with the stewards and firemen, in fact some of them didn't know the difference between port and starboard. They were pulling all ways at once.' Soon the lifeboat took on water much more quickly. When it reached a critical mass, the fragile craft capsized, tipping all the men into the icy North Atlantic swell with only their lifebelts for protection.

Radio Operator Nichols was among those who managed to stay with the capsized craft, along with six other survivors trying to hang on. The remainder were washed away and never seen again. After clinging to the boat for about thirty minutes, a raft, which had drifted off the *Coulmore*, floated past; the seven remaining survivors swam to it and climbed on board. But with so many men desperate to get on it at the same time the raft capsized twice, throwing everybody back in the water. Triggs, who could not swim, clung to Able Seaman Chalecroft to save himself from going under. After several hours some of the men were aboard while others clung to the raft's edges. They were desperately in need of energy, but as Nichols remembered, 'We tried to get at the bottle of brandy, but the stores, which were kept in a tank in the centre of the raft, were battened down with a cross piece of wood. As we did not have a knife, and our hands were much too numb to break those wooden fastenings, we had to give up the attempt, and stretched ourselves on the raft until picked up.'

At 9.00 am the next morning the USS *Bibb* spotted the raft. The last thing Nichols remembered was being hauled aboard a ship, then waking up in a bunk, safe, warm and alive. Forty out of her 47-man crew were killed, many bodies never being found – if they had remained on board all would have survived. In hindsight their true mental state after more than ten days of poor conditions, frequent false alarms and the trauma of seeing many ships explode and disappear around them must have made going into the water preferable to risking another torpedo strike.

When the wolf pack ceased attacking on 11 March, due to bad weather, twelve ships had been sunk with more than 300 lives lost. The dead included Commodore Birnie and his entire staff who froze to death before help could reach them. Among the forty-seven men who went into the water, Nichols noted only one act of bravery. 'I wish to place on record the fine behaviour of deck boy Triggs, who could not swim, clutched A.B. Chalecroft, for support. When he found he was pulling this man beneath the water, he deliberately released his hold and was drowned. His unselfish action undoubtedly saved Chalecroft's life, but at the sacrifice of his own.'

Later that day the *Bibb* picked up two more survivors, including the *Coulmore*'s carpenter, Harry Smith. As the *Bibb* cruised around the area Smith was able to positively identify the *Coulmore*, which unlike the other twelve ships attacked, had not gone down. The *Bibb*'s master asked Smith if he would like to rejoin his ship until a salvage party arrived, adding that the cutter could not stay and wait. Still frozen with his hands and legs cut open and peeling after his ordeal, Smith declined the offer, a decision that would make the salvage party's job all the more hazardous when they found the *Coulmore* five days later, in the same storm that had shown no signs of letting up.

The 980-ton Flower Class corvette HMS *Aubrietia* was known as a 'canteen ship', meaning that she could be called upon for any kind of work, usually at very short notice. The Flower Class was derived from a whaler design, which gave the type the distinctive look of a merchant vessel painted grey. Their primary task was as convoy escorts, but, although they were slow, poorly armed and had a tendency to pitch and roll, the 'Flowers' sank or captured more than fifty U-boats. After the war at least one was converted into a salvage vessel. The *Aubrietia* contributed more to the war effort than any of the other 267 Flower Class corvettes built in both Britain and Canada. On 9 May 1941 she sighted and depth-charged the *U-110* before HMS *Bulldog* and *Broadway* closed in to finish the job. But the *U-110* failed to sink and among many items recovered from her was the first ever Enigma

113

machine, complete with its codebooks. This important find enabled cryptographer Alan Turing to crack the code at Bletchley Park, giving the Allies the edge in the Second World War.

Just after lunch on 11 March, the *Aubrietia* sailed from Londonderry along with the rescue tugs HMT *Eminent* and *Samsonia* to find and save the *Coulmore*. For two days and nights all three ships were heading 400 miles into the North Atlantic through gale-force headwinds. The sea hammered so hard against the *Aubrietia* that her forward gun shield was buckled and one of her two dinghies was smashed. On her open bridge, her watch found that driving hail was the new enemy. An Able Seaman later described how he had to look for the *Coulmore* through his fingers in a bid to stop the bullet-hard pieces of ice stinging his face like 'gravel in a blaster'. As the lashing hailstones stung his sore flesh, they felt more like hail rocks as blood rushed to the impacted area beneath the skin, deepening the raw pain as another hit the same spot.

The three ships were pounding head-on into a Force 9 gale. On land such a wind speed would be ripping off roof tiles and branches from trees. In the North Atlantic the waves had reached more than 22ft and visibility was obscured by the 50mph wind whipping up the dense foam and sea spray as it curled off the wave crests. Amid all this uncontrollable energy the HMT *Eminent* sighted the *Coulmore*. The *Eminent*'s commanding officer, Lieutenant R. Coleman, recalled, 'She was abandoned and wallowing in the trough of a rough sea and westerly swell. By first inspection it was noticed that she was badly holed forward of her collision bulkhead, Number One Hatches were nearly all off and water was spouting from her hold at times.'

At dawn the following day Lieutenant Commander Gerald Ducat Fowler aboard the *Aubrietia* planned to put a party of thirteen ratings and two officers on the *Coulmore*. A skeleton crew had to get on to her and secure the towlines as well as keep normal duties such as steering, watches and anything else needed to maintain salvage control. Fowler began transferring the boarding party at 8.15 am. 'This necessitated three trips in very bad weather as the only available boat was *Aubrietia*'s 14ft dinghy. My other dinghy had been damaged by heavy seas the previous day.' Twenty-two-year-old Sub Lieutenant Patrick Charles Coyne led the boarding party, which was no easy task as the Jacob's ladder, which the *Coulmore*'s crew had used to abandon ship, was more than 14ft above the waterline and blowing around wildly in the gale. Had carpenter Harry Smith returned to his ship, lowering the ladder to sea level would have made this crucial stage in the salvage operation much easier.

Judgement and timing were everything. Coyne had to wait until the *Aubrietia*'s dinghy was right alongside without smashing into the *Coulmore*'s steel hull, then grab for the flailing rope ladder while riding on the very peak of a wave. After grabbing the ladder he then had to haul himself up to the main deck and lower the ladder back down far enough for the rest of the landing party to make the same hazardous journey. Chief Engine Room Artificer Maurice William Scanlan was among the boarding party. His first job was to get the engines and boilers working if at all possible. Scanlan made for the engine room where he found that, like the disrupted electrics in the accommodation block, the *Coulmore*'s engine room had suffered similar neglect. In the dim, flickering light of his oil lamp, Scanlan noted that the machinery was generally in a worn condition. The bilge suctions were badly choked and their valves were, in some cases, very worn and scored. Stripped threads on the engine-room direct bilge suction strainer prevented tightening and air leaking into the space was a major problem.

Scanlan and a few men worked for more than twenty-two hours, sometimes up to their chests in freezing water, to try to get the cold boilers working. Eventually mattresses had to be burned to get them back on line. Once the boilers were lit, pressure gradually built up. The starboard after boiler soon had 30lb of steam pressure, which crept up to 50lb by mid afternoon before the boiler developed a bad leak. By 10.00 pm Scanlan had 50lb of pressure on the port after boiler, giving enough power to turn the propellers. After ninety minutes the inboard dynamo was started and, shortly afterwards, at last they had electricity. By now the water in the engine room was slightly above the bottom plates. The bilge pump was started, but Scanlan was unable to get suction due to the choked bilge pipes and strainers – the bilges were thick with coal dust and clinker. He added, 'The bilge suction pipes and strainers were, moreover, becoming rapidly inaccessible, due to the heavy rolling of the ship. Pipes and strainers were no sooner becoming cleared than they again became choked. The situation was becoming very serious.'

Above decks, Coyne's first job was to conduct a full damage assessment. The torpedo had put a hole through the stem, blowing away the forepeak collision bulkhead and the bulkhead of Number One Hold. The starboard anchor chain had fallen out through the bottom of the

115

ship, the cable parting at the windlass. A great deal of cargo had floated out through the same hole and the blast had blown off the hatch covers. He was deeply concerned. 'At this time I did not know how long *Coulmore* would stay afloat as she was badly damaged forward and was labouring heavily.' Towing her bow first created a problem. Pulling about 9,000 tons of combined cargo and ship head-long into gale-force winds could well cause too great a pressure against her already weakened fore end, which could break away. The only other alternative was to tow her backwards all the way to England. One hour after boarding, the *Eminent* prepared to secure her towline.

The wire towline was made with a 4in diameter rope tail, or 'messenger'. Once the messenger was aboard the wire would be let out to 1,500ft. To get the messenger aboard, the *Eminent* steamed as close to the *Coulmore* as possible so that a crew member could throw a heaving line across to the derelict ship. Trying to tether a sinking ship that was out of control in a raging sea took a certain amount of skill and courage to even attempt, let alone to achieve successfully. The storm was so bad that at times the tug was above the *Coulmore*, with her crew looking down into the eyes of the boarding party, only for the *Coulmore* to be soaring up the side of another massive wave for the same men to be looking down at the outstretched hands of the tug men who were now looking up. The split-second timing involved judging the wind speed and direction as well as the violent pitching and rolling of both vessels. After struggling for an hour, the 1,500ft towing line was secured, paid out to its full length and the *Eminent* was ready to make for England, once the *Samsonia* was in position.

The first line from the *Eminent* was secured on the ship's port side. Coyne remembered, 'At approximately 11.30 a line was taken from the second tug and passed through the starboard after fairlead but it was found that the weight of the wire in the water (60 fathoms, 41½in) was too heavy to manhandle and eventually caused the mes-senger to part in the water.' While the *Samsonia* was recovering her wire for a second attempt, Coyne, fearing the *Coulmore* might go down, ordered his men to make an emergency raft out of the shattered hatch covers that littered the deck. The *Samsonia* soon returned for another attempt. The tug's line was again taken but again, owing to the amount of wire let go in the water, it was impossible to heave it up to the deck. On the third attempt the messenger was fed from the *Coulmore* back to the *Samsonia*, which was now alongside, and the wire heaved aboard using her capstan. It was dangerous, but worked.

116

Later that afternoon both tugs gradually eased their engines forward and the *Coulmore* was going home, albeit backwards.

For the next six hours the two tugs could only manage 3 knots to save any undue strain on the wires. As the men settled down for their first night aboard the *Coulmore*, finding somewhere fit to sleep was the first problem. With so many cabins flooded, many chose to sleep in and around the ship's saloon. And for their first few meals, all that could be found were tins of fruit, eggs and oranges, which the men, in the same filthy and wet clothes, had to live on until the *Aubrietia* could ferry across fresh food and supplies a few days later. When the *Aubrietia* signalled the *Coulmore* to ensure all was well, the reply was: 'OK big eats, but no spuds.'

Like all rescue tug commanders Lieutenant Coleman had to write a report on each salvage operation the *Eminent* carried out. Tug commanders were well known for their brevity when explaining how and why events during any given operation had happened, often giving nothing away regarding the skill and danger that came with the job. Between 10.00 pm on 14 March and 7.30 am the next morning, Coleman's account of what happened was typical of a Rescue Tug captain:

22.00/14 Wind veered to SW 6/7. Rough sea short swell. Towing wire inspected and nip changed hourly.
02.30/15 Vessel took violent sheer, decreased revolutions.
06.00/15 Tow sheering badly.
07.30/15 Wire parted from vessel's quarter. Commenced to heave wire aboard. Weather not good for reconnecting.

Aboard the *Coulmore* Sub Lieutenant Coyne did not see events in such a crisp and clear-cut way. His version began: 'At 02.45/15 the port wire jumped the fairlead and parted, carrying away the guardrails and one support to the gun platform. The wind was blowing at about Force 6 and the ship was rolling heavily. By 07.30 the wind had increased and the rising sea caused the starboard wire to wrench its fairlead out of the deck, carrying away the starboard guardrails.' By some miracle the wire, although under incredible strain, still held. If he could get the *Eminent*'s port wire back on board in time they still had a chance to ride the storm.

The *Samsonia*'s wire was now lying across the edge of the starboard quarter at deck level, and chafing badly on the sharp corner where the deck met the ship's side. 'Before this could be packed,' Coyne continued, 'the starboard bollard cracked across the middle and the inboard half began to lift out of the deck. I considered it too dangerous to work on the wire in case the bollards gave way altogether.' Although hanging on by a 4½in thread, the *Coulmore* stayed in tow, ploughing and buffeting her way a few more miles closer to home. In the engine room, Scanlan managed to get steam power to the after winches. Getting the port line aboard would now be very much easier.

This time the *Eminent*'s crew fired a rocket-propelled heaving line that successfully landed on the *Coulmore*'s after deck, but the rope messenger attached to the main towing wire parted twice before being made fast. Coleman let out 1,800ft of towline this time, greatly reducing the load on the *Samsonia*'s starboard wire that had been grumbling and singing under the strain for some time. Although the seas remained heavy throughout the night, slow but satisfactory progress was being made. Just before lunchtime the starboard wire finally parted. Later that evening, again in his usual brief manner, Coleman said of his port towline: 'Parted tow. Wire was not broken, it had rendered round the *Coulmore*'s bitts.'

For Coyne, 'rendered round the *Coulmore*'s bitts' meant: 'At 18.45 the bollards holding the port wire snapped throwing the broken bollard 12yds away. The ship was now adrift and in view of the adverse weather conditions, I decided to use main engines, the assistance of which had been refused by the tugs.' With the light failing and the sea rising the *Samsonia* and *Eminent* simply could not risk another attempt at getting lines aboard that day, neither could Coyne drift aimlessly in such a severe storm. Her engines had to be running or she was lost and very probably the boarding party with her. The two rescue tugs stood by while the boarding party planned to raise steam and, with the engines astern, take the *Coulmore* backwards throughout the night.

Getting the propellers turning was now critical. Coyne directed Scanlan to use her main engines going astern. They were only running until 6.00 am the next morning, but not because Scanlan and his men were unable to overcome any mechanical failure – they had increasing difficulty trying to keep enough steam pressure up because the coal they were using was mainly dust. The stokeholds were also becoming full of red-hot ashes and there were not enough personnel to get them out.

Dropping pressure rendered the engines useless, but they had done their slow job admirably, having kept the *Coulmore* on a relatively straight course throughout such a bad night. At daybreak on 17 March the weather had eased and both tugs were able to reconnect their towlines. Since her stern bollards had been ripped out of the *Coulmore*'s deck, this time the towlines were made fast just behind her accommodation block in the well-deck area, but not without difficulty. A line was taken in through the port after fairlead and the wire secured on the well deck's towing bollards. About twenty minutes later the second tug's line was through the starboard fairlead, but once more the weight of the wire was too great and it parted with a mighty crack as the two ends flailed around in the air until all their energy was spent and they dropped back into the sea. On a second attempt the wire was got inboard again, but the *Eminent* ran over the wire and the *Coyne*'s men were ordered to let it go. After considerable difficulty both lines were eventually secured aboard, both tugs were in position and they gradually steamed in unison. Coyne, who by now was exhausted, recalled: 'At 0900/18 starboard after bollard on after well deck cracked but held. Tow wire on port quarter began to chafe owing to play of rudder chain. This was chocked up clear of tow wire.' The rudder chain was damaged when the *Eminent*'s towline had ripped out the *Coulmore*'s gun platform support three days earlier.

Although the *Samsonia*'s line was giving every sign of threatening to part, it did hold. After a couple of hours the *Aubrietia* informed Coyne that he was only 20 miles off Donagree Point in Northern Ireland. She had been shadowing the salvage operation since putting Coyne's party on board. Now, along with the added protection of the Flower Class corvette HMS *Clover*, she steamed back towards Londonderry. The two tugs were ordered to proceed to the Clyde where the *Coulmore*'s precious cargo could be unloaded and necessary repairs made. At last the salvage team could count down the markers home. Just after midnight they passed within a mile of Altacarry Head near Northern Ireland's extreme north-easterly tip. Then they approached Sanda Island near the Mull of Kintyre; Scotland was only 4 miles away. After another two hours Fladda Island, just off the Scottish coast, was 1½ miles off the port bow. At 4.40 pm on 20 March the *Coulmore* was safely in Rothesay Bay, having been claimed and lost more than twelve times since being sighted eight days earlier. Her spectacular salvage led to Fowler, Coyne and Scanlan being decorated. With the three crews now qualifying for salvage award under the new Salvage Act they all shared in the prize. The combined value of the ship and cargo was £171,000; the whole salvage award was calculated at £25,000. In July

1947, the crew of the *Aubrietia* were awarded £2,000, of which the boarding party were awarded £1,200. The crews of the *Samsonia* and *Eminent* were awarded £1,500 each.

Merchant shipping casualties needing salvage assistance dropped significantly from May 1943, but more salvage ships were already planned. By September there was a commitment for another ten craft, at a cost of £1,662,500, bringing the Admiralty's salvage fleet up to forty vessels. Although the continued building programme might seem a little extravagant, considering the need to divert resources elsewhere and the ever-shrinking need for salvage around the British coast, its expansion was just in time for the Salvage Department and Rescue Tug Service to play their greatest and most decisive role in the biggest seaborne invasion in history.

Chapter 13

'Polland's Circus'

Early in April 1944 the War Office telephoned Room 45 with an urgent request for the Admiralty to recover a vessel that had broken its towline and run aground near Littlehampton, Sussex. Salvage Officer William 'Bill' Robinson was soon on site to assess the requirements necessary to refloat the stranded craft. He had expected to see a cargo ship or tanker on the shoreline, but was confronted with a large concrete caisson about 200ft long, 56ft wide and 60ft high. The box-like construction had an open top with an internal area divided into two halves down the centre line, subdivided into twenty-two smaller compartments, and the walls were built with 15in reinforced concrete. Throughout his many years as a salvage officer, Robinson had never seen a seagoing vessel like it.

With no familiar reference points to even begin the recovery operation, Robinson contacted Deputy Salvage Director John R. Polland for advice but, on hearing Robinson's account, Polland had no more idea than his colleague of what the concrete block was for. However, as the matter seemed urgent he requested plans from the War Office for what was called a 'Phoenix Unit'. Polland studied the plans in detail and could see that the pumping arrangements were very well designed. The main central wall was watertight throughout, but the many crosspieces forming the twenty-two sections had openings called 'limber holes' to allow the water to flow freely inside the structure. Thin guide wires on the surface were attached to 'penstock' or sluice valves to allow for easy opening and closing from above. Halfway up the caisson's side was a gangway slab, a 6ft ledge that ran all the way around the concrete block. Polland could see that dividing the caisson into compartments allowed for greater strength, and it also broke up the free-flowing water mass, thus giving the vessel more stability.

Even though the Phoenix Unit was stranded above the spring high-tide mark, Robinson should have been able to refloat it much faster than he was reporting, so Polland visited Littlehampton to see for himself what the problem was. Finally, the younger salvage officer had the opportunity to show his superior that there were significant differences between the design on paper and the final build. Polland saw at once that the outlet holes were 6in diameter to take a 6in pump, which in theory seemed correct. But in practice each pump required a 9in flange to bolt it on with; a crucial point missed by the designers. Then reinforcing bars within the concrete blocked some of the vital outlet holes. These bars had to be cut through before pumping could even begin to take place. Salvage divers were already widening the holes with sledgehammers and chisels, but more was wrong. Polland and Robinson climbed the ladder to the top of the caisson to peer into its vast interior. Divers were in some of the compartments, which, according to the plans, was not necessary. The all-important guide wires connecting the penstock valves to the surface had never been installed, and when the divers tried to find the valves on the caisson's bottom, builders' debris such as chunks of masonry and scaffolding blocked their way. Many of the free-flowing openings in the cross-sections were also blocked with the same rubbish.

While in Littlehampton Polland had time to view the surrounding area, as the War Office wanted the caisson towed to nearby Selsey Bay once it was raised. When he travelled to Selsey by motor launch there were many more Phoenix Units in a sunken state. Altogether he identified about six different sizes randomly sunk in the Bay, some of the larger ones in shallow water, with smaller ones sunk more deeply. Polland later recalled:

> There, sure enough, were dozens of these monstrosities, sitting on the bottom, and moored to them were other fantastic pieces of equipment floating on small pontoons. There were also a number of huge steel barges with square-section steel legs standing up at each corner. The whole area of the Bay, for 3 miles offshore, was cluttered up with concrete and steel equipment resembling nothing I had ever seen before, ashore or afloat.

Polland had no idea how vast the Phoenix building programme had been, or what their real purpose was. Production had begun in October 1943 and twenty-four contractors were employed all around the United Kingdom to make them. They were supposed to have been built in dry dock, but there was not enough space available in the whole country to accommodate their building. Many units had to be made on the foreshore along the south and south-east coasts and then towed to assembly points such as Selsey Bay. There were about 100 Phoenix Units parked at Selsey and another twenty-five were sunk between Dungeness and Sheerness. More than 600,000 tons of concrete and 31,000 tons of steel had been used to make them, involving 25,000 workers. The six types varied from 25ft to 60ft high, some displacing 1,672 tons, considerably more than the latest T Class submarine. Others weighed as much as 6,044 tons, or equivalent to a large trans-Atlantic merchant ship. The Unit ashore at Littlehampton was of the latter type.

These sites were chosen because they had flat, sandy bottoms, and were a relatively short distance from France. What Polland did not know was that the Allies needed a port near their invasion point to put ashore all the tanks and jeeps, men and other battle supplies. The Phoenix Units were needed to underpin two artificial floating ports called Mulberry Harbours, one for the American forces and one for the British. Each Unit was designed to be sunk end to end in two long strings a mile offshore in 30ft of water, leaving 10ft above the high-water mark. In order to keep the invading force adequately supplied, both harbours would have to land together 12,000 tons of cargo and 2,500 vehicles by the first two weeks after the invasion. This included berthing and accommodation facilities for deep-draft Liberty ships and shelter for smaller craft.

The Mulberry Harbours were built in three main layers. Firstly, about sixty blockships, or Gooseberries, were sunk to form a break-water. Then the Phoenix Units were sunk in position to form a solid foundation, and finally floating breakwaters were attached, followed by piers to disembark some of the vehicles under their own power. When they were completed, each artificial port was about the same size as Dover Harbour. The units had to satisfy several core conditions: they had to be seaworthy and able to be towed with relative ease. They also needed to be quick and easy to sink, stable when 'planted' and strong enough to stand up to normal summer weather. The units also had to be built in the quantity required within the time available. On paper all these criteria had been met, but their mass production was their greatest weakness. Now simple design flaws and poor building standards threatened this vital component of the impending invasion.

With the planning for Operation Overlord well advanced, the Units' successful delivery to bolster Mulberry A at St Laurent in the American

123

Sector and Mulberry B at Arromanches in the British Sector was now extremely important. Dutch ships called *Schuyts* had been allocated to pump and raise the units. *Schuyt* means small steam coaster, and these craft worked in and around the canals of Holland. Two *Schuyts* had escaped before the German invasion and were now employed by the Royal Engineers. Massive centrifugal pumps had been placed into the bow of each craft, but War Office Director of Transport Major General D.J. McMullen later explained why they were still not suitable to raise the Phoenix Units: 'When originally planning Mulberry it had been anticipated that only a proportion of the Phoenix Units would be sunk in the assembly area and that the remainder would be moored in sheltered waters.' The planners seemed to have forgotten that the more Units sunk meant that the more had to be raised. Although tidal conditions played a major part, refloating the Littlehampton Unit alone took nine days. At that rate, a worse-case scenario of refloating all 125 caissons would take more than three years.

From Prime Minister Winston Churchill down to the designers and builders of the Phoenix Units, no one knew that each caisson shared the same mixture of design flaws and poor workmanship as the one aground at Littlehampton. And the two small *Schuyts* were simply not going to cope. Polland informed Admiral Dewar that to raise all the Units quickly would be an engineering impossibility unless drastic measures were taken to resolve the design flaws. Most importantly, ships and pumps were needed desperately at Selsey – with more than 5,000 vessels already committed to Overlord, finding a few more was going to be very difficult indeed. Polland was sure that eighteen ships, two to each of nine units, with three 6in pumps per vessel, could do the job, although that meant finding in excess of sixty pumps. Two suitable ships fitted out as repair vessels were known, but they belonged to General Bernard Montgomery's 21st Army Group who were hesitant to release them. Their rationale was that the ships were needed for the initial assault phase and the Phoenix programme was to last until about D-Day+14. The Army, however, did have large pumps capable of moving many tons of water each hour.

Dewar passed Polland's concerns to First Sea Lord, Admiral Sir Andrew B. Cunningham, who raised the matter at a War Cabinet meeting at 11.00 am on 22 May 1944. Cunningham told the Chiefs of Staff, '[Dewar] has not seen any of the Army equipment working and is doubtful if it will be ready in time or in sufficient quantity to assist in the Operation. The army equipment, if it proves satisfactory, is about equal in capacity to the naval equipment, which is now being made available.' Cunningham felt that it should be possible by 1 June to raise Phoenix Units at the rate of three or four per day – less than half that required by the Allied Naval Commander Expeditionary Force (ANCXF), Sir Bertram Ramsey. If all preparations were completed, and all the army equipment happened to work, the rate of raising Phoenix Units would increase to about six to eight per day. However, he was adamant that the work could not be maintained indefinitely as the ANCXF wanted at least nine units per day, especially for the initial D-Day assault.

That same evening, General Sir Hastings Ismay, one of Winston Churchill's closest advisers, wrote to the Prime Minister: 'The Chiefs of Staff considered the attached note by the First Sea Lord at their meeting this morning. They were assured that everything possible was being done to overcome the bottleneck which it discloses, but at the same time they felt that you should know the position.' Churchill summoned both Cunningham and Ismay to the Cabinet War Rooms to discuss the situation in more depth. Sitting in his Map Room, deep beneath King Charles Street, London, Churchill chaired the meeting with five other Chiefs of Staff.

Surrounded by maps covering all the available wall space, many with frayed, coloured pieces of string pinned into the paper, denoting various stages of advancing armies or shipping movements, the eight men discussed the Phoenix problem until well into the night. Churchill expressed his deep concern at Polland's findings. Knowing how many of the ports from France to Germany would be blocked, he pointed out the advantage gained by the operational surprise the Mulberry Harbours represented. Ever the man for good ideas, he asked the Chiefs of Staff if pumps belonging to the London Fire Brigade could be commandeered and sent to Selsey. Major General D.J. McMullen answered the Prime Minister, saying, 'The Army has mobilized all possible resources, including heavy fire brigade pumps, and the difficulty now is not one of provision of pumps, but how to find suitable ships for the operation.' Field Marshal Sir Alan F. Brooke offered to speak personally to Montgomery in a bid to secure the much-needed extra ships.

Director of Ports, Brigadier Bruce White, was confident that the necessary Army pumps could be in place on time aboard any coaster not immediately required for the invasion. He also suggested that, perhaps, one of the pumping units was not even necessary. White was well positioned to know – he had passed the final design for the construction of the Phoenix Units in October 1943. Rear Admiral E.J.P. Brind listened carefully to what White had to say, but he was strongly opposed to the Brigadier's optimism. Brind emphasized that Dewar, and thus Polland, were depending absolutely on having enough ships and pumps available to do the job – on the day – as nine Phoenix Units had to be ready to go during the first assault phase. Any less could mean unacceptably heavy losses during the first crucial days while the build-up of men and supplies into Normandy was in progress.

After hours of discussion, all Churchill and his Chiefs of Staff could agree on was to try to obtain adequate shipping without drawing on pre-designated vessels, and for Brind to submit progress reports to the War Cabinet every seventy-two hours. Their next decision resulted in another headache for Polland. He remembered: 'Following various meetings between the Admiralty and the War Office, the Allied Naval Commander of the Expeditionary Force requested that the Admiralty should take over the whole operation of pumping and re-floating, and at the eleventh hour this formidable responsibility was shouldered by the Salvage Department.'

Polland had no plan, no date to work to and as yet very few resources. He added: 'There was only one practical method of carrying out the task in time and this involved the setting up of a complete organization.' Although most of the Salvage Department's fifty or so vessels were either already committed to Overlord, or trying to cover the British coast for normal salvage duties (some coastlines had no cover at all), Polland managed to obtain three ships from the salvage companies already on agreement. The Liverpool & Glasgow Salvage Organization loaned a Belgian mooring vessel, the Port of London Authority a converted trawler and Risdon Beazley lent Polland an old Dutch dredger. Men were also offered to crew the ships, including salvage officers deemed too old for active service on the main assault.

There might just be the required number of pumps in the various army and naval bases around the United Kingdom, but their utilization depended on whether there was enough time before the invasion took place. Polland sent orders to salvage bases around the country to send all available equipment as soon as possible; diving gear, motor launches, welding gear air-compressors etc. were also sent down to 'Phoenix Park'.

Admiral Brind's first report reached the War Cabinet as agreed on 27 May, D-Day-8. Even though Field Marshal Brooke had spoken personally to Montgomery, he confirmed that the Army could (or would) not allocate the two ships. However, he was assured two other suitable vessels could be found, adding that although the two ships had not yet been allocated, they 'should' be available by D-Day. Three weeks earlier, on 8 May, Allied Supreme Commander Dwight D. Eisenhower set D-Day at 5 June. Polland was never informed, as his security clearance was not high enough. On 30 May, D-Day-6, Brind's second report stated: 'The situation remains substantially unaltered.'

Meanwhile Polland was formulating his mass Phoenix rescue plan. He now had an assortment of support craft, including coasters, repair ships, a collier and a water boat as well as eight mechanics repairing pumps, twelve salvage officers and fifty ratings. The collier and water boat were essential to replenish the ships, ensuring they could work around the clock, but still ships and men were needed. Polland was sure that the Phoenix Units inshore would be easier to lift. Those further out were more of a problem – and their 6ft gangway slabs that prevented the salvage ships from getting too close were not the only one. The salvage ships had to be moored alongside on a falling tide and land the pumps as soon as the slabs were just awash, otherwise the pumps on the Unit's ledge did not have enough time to raise the Unit before being swamped once again on the rising tide.

For the pumps to work efficiently, standpipes had to be made and fitted to each one, through apertures in the gangway slabs. Steel piping was collected and a workshop set up ashore in Littlehampton where military and United States Navy personnel mass-produced the lengths ready to install on the Units prior to pumping. Fixing the standpipes saved crucial time compared with trying to secure a pump's suction pipe under water. Now it was simply a case of bolting the pump to the standpipe and the water would soon be gushing over the side. The pumps had to maintain a discharge rate of about 1,200 tons per hour without interruption. Polland recalled: 'The operation in the case of each Unit was a race against time. Any delay in fitting and connecting up and starting the pumps, or any subsequent interruption through breakdown would result in the Unit failing to rise on that tide.' And with only days to go before the invasion, every hour counted.

As the Units came up, Polland hit one problem after another. Men had to plug many of the Units' scaffold holes as they came above water, either standing waist-deep in freezing water, or hanging from bosun's chairs as the holes became visible. When divers tried to replace the wires to the penstock valves, they sometimes found only holes where the valves were supposed to be. The so-called watertight fore and aft bulkheads also leaked. Other misplaced holes meant that anything apart from perfect sea conditions could mean some of the caissons might sink during their 100-mile or so voyage rather than just off a Normandy beach. On 2 June, D-Day-3, Brind reported:

> Satisfactory progress has been made in preparing the pumping units: eight out of ten have arrived. Two others are expected within days and an eleventh is being provided by the Director of Salvage in case of failure of any of the above units when tested. Two of the above units referred to have still to be proved operationally. Work is progressing at full speed and it is hoped to meet operational requirements, but it is not possible to say this with certainty, until the two outstanding pumping units have been fully tested.

The first caissons Polland tackled were those sunk in deep water with their gangway slabs completely submerged. Two salvage vessels and two diving parties were tasked with doing the job when the divers sealed the standpipes into the pumping compartments. Some Phoenix Units were listing so far that the pumps were out of the water and prone to sliding overboard if they were not lashed in place. Meanwhile two vessels were carrying out pumping tests on other Phoenix Units to see if badly cracked caissons could still be pumped and towed. Once they were off the bottom, some were towed with the pumps still running into the anchorage ready for quick use, should Polland need to make up numbers if some days the nine-a-day quota could not be met. Securing these spare Units was not an easy task, as they were clearly not designed for mooring like a conventional ship – with no power or winches on board, their large, flat sides could easily act like a giant sail. Sixteen moorings were needed for each one to ensure that they neither drifted on the tide, nor were blown into each other.

Many of the Units proved to be very unstable once they were raised and refloated. Their centre walls were not as watertight as they should have been so that the water mass was flowing freely around the inner space, causing massive and ever-changing weight displacements. One Unit even broke its back after being successfully pumped out and towed further inshore. The date was now 3 June. When Polland was at last formally notified that Operation Overlord was due to commence on 5 June, only four Units had been successfully raised. Polland wrote at the time: 'Dear God, how many more difficulties shall we discover

128

before time runs out on us?' He had forty-eight hours to finish the job and be able to deliver approximately nine units a day for the next two weeks.

On 4 June, many men were hard at work, but raising the caissons was still going too slowly. Polland now had the ships, the equipment and the expertise on site with all available salvage craft, officers and men already down at Selsey. Much of the expertise, though, was tied up with the more menial tasks rather than getting the Units up and out. Now, with only hours to go before the invasion, the true resourcefulness that is integral to a salvage officer's make-up was tested to the limit when Polland made one of the boldest decisions in the Admiralty Salvage Department's history. Calling on the spirit of Dunkirk seen four years earlier, he made an urgent call for all available able-bodied men ashore – volunteers from the local yacht clubs and boat clubs along the south coast – to come forward and lend a hand. The response was fantastic and as they took over the more menial, but no less important tasks, those more qualified were released to get on with the more technical aspects of lifting the Units and preparing them for tow. Untrained civilians were now fitting standpipes, plugging holes and helping to refloat the Units.

Admiral Brind's last report said that the required Units could leave Selsey on D-Day, Monday, 5 June, D+1, 6 June, and D+2, 7 June – but after that he could not say. For Polland down at Selsey this forecast was a little too optimistic. Not until D-Day, 5 June, were all the pumps and vessels necessary actually in place. As so often in British naval history luck, or fate, was about to change everything. On 3 June a low weather front moving in from the Atlantic was pushing a high away from the Channel. The next day, the south coast of England was under heavy wind and rain, with visibility poor. Low cloud and storm-force conditions were forecast for 5 June, meaning that deploying the essential air cover necessary – in advance of the invasion – could well be hampered. Many men were already aboard the myriad assault craft ready to leave. If weather conditions did not improve over the next few days the invasion would have to be delayed for some time with all the logistical problems of disembarking the men and refuelling the thousands of ships. With his Chiefs of Staff divided between launching and delaying, Eisenhower decided to put D-Day back to 6 June. Polland had a vital extra twenty-four hours. The first nine Units would now be ready.

On 5 June, now D-Day-1, eighteen assorted craft moored alongside the first nine Phoenix Units to tow them across the Channel. The pumps were placed on their gangway slabs and connected to the stand-pipes that Polland's men had fitted previously to keep removing the water. Between three and five hours later, the first nine Units were on their way out to deeper water. The tugs due for the next day's work had to be carefully selected depending on draught and the depth of water in which the particular Unit was lying.

All the invasion vessels sailed for Position Z between England and France. Just behind this vast armada was Force Mulberry, towing the components to build the artificial harbours. Position Z was called Piccadilly Circus and was marked with a black and white buoy at its centre, flashing four lights every fifteen seconds. The swept area at Piccadilly Circus was 10 miles wide, opening up to 30 miles wide at the French coast to avoid congestion. Each beach area had two cleared channels, one for fast-moving traffic and one for slow. Dan buoys were laid to mark the swept channel leading to the beaches. Finally, float-ing beacons were laid where the Phoenix Units were supposed to be dropped.

The first-phase Phoenix Units moved at 3 knots. For most crews it took thirty hours to reach Normandy, although some tugs managed the journey much more quickly. On 6 June, crew member Deane Stuart Wynne was aboard the rescue tug, *Samsonia*, one of the tugs taking the old French warship *Courbet* across to be sunk as a block-ship. Then the *Samsonia* was ordered to Selsey Bay. In 2002, Wynne remembered:

These massive 6,000-ton blocks were hollow inside. A platform across the middle carried an anti-aircraft gun and a small crew was put there to fire it. Their big square fronts made it difficult to keep them steady under tow. The marshalling officer came over to us in a boat and soon had us organized with our first hitch. We were on our way back to Normandy in no time at all. In fact, such was the power of the *Samsonia* that we had soon caught up with some of the small tugs we had seen going over on our way back. We overtook some of these and I believe established a record of delivering, positioning and sinking the caisson and getting back to Selsey in eighteen hours.

Although the Units were on their way, there were still problems during the tows across to Normandy. On one occasion an ocean tug had to turn back with a heavily listing Unit. Then a small tug rammed and sunk another Unit while trying to hand it over to an ocean-going tug. On another occasion a Unit was found to be badly leaking and thus useless, at least for a while. In less than two weeks, Polland's Circus, as his team became known, raised sixty-five units. After Selsey had been cleared the same procedure was carried on at Sheerness and Dungeness. He remembered the work of his circus: 'It was extremely fortunate that the Department, even at such short notice, was able to cope with this situation, otherwise a last-minute breakdown might have occurred in a vital part of the impending invasion operations.'

One wonders what might have happened had a Phoenix Unit not grounded at Littlehampton when it did, or perhaps a few days later, putting a vital part of the D-Day offensive in jeopardy. What if the weather had been fine on 5 June, and Eisenhower had never put Overlord back twenty-four hours? But the ability to exploit that luck was present too, and this was never more obvious than when Polland and the Admiralty Salvage Department were tasked with solving the Phoenix problem.

The Rear Admiral in charge of Mulberry, William (Dunkirk Joe) Tennant, had been the Beachmaster at Dunkirk in 1940 where he had played a key role in the evacuation of more than 300,000 British and French troops off the beaches. He was also heavily involved with the planning of Overlord. He later recalled: 'The Salvage Department stepped into the breach and performed, in a very short time available, a Herculean task in getting the pumping station under control and the thanks of the Allied Commander-in-Chief Expeditionary Force are due to them, and particularly Captain Polland for their great assistance.'

As Polland saw the Phoenix Units off from Selsey, the rest of the Salvage Department were scattered among the invasion fleet heading directly into the heart of determined German resistance. While the first waves of men fought their way over the bodies, barbed wire and mines to retake France, the Chief Salvage Officer for Northern Europe, Thomas McKenzie, was about to command more than fifty salvage vessels and hundreds of men urgently needed to clear the beachheads and blockaded ports, and get as many ships as possible back into the war.

Chapter 14

Overlord

A salvage policy was established for Operation Round Up in 1943, General Eisenhower's first blueprint for an early invasion of France, which was cancelled due to lack of resources and military commitments in other theatres. Parts of its planning still formed the basis of Operation Overlord the following year, but its salvage element certainly did not. Admiral Dewar was heavily involved in organizing Round Up's salvage strategy. At a time when nearly all the Department's resources were committed to the Battle of the Atlantic, he minuted somewhat bleakly: 'The whole success of the expedition will be jeopardized, unless we prepare an effective salvage organization. There is not the slightest hope of providing enough [ships] from the existing salvage fleet.'

Dewar first broached the subject of a salvage facility for Operation Overlord later that same year. He knew that it would call for many more ships, equipment and men than Round Up, but the number and types of vessels, and the location of the invasion needed to be defined if he was to develop a competent salvage venture this time. Dewar saw a little more clearly what he was up against after discussions with the Admiralty's Research and Development Department, and made his views known to the Director of Plans. 'It transpired that the rapid salvage of a large number of big Tank Landing Craft would be a requirement, although this fact has never been communicated to DS/VD [Dewar himself]. It is, therefore, requested that information on the following points may be furnished to DS/VD as soon as possible.'

Dewar's first two questions were certainly the most controversial and, although they were intrinsic to Overlord's salvage strategy, he received no answer whatsoever. He knew that it was essential 'to know which ports we have to deal with to enable the most suitable type of salvage craft to be allotted'. His next question was even more contentious when he requested 'an indication of the number of landing beaches and their distance from the nearest ports'. Dewar then wanted to know how many major assault craft and merchant vessels would be allocated to each beach to estimate the numbers of salvage craft required, and a rough guide as to how the invasion would progress to other, perhaps blocked, harbours.

Director of Plans Staff Officer, L.L. Hughes Hallett, confirmed that there would be a salvage requirement for the recovery and dispersal of a variety of ships blocking ports, berths and fairways, as well as coasters and major landing craft. There was no indication of where, when and how big the assault was going to be, but Hughes Hallett did give some indication of expected losses during the initial assault phase. He replied: 'Director of Plans suggests that something in the order of thirty LCTs [Landing Craft Tanks], ten LSTs [Landing Ship Tanks] and eight coasters or ships requiring assistance concurrently may be a reasonable estimate.'

Altogether a fleet of fifty-five salvage vessels was finally assembled for the invasion of Normandy, including lifting lighters, wreck dispersal vessels, Rescue Tugs and store carriers. Some consideration was given to identifying salvage craft and Rescue Tugs to separate them from other non-combatant vessels. Salvage ships had a large white 'S' painted on their funnels and Rescue Tugs had a large white 'R'. In the thick of battle their easy identification was necessary, both for beachmasters and disabled vessels alike. Fifteen salvage vessels were allocated for the initial assault phase and the next few days thereafter, two each for Juno, Sword and Gold Beach and two for each Mulberry Harbour arriving on D-Day to D+5. This left five in reserve as necessary and for captured ports. One wreck-dispersal vessel was also allocated to each beach area, leaving one in reserve. Thomas McKenzie was appointed Principal Salvage Officer with eighteen key officers below him, including Commander Kay who had excelled himself during the First World War. The United States Navy had their own salvage organization but, as history would soon show, it would be far too small to cope with severe losses, especially those on Omaha.

McKenzie had to be on the beaches from the earliest stages to coordinate the necessary salvage work and to keep in touch with his officers at all times. Each vessel's captain was informed that the presence of an Admiralty salvage officer on board a salvage vessel directing the operation did not at any time relieve the master from the obligations or responsibilities regarding care and control of his vessel. But at the same time, the salvage officer was in charge of the actual operations and it was the master's duty to assist him in every way by working his ship and crew to the salvage officer's needs. Once ashore small salvage parties were supplied with tractors and bulldozers to push some stranded craft back into the sea.

The Germans had poured millions of tons of concrete into Hitler's Atlantic Wall, primarily along the Pas-de-Calais, a 70-mile stretch of the French coast running from south of Le Touquet to just north of Dunkirk. The Pas-de-Calais is directly opposite Dover and Folkestone, and only about 20 miles across the Channel, where the Führer believed an invasion might land. When Field Marshal Erwin Rommel was tasked with strengthening the Wall, he had a fixed idea of how to begin:

> I want anti-personnel mines, anti-tank mines, anti-paratroops mines. I want mines to sink ships and I want mines to sink landing craft. I want some minefields designed so that our infantry can cross them, but no enemy tanks. I want mines that detonate when a wire is tripped; mines that explode when a wire is cut; mines that can be remote controlled; and mines that will blow up when a beam of light is interrupted.

Altogether Rommel had more than 6.5 million exploding devices sown along the Normandy beaches, and for some distance out to sea. In the early hours of 6 June the LCTs, LSTs, destroyers, supply ships, Rescue Tugs and salvage vessels began their 100-mile or so voyage to Normandy. It was essential that the landing craft hit the beaches on a rising tide to allow for a rapid exit. About 500ft out from the high-water line, Rommel's underwater beach defences began. Some, called Belgian Gates, were 10ft-high iron structures dug into the seabed, pointing out to sea like seventeenth-century pikes. They were clustered with Teller mines and old French Navy shells armed and ready to annihilate any craft that touched them.

One Canadian infantryman, Private G.W. Levers, described the events in his diary as he headed for Juno Beach: 'We are within half a mile from shore by now and several of the chaps are quite seasick. The engines are speeded up and making a run for the shore.' Having got past the Belgian Gates, about 160ft further in, logs were driven into the seabed, again pointing out to sea, with more Teller mines strapped to their tops. Levers continued: 'We can see the beach although the

134

seas are running high. We can see a big pill box with the shells bursting around it and apparently doing no damage at all.'

Having got this far without being hit, on the seashore itself were hundreds of hedgehogs, 6ft-high X-shaped steel obstacles capable of punching a hole through any landing craft with ease. Levers finished his diary entry by saying: 'The machine gun bullets are starting to whine around our craft and the boys are keeping their heads down. Here we go, the ramp is down.' When the ramps dropped on the beaches the soldiers were faced with mortar, sniper and assorted small-arms fire as well as more mines, including S mines or Bouncing Betties. When triggered they sprang up to waist height before exploding horizontally, indiscriminately shredding steel and flesh alike. Many landing craft on Juno were damaged on or near the beach.

The first British troops landed in a hail of machine-gun fire and 88mm shells on Sword Beach at 7.26 am. German mortar fire put at least one LCT out of action as it burned furiously on the water's edge. Many others were mined further out to sea as they tried to dodge the obstacles in order to reach the beaches. The British 50th Division landed on Gold Beach ten minutes later. Cold, wet and skidding in each other's vomit, they immediately ran into trouble as a rising tide had covered the Belgian Gates. These proved to be more hazardous than the German gun emplacements as some craft were impaled on them and blasted. By the time the first wave of landing craft had hit the sand, twenty were mined on either the Belgian Gates, wooden pikes or on the beach itself. During another wave later that day, fifteen out of sixteen landing craft carrying the 47th Royal Marine Commandos were damaged in one way or another.

The Canadian infantry landed on Juno Beach twenty minutes later, after Bomber Command had dropped more than 5,000lb of ordnance on German gun emplacements the previous night – grossly missing their target. A daylight naval bombardment caused even more chaos as smoke obscured much of the beach area. The heavy swell and fear of running into shoals meant the landing craft collided on their way in, many tripping Teller mines that either crippled the craft or jammed some of their ramps shut. Altogether more than half of all the landing craft running into Juno were damaged and a quarter of them were sunk. The Canadian forces suffered the second-highest casualty rate behind the Americans on Omaha Beach, but they still managed to take

Bernières-sur-Mer, which was the first village to be liberated on the main D-Day assault.

Many of the soldiers landing in Normandy had just completed at least two years' intensive training for this one, big day and were naturally well armed and extremely well prepared. Admiralty Salvage personnel had no such combat training, many were unarmed, and yet they were caught up in some of most savage fighting, witnessed and documented by surviving military personnel. They were also some of the only civilians involved in the entire D-Day operation and were on the beaches from the very beginning until many of the armed forces had advanced well into occupied territory. Sadly, as so often happens when military history has been officially recorded, analysed and theorized, there is no mention of the vital part salvage men played in a frontal assault that some historians have called the ultimate battle to decide whether Europe was to be a free or fascist state.

From D-Day onwards the Salvage Department raised or cleared three times as many ships than during the whole of the First World War, right up to the end of the second Battle of the Atlantic. Casualties attended to during the beach phase alone (June to August 1944) amounted to more than 1,250 vessels, caused mainly by mining and weather damage. These figures are truly striking, but what was it actually like to be salvaging ships under the most trying of combat conditions?

Throughout the First World War, right up to May 1944, all shipping needing salvage assistance was recorded in great detail, including reports from salvage officers, tug masters, pilots and surviving crew members. Once D-Day had started there was simply no time for such attention to detail, a bureaucratic deficiency that would eventually lead to a difference of opinion between the men saving ships in the blood and sand on Juno, Sword and Gold, and the Admiralty in White-hall. However, there are two surviving sources to give some indication of the working conditions. The very brief salvage reports, that were barely more than a few sentences long are one source, and the decoration citations earned for bravery on the beaches during the invasion and the port clearance work are another.

Casualties attended by the first wave of salvage vessels were much higher than the Director of Plans had estimated, and not only for landing craft. On Juno, from 6 June 1944 to 17 July, fourteen merchant ships were mined, bombed or torpedoed. All but two of the vessels were salvaged, the latter having hit mines and broken their backs. A typically brief salvage report on the 638-ton ammunition ship *Dunvegan Head*, says: 'Ammunition ship shelled & burned out. Surveyed & considered a constructive total loss.' The *Kyle Gorm* ran aground on Gold. 'Attended & repaired by *Sea Salvor*. Refloated. Towed to UK.'

At times a little more detail survives, such as the 7,093-ton troop-ship *Derrycunihy*, mined on Sword. Her salvage report only comments: 'Back broken, after end sunk, fore end floating – 109 army vehicles and other material salvaged undamaged from fore end, ship total loss.' Such a brief account gives nothing away of what actually happened to this ship, and the conditions the salvage men had to work under to clear her. Bad weather had delayed the *Derrycunihy*'s berthing for a week. On her first night at anchor the Luftwaffe dropped some of the newly developed oyster mines in the area. The following morning she weighed anchor to steam round to Gold where it was more sheltered, but when her engines were started an oyster mine ripped the ship in half and killed nine of her crew. The stern section sank in a matter of seconds with many troops still in their bunks. Heavy vehicles were stored on the deck above and, as the stern broke off and went down, the severely weakened deck collapsed, tipping the heavy trucks and trailers onto the struggling men below. More than 150 were crushed or drowned. The fore end was saved and towed back to Britain as a possible 'spare', but the after end is still lying off Sword, where McKenzie's men abandoned it more than sixty years ago.

The same storm that delayed the *Derrycunihy*'s arrival caused much more collateral damage than any German resistance. Hurricane-force winds reaching Force 12, or 80mph, piled an unusually high spring tide into the Mulberries and beaches. Small onshore trees were being blown over or even uprooted as roof slates and masonry were tossed around like playing cards. Offshore, the sea level rose 10ft above normal high water and the air was thick with spray and foam. The American Mulberry A was lost, mainly due to the poor alterations made beyond its design capabilities. On 19 June the weather worsened. Landing craft wires parted, leaving them to thrash about in the raging sea until they sank, or were rammed into the harbours. The British Mulberry B was much luckier, having been better constructed and because the nearby Calvados Reef offered some protection. Altogether more than 150 ships were able to shelter within it.

When the storm abated, more than 800 landing craft were stranded and 300 were destroyed in the American harbour alone. The Salvage Department repaired 553 ships, of which 90 were HM vessels, 80 were naval units, 27 were unclassified, 13 were merchant ships and the remaining 315 were small landing craft and barges. During the gale many ships were at sea, bringing supplies or sections for the Mulberry Harbours.

Among the awards and decorations earned during the summer of 1944, scant details can only leave to the imagination what these men achieved. Commander Frank Scurr was awarded the DSC. He was a senior salvage officer on Sword. The Honours and Awards Committee noted that Scurr was 'frequently under shell fire, and it is due to his efforts that before Sword Beach was closed everything salvageable was salvaged'. McKenzie said of Scurr:

> Though by no means a young man, to him fell some of the most difficult and hazardous salvage operations in Overlord. During the first few days he and his men were constantly on the beaches, or operating close inshore, frequently under enemy shellfire. When all the work had been done, Commander Scurr was forced to return to the UK and hospital suffering from overwork and exhaustion.

Lieutenant Victor Campbell was made an MBE for the salvage of three HM ships, three merchant ships and a number of landing craft. McKenzie wrote: 'Although this officer has only limited experience of salvage work, he showed great zeal and resourcefulness which commanded the respect of the men under his command and of the senior officers.' Lieutenant Commander Herbert James Lott was decorated 'for major salvage operations in North Europe'. For salvage operations on the Normandy beaches and port clearance work in the United States sector, he showed 'outstanding skill and initiative on major salvage operations in the Seine at Antwerp and in the outer Schelde. Strongly recommended for decoration.' Acting Lieutenant Commander David John Roger Davies was decorated for salvage operations on the Normandy beaches and port clearance work assisting the Americans on Utah and Omaha beaches.

Temporary Lieutenant John Archer Scott was also decorated for salvage operations on the Normandy beaches, and port clearance work. During the operations and thereafter Lieutenant Scott also served under orders of the United States salvage organization. His citation reads: 'Through initiative, co-operation and unfailing will-ingness to undertake unusually difficult tasks even under most difficult physical conditions, he has been responsible for raising many sunken ships and obstructions and contributing materially to the clearing of continental ports vital to the successful build-up of the Allied Forces in France.' Thomas McKenzie was awarded the CBE in 1943 and the CB in 1945 for his contribution to marine salvage.

The Admiralty had to loan the United States salvage organization six vessels and personnel to help clear the debris from Utah and Omaha beaches from D-Day onwards, under Commander W.I. Wroten, United States Navy. McKenzie was pleased with how Wroten operated the vessels. A year after D-Day the six ships were still in the American Sector. McKenzie wrote fondly: 'Largely due to his [Wroten's] leadership and cheerful personality, the combined British and US salvage parties have worked, and are still working, in complete harmony and make a first-rate salvage team.' The shipping casualties on Omaha were very high indeed. The beach was divided into five sectors. The largest, Easy Red, lay in the centre flanked by two other sectors on either side, and saw by far the most vicious and bloody fighting throughout the main D-Day assault. Four hours after the first troops landed, the 18th Infantry Regiment alone lost twenty-eight assorted landing craft to mines and shellfire as they tried to reach their ¾-mile stretch of the 3-mile long beachhead.

For all the good the Salvage Department were doing on the beaches, the Admiralty kept pressing McKenzie for more detailed reports of the ships his men were clearing. By February 1945 their demands were becoming more insistent. In response to their enquiry the Admiralty were informed: 'With his existing staff and without prejudice to his primary duties of superintending the salvage of valuable shipping and the clearance of liberated and occupied ports, it is not possible for the Principal Salvage Officer to produce further or more detailed reports than those at present rendered.' All that could be managed were a couple of token detailed reports to appease London. Ironically, from all the salvage success stories that could have been chosen, for some reason the two submitted concerned vessels that did not really help the invasion.

McKenzie submitted one and Commander Kay the other. McKen-zie's was a detailed account of a 4,702-ton Liberty ship called the *Alan A. Dale*. A Biber one-man midget submarine hit her on Christmas Eve 1944 (the Biber having just been developed in response to a possible

139

Allied invasion with the sole intent of crippling Allied shipping). The *Alan A. Dale* was in the River Schelde, inbound with a general cargo of heavy motor vehicles, trailers and a considerable amount of mail. Two hours later the Admiralty salvage vessel, *American Salvor*, one of the new salvage vessels that had been built under the United States Lend-Lease agreement, reached her and found that the amidships section was burning furiously.

Salvage personnel tried to save the ship throughout the Christmas period, but on 27 December she developed a 24° list. McKenzie reported, 'There being nothing substantial for any craft to moor against even at low tide, I considered it was not prudent to risk any more craft alongside. In my opinion further discharge was now impracticable and on account of above conditions the vessel would have to be considered a total loss.' She was only removed in June 2003 as part of an operation to improve shipping access to Antwerp.

Kay's report ran to a little more than one page and covered the raising of the American Hog Islander (a type of cargo ship mass-produced during the First World War) *Alcoa Banner* that had been bombed while moored alongside a quay on 24 January 1945. Kay does not even say how she was damaged, where she was or what efforts in detail were made to save her. There is only a brief list of dates and times when events took place, such as on her last day when he wrote: '28th January 1945. 14.00 contractors commence shoring vessel. 16.00 vessel takes the blocks. 17.00 vessel dry.' She eventually had to be scuttled. The Admiralty in Whitehall did not press for any more detailed salvage reports.

Many of the ports on the way to Germany were packed with scuttled ships in a repeat of Zeebrugge and Ostend in 1918. They were also heavily booby-trapped. To remove the ordnance 'P' Parties of specially trained men went ahead of the salvage teams to find and make it safe. Cherbourg was one of the worst affected ports, where the retreating German Army scuttled sixty-seven ships. Even the quays were demolished and hundreds of submarine mines were dumped into the water; railway trucks were piled on top of the wrecks to add to the chaos. Three weeks were needed to clear a narrow channel through all the mines. Because the port was in the American Sector, McKenzie assisted Commodore W.A. Sullivan, United States Navy Chief Salvage Officer, to plan the Cherbourg clearance, which then became another joint British and United States project. The Admiralty Salvage Department cleared the wrecks while the United States salvage organization cleared the jetties and landing stages.

Within a few days the first DUKWs (the ultimate in seaborne 4 × 4s) and LCTs were unloading cargo, and the first Liberty ship had entered the port by 16 July. Cherbourg was working at half its capacity within four months and by the end of September the port was handling more cargo than in its pre-war life. As the Allies advanced, so did the Salvage Department. When Dieppe was liberated on 1 September, there were twenty-one wrecks jamming the harbour. With no mines to contend with, it was one of the first French ports to handle convoy supplies and was soon landing 7,000 tons of goods per day. Le Havre fell eleven days later when 165 ships and the usual assortment of toppled cranes and booby traps were removed. McKenzie was in charge of clearing Ostend. The port was so choked with sunken ships that more than six months would normally be needed to clear the debris. For the sake of speed he resorted to blasting them out. Within four days, enough of the port was reopened to allow vital army supplies to be unloaded while the shattered steel was being cleared away around them.

Le Havre was to be the main unloading port for all supplies, but it was too badly damaged and Rouen took its place. Reaching the inland port meant steaming up the River Seine, but it was heavily mined and blocked at the village of Sours, north-west of Rouen, by a sunken 12,000-ton whale-oil factory ship and several other vessels. A passage wide enough for small ships was cleared past the whaler and by the time the river was free of mines, Liberty ships could proceed. Eventually the whaler was raised, towed to Rouen and fully repaired. A combined British and French salvage team cleared more than eighty sunken vessels from Rouen, giving the Army all the unloading space they needed. The port clearance was so successful that shortly afterwards, when the American forces also needed to use Rouen, their ships were also able to berth with ease.

After Ostend was liberated, Wreck Dispersal Vessels blasted a way through the blockships at the entrance so that salvage vessels could enter and clear more than sixty wrecks from the quays, allowing the port to become the main point for troops coming to Europe or going home on leave. In November, Antwerp fell and soon became the principal deep-water port for Europe. Although there was very little damage to the port installations and quays, for many months Antwerp became the main target for V1 and V2 rockets resulting in nearly fifty more shipping casualties.

Salvage operations were started in Hamburg after Germany surrendered. Allied bombing had annihilated the port where more than 620 wrecks of all sizes were sunk alongside and around the demolished quays. In six months, before the responsibility for salvage was handed over to the Control Commission, more than 320 craft – 120,000 tons of shipping – had been raised and ample berths were provided for all subsequent shipping requirements. In Kiel seventeen ships were salvaged, in Wilhelmshaven twenty-one, as well as others in many other German ports. More than 125 U-boats were also raised or removed, taken out into deep water and scuttled.

Many decorations were awarded to salvage personnel for this important port clearance work. Deputy Chief Principal Salvage Officer James Fenwick McKenzie was decorated for 'Salvage operations, for opening up the port of Ostend and outstanding courage, leadership and skill as Deputy Principal Salvage Officer, North-west Europe'. Thomas McKenzie wrote: 'This officer showed quite outstanding energy, leadership and devotion to duty in salvage operations in the port of Ostend and the rapid opening of this port was largely due to him. He has also been responsible for saving a number of ships mined or torpedoed off this port during the past six months.'

Salvage administration staff members were recognized as well. Lieutenant Commander Ian Clarence Trelawny, who was Thomas McKenzie's assistant, was heavily involved with salvage organization and port clearance. Trelawny had already been awarded the DSC in May 1943, and bar in December of the same year. He was a very competent assistant, of whom McKenzie noted: 'During my frequent absences on detached duty he has been responsible for the movement and administration of over fifty salvage vessels, Wreck Dispersal Vessels and Rescue Tugs, and by his devotion to duty has been in a large measure responsible for the success of the Overlord salvage operation.'

The Flag Officer for the British Assault Area, Admiral Harold Martin Borough gave some indication of the fighting on the beaches during and after the Allies gained their first foothold.

The enemy tried every means in his power to sink our shipping and disrupt the unloading. Attacks were made by e-boats, mine laying aircraft, mine laying coastal craft, torpedo aircraft, bombers, composite aircraft, long-range shore guns, human torpedoes, explosive motor boats, swimming saboteurs and very long-range torpedoes. During this period five E-boats, sixty-four explosive motorboats and forty-two human torpedoes were sunk. Ten enemy aircraft were shot down and 609 mines were detonated. This result was only made possible by the constant alertness, courage, skill and determination displayed by all concerned. The work of the personnel engaged on salvage and repair operations was equally outstanding and a large number of ships and craft, some of them very seriously damaged, salved and repaired during the period under review are evidence of the skill, resourcefulness and endurance of the officers and men concerned.

The size of the merchant fleet at the beginning of the war was 17½ million tons. From September 1939 to the end of 1943 the losses amounted to 11½ million tons. During the same period, 4½ million tons of new merchant ships were produced in the United Kingdom, and a further 2½ million tons were salved, repaired and restored to service. The Admiralty's responsibility for salvage continued until 30 September 1946, by which date more than 3¾ million tons had been dealt with by the Salvage and the Rescue Tug Departments. Broken down into shipping numbers this equates to more than 1,000 vessels salvaged, towed or removed. This does not include port clearance work after D-Day where a further 1,700 ships where cleared from more than fifteen European ports, of which more than 900 were from the Normandy beaches alone. Services were also rendered to over 800 naval vessels between 1939 and 1945.

At the end of the war the Admiralty's combined salvage arm, including Rescue Tugs and Wreck Dispersal Vessels, came to more than eighty vessels, as well as sixty-four submersible pontoons of various types, crewed by more than 2,500 officers and men. The list of equipment ran to thousands of assorted pumps, tools, shackles, generators and the myriad tools needed to lift stranded ships. It was bigger and better equipped than the salvage fleets of all the other Allied nations put together. Maintaining such an organization in time of peace was a heavy financial drain on the Admiralty coffers.

In July 1946 the Phillips Report 'On Peace-Time Policy for Salvage and Deep Sea Rescue Work' was published. Fearing a repeat of 1919 when the last salvage organization was broken up and lost, Vice Admiral Henry C. Phillips stated:

We are of the opinion that a salvage service should be maintained in time of peace as part of the country's naval defences to maintain and develop the technique not only of ship salvage, which is part of the defence measures always required by a maritime nation, but also of the port clearance work which is an important factor in modern amphibious operations.

To maintain a trained nucleus organization, which would be instantly available to prevent severe losses from sudden attack, Phillips recommended that only four salvage ships should be retained in commission under the White Ensign. Due to the lack of salvage work in time of peace, the Report stressed that all salvage vessels and tugs should remain in British hands to ensure that British commercial salvage firms retained the very best equipment when it came to competing against foreign companies for lucrative contracts. Every effort was made to dispose of the surplus vessels, strategically, around the Empire, such as Singapore, Aden and the Mediterranean. All could then be requisitioned in time of war. The remaining salvage vessels were put into care and maintenance. Twelve rescue tugs were also maintained in service, while the remainder, like the surplus salvage vessels, were sold within the British Empire or transferred to care and maintenance. But they, along with the redundant salvage vessels, were not allowed under any circumstances to be sold abroad.

Phillips also recommended that the Salvage Department should be transferred from Admiral Dewar to the Boom Defence Organization, along with the Rescue Tug Service and Wreck Dispersal Department. The Boom Defence Organization was mainly responsible for navigation buoys, moorings and port protection throughout the Empire. By the end of the war most countries were willing to accept salvage clearance from United Kingdom companies operating abroad, although Turkey and the Soviet Union flatly refused to allow British-flagged vessels into their territorial waters. Phillips wrote, 'We are of the opinion that it is desirable to ask these two countries to withdraw their restrictive legislation and we recommend that the Foreign Office should be invited to make representations accordingly.' For the Soviet Union, at least, Western salvage vessels did not enter Russian naval bases until 2006.

Although the Admiralty's massive Salvage Department was now broken up and scattered throughout the Empire, this time it could be called back, in full if necessary, a point stressed by Admiral Phillips

144

when he criticized Admiralty Salvage in 1939:

When war came, in spite of the magnitude of our seafaring interests, only five ocean-going commercial tugs were available in the country and we had no modern salvage vessels and equipment. In consequence a large number of lives, ships and valuable cargoes were avoidably lost, the nation unnecessarily imperilled and the war indirectly prolonged. We regard such a situation as most deplorable and urge that it must not be allowed to recur.

Chapter 15

Operation Elba Isle

Some of the salvage vessels, retained after Phillips's recommendations, were transferred to the Mediterranean, based in Malta. Seven years after his report was published the Admiralty Salvage Department, now known as the Admiralty Salvage Service, became involved in one of the most historic peacetime salvage operations throughout its hundred-year history, requiring the use of new techniques. The British Overseas Airways Corporation (BOAC) de Havilland Comet G-ALYP Yoke Peter was the world's first commercial jet airliner. Just after the 1953 Christmas holidays she was en route from Singapore to London via the Middle East and Rome.

Heavyweight boxing champion John Steel boarded Yoke Peter in Singapore for the flight to Bangkok and then onwards to Rangoon, where veteran war correspondent Reginald William Winchester (Chester) Wilmot boarded. Australian-born Wilmot was regarded as one of the finest correspondents of the Second World War and was on his way home after attending the BBC's Round-the-World Christmas Day broadcast from Sydney, Australia.

Yoke Peter flew northwards via Karachi, Bahrain and Beirut before arriving at Rome's Ciampino Airport to pick up one last passenger for the final leg to London. There were now twenty-nine passengers aboard, including ten children and six crew members. On 10 January, 31-year-old Captain Alan Gibson DFC took off for the two-hour journey home. About twenty minutes into the flight, Wilmot, Steel and the other passengers settled down as one of Yoke Peter's crew members, stewardess Jean Evelyn Clarke, was in or near the after galley area preparing to serve drinks.

What happened during the next couple of minutes took many months to piece together, but as Italian magistrate Dr Antonio Maria Perri said, 'Its outstanding importance from a social viewpoint' became essential, 'and perhaps also improvements, or modifications, to that type of aircraft and to hopefully save human lives'. Yoke Peter was a first, not only in salvage recovery, but also in understanding high-altitude crash dynamics. Never before had commercial fare-paying passengers been subjected to such a scenario – the combined forensic evidence and salvage operation ultimately lead to much safer commercial jet travel that is still enjoyed worldwide today.

After collecting a great deal of evidence BOAC Director of Medical Services, Sir Harold Edward Wittingham, was in a strong position to recount the following events. This included investigating a strange phenomenon found on all recovered bodies, except Jean Clarke. Unusual burns, also noticed on passengers aboard a McDonnell Douglas DC6 that had broken up over the Mexican Gulf the previous year, were on the dead. What made these so odd was that the burns were beneath the passengers' unmarked clothing, and hair as well as fine down on the bodies had not been singed or charred.

As Yoke Peter passed 26,500ft, Gibson began climbing to 36,000ft where he made radio contact with a fellow captain aboard a BOAC Argonaut passenger plane some distance below. Just after his eleventh word, nothing but static replaced the rest of his otherwise calmly spoken transmission. Part of the fuselage just behind the flight deck had been torn out, causing an instant explosive decompression. Many passengers were ejected from their seats upwards and forwards into the ceiling and luggage racks, causing severe skull fractures in some, while others were merely stunned. Yoke Peter, screaming like a banshee, was now in a steep dive, pitching, yawing and spinning so violently that the passengers struck various hard surfaces, causing more skull fractures to the sides of their heads this time, as well as ribs, and severe internal injuries. Effects of sudden explosive decompression made their lungs expand, causing internal lacerations as the cabin pressure fought to adjust with the now exposed stratosphere. In an ever-increasing dive attitude the passengers, some already dead, others dying or uncon-scious, lay slumped across the seats and in the gangway.

Many reasons for the strange burns were put forward, including radiation, ultraviolet, acid, friction, even kerosene mixed with sea-water, but why were the burns beneath their clothing? And why was hair and fine down on the bodies not affected? Sir Harold Edward Wittingham stated:

Their clothing and bodies then became contaminated with scald-ing or very hot fluid (possibly hydraulic fluid at 90°C or lubri-

147

cating fluid at 100°C) which had been pumped in considerable quantity over the floor of the cabin. This fluid may have entered along an air-conditioning trunk or ruptured piping and been aided in its spread by the dive position of the aircraft.

The oil soaked through the passengers' clothes onto their skin as it was literally pushed up through Yoke Peter, coating everything in its sticky, boiling path.

At about 20,000ft, an explosion, possibly fuel-related, concentrated the fire outside the aircraft rather than within while Yoke Peter now sped like a flaming meteor towards the Mediterranean. The fuselage then broke in two just behind the main wing spar. Many more passengers were ejected, skirts, shirts and even trousers being ripped off in their rapid descent, aided by somersaulting at a speed in excess of 170ft per second. The worst injuries were in or around Row 7, just behind the hydraulic oil tank near where Steel was sitting. Necropsy investigation showed that from this point passengers bled more the further back they were, explaining that 'the more they bled, the longer they lived'. All life was extinct from within seconds to two minutes, but loss of consciousness is likely to have occurred much sooner. Chester Wilmot and Captain Gibson were among the twenty bodies never recovered. The remaining passengers in the tail section, including stewardess Jean Clarke, were spilled out near, or on impact with the water as Yoke Peter's shattered remains speared into a disused German minefield off the Italian coast – gauging a 65ft scar along the seabed.

Elba fisherman Giovanni di Marco was working his boat just south of the island. It was a beautifully calm Sunday morning with a cloudy sky. He later recalled:

I heard the whine of a plane above me. It was above the clouds. I could not see it. Then I heard three explosions, very quickly, one after the other. For a moment all was quiet. Then several miles away I saw a silver thing flash out of the clouds. Smoke came from it. It hit the sea. There was a great cloud of water. By the time I got there all was still again. There were some bodies in the water. We began to pick them up. There was nothing else we could do.

Britain's de Havilland Aircraft Corporation had beaten Boeing to introduce the first passenger jet aircraft and in doing so had cornered the market in the new jet age. Now all that was left of their flagship

148

Comet was the remains of fifteen passengers scattered amid light wreckage over about one square mile of the Mediterranean. With the Comet's future threatened, BOAC grounded its entire fleet for examination by de Havilland, BOAC and government personnel to try to discover what had gone wrong. The situation was deemed so important that Prime Minister Winston Churchill called a crisis meeting with Minister of Transport, Alan Tindal Lennox-Boyd, after he flew back from Italy, having met with Admiralty salvage officials.

Lennox-Boyd had met with Chief Salvage Officer for Malta, Victor Campbell, who was decorated as a young officer for his actions during Operation Overlord. He wanted to know if recovering the wreckage was possible. Campbell was sure that the wreckage could be salvaged, provided it was no deeper than about 180ft or 200ft at the very most – the salvage divers could not descend any further. If they did the compressors would be unable to sustain an adequate airflow beyond that depth. Yoke Peter had hit the seabed about 600ft down and, being well out of salvage range, finding the flaw that had destroyed the Comet, and so Britain's edge on international jet air travel, looked very bleak indeed.

At the same time that Churchill's meeting took place, Commander-in-Chief, Mediterranean, Earl Mountbatten of Burma was at his private home, Broadlands in Hampshire, after attending an Admiralty meeting. Lennox-Boyd telephoned the C-in-C immediately after the crisis meeting had finished. With Mountbatten having to get out of his bath to go to the phone, the Minister of Transport explained why he had called him at such an inopportune time. 'The Government consider it vital to salvage the Comet that crashed off Elba. Can you tell me a salvage firm, which could do this?'

Mountbatten replied, 'What depth of water is it in?'

Lennox-Boyd said succinctly, '600 fathoms.'

'I didn't know there was a depth of 600 fathoms in the Mediterranean,' said Mountbatten.

'Sorry,' said Lennox-Boyd, 'I meant 600 feet. What salvage firm do you think I could approach?'

'My own, of course,' replied Mountbatten.

Having already received Campbell's pessimistic report, Lennox-Boyd was at a loss. He said, 'What do you mean?'

'The Mediterranean Fleet of course.'

'Do you think you can do it?'

'If anyone can salvage the aircraft, the Navy can certainly do it,' said Mountbatten, 'I'll issue orders right away.'

Malta was instructed to recover Yoke Peter, regardless of the obstacles involved. Malta Chief of Staff, Commodore W.W. Woods DSO, discussed the situation in more detail with Salvage Officer, Commander Gerald Forsberg, who was to direct the salvage operation, and Campbell. Regarding details of the crash they did not have much to go on. Forsberg said rather tartly, 'Up to this point the sole source of information had been from reports in *The Times*.' Without standard diving equipment a completely different salvage method had to be utilized, including the use of specialized resources from the commercial sector. Then the basic search and recovery plan was based on a pioneering salvage operation conducted three years earlier.

The A Class submarine HMS *Affray* had gone missing while on a simulated war patrol in the Western Approaches, her last reported position near the Isle of Wight. After a search covering more than 1,500 square miles of the Channel, by twenty-four ships from four nations, she could not be found. The Admiralty Research Laboratory at Teddington offered an experimental Marconi underwater television camera to widen the search area and the original search pattern was repeated, but with no luck. The next two contacts outside the area were immediately disregarded after the grainy black and white image showed that they were not the *Affray*. The Marconi camera then located another wreck the following day. As the camera panned around the steel hulk, the name '*Affray*' was clearly seen on her conning tower. She had sunk a considerable way from her estimated position, within sight of Alderney, in the Channel Islands, where she still lies today as a protected wreck. Not only was she found, but the camera also clearly identified that her snort mast, similar to a snorkel, for venting the submarine while submerged at periscope depth, was hanging off. The device was removed using cutting gear under the direction of the camera operators, was later inspected in Portsmouth and is thought to be the reason for the *Affray*'s loss.

Two phases to the Comet salvage operation were identified, which might seem obvious, but both needed very careful consideration. Firstly the wreckage had to be found, somewhere in 100 square miles of ocean, and secondly, it had to be raised from record depths. The ocean-going salvage vessel *Sea Salvor* was one of two vessels deployed for the operation. She was a hybrid of a Rescue Tug and an ocean-going salvage ship, and was well suited to the role. She could tow a vessel in distress, fight fires, as well as carry out the patching and pumping methods needed for all types of ships requiring salvage assistance. The boom defence ship HMS *Barhill* was also deployed, as every time *Sea Salvor* needed to relocate above a new contact, she had to be securely moored in place.

The only way to pick up the fragmented wreckage was to literally scrape Yoke Peter off the seabed using a grab. The Southampton salvage firm, Risdon Beazley, was known to have one with a lifting capacity of 4.5 tons. The firm also supplied an observation chamber, which was long and narrow with toughened windows at 60° intervals, with additional ones to give a full vertical view. The observer sat on a revolving seat giving quick access to each window, allowing him to telephone the ship above to give details of what he saw. Commander John Polland, who had returned to Risdon Beazley as a senior salvage officer after the war, oversaw the necessary changes to the equipment aboard *Sea Salvor*, such as fitting the grab, the observation chamber and six new mooring points to hold the 4 tons of 4in wires necessary to keep the *Sea Salvor* rigidly in position over each search area. His main job during the salvage operation was to oversee the grab operation in conjunction with the observation diver and camera operators.

The bottom of the Mediterranean near Elba is a flat, featureless moonscape littered with more than 2,000 years of wreckage from hundreds of large and small craft. The only way to find anything of possible value was to use ASDIC and simple trawling. The W Class destroyer, HMS *Wrangler*, was deployed to make the ASDIC sweeps and HMS *Sursay* to lay marker buoys on any contacts *Wrangler* located. The ASDIC could pinpoint contacts, but could not classify them as the system was designed to locate moving targets, not those quiet, stationary or scattered over a large area. Accurate identification was crucial to separate aircraft wreckage from two millennia of man's sunken debris.

To augment the ASDIC contacts, the deep-sea television cameras were used to identify targets positively before the *Sea Salvor* spent valuable time mooring above a contact. The standard studio-type Pye camera, modified for underwater use, was installed aboard *Sea Salvor*, and the equipment was lowered from one of her derricks with a shackle dangling below the camera on a line to enable the monitor operators to gauge when the camera was at the right distance from the seabed. It was primitive, but it worked. Two more television cameras were introduced later in the operation, including another Pye camera designed and built in only nine days specifically for Operation Elba Isle. Its field of vision was 10ft by 11ft so objects as small as a shoe could clearly be seen and then focused through a servomotor system. The grainy images were sent back to a bank of six black and white television sets. Simply adjusting the contrast on a black and white screen greatly improved the poor visibility.

A Marconi camera was installed in HMS *Wrangler*'s relief, *Wakeful*, and later transferred to the *Sea Salvor*. This camera was similar to that used to locate the *Affray*, but with several optical improvements. The somewhat bulky camera was housed in the middle of a sphere and surrounded by eight adjustable and very bright mercury-vapour lights, the whole looking rather like a surgeon's lighting system above an operating table. The Marconi set had greater magnification with remote control and trainable periscope eyepiece, but this meant a limited field of view over the latest Pye machine.

Finally, two trawlers were chartered. Lieutenant Commander M.G. Fowke was the designated 'trawler boss' and he taught the Italian fishermen minesweeping techniques to gently locate and lift the wreckage to the surface. The trawlers dragged up much smaller, but no less significant, wreckage such as maps, personal effects and some smaller pieces of fuselage. Three more trawlers were added to the small fleet and, under Lieutenant M.R.D. Hooke's direction, one chunk of wreckage trawled up proved to be a vital clue in understanding Yoke Peter's demise.

With the right salvage ships, equipment and mooring facilities in place, Operation Elba Isle could now begin – firstly by finding the wreckage. Elba harbour master, Lieutenant Colonel Lombardi, tried to find Yoke Peter before the Malta salvage party arrived. He spoke to all the eyewitnesses he could find to gauge as closely as possible where she had hit the sea, and even took witnesses back out to the exact positions they were when the plane crashed. Through sextant angles he then plotted the sixteen observer lines to narrow down the crash site, but it was not completed by the time the salvage team arrived. Another position was calculated from a photograph taken by a crew member aboard another plane that had flown over the area later that same Sunday. The picture showed fishing boats recovering bodies, with part of Elba in one corner of the frame. Photographic interpretation narrowed down the land mass. With this and Lombardi's plotting lines 'Elba Force' began their search, but immediately ran into problems. Both the picture and Lombardi's incomplete search data did not allow for the bodies' and wreckage's drift of about 7 miles further south, meaning more time was spent trying to locate the crash site.

HMS *Wrangler* ran ASDIC sweeps, traversing lanes 300yds apart, making her turns outside the search area to prevent missing a possible target. *Sursay* then marked any target of interest to be checked by *Sea Salvor* and her camera. All contacts were given code names and every one would have to be inspected. HMS *Wakeful* soon arrived to relieve the *Wrangler* and was a great deal more successful. She also carried the advanced Pye television equipment, but her speed meant targets were easily missed – she had to steam at three quarters of a knot to use the camera effectively while under way.

The *Wakeful* was positioned to windward of a contact, the camera was lowered and the ship was allowed to drift over the find, very slowly, three times. Forsberg said, 'Results were only obtained by a pinch of luck, superimposed on constant and precise plotting, super-imposed on patience and steady handling. There is always a tempt-ation to adjust the ship's approach by engine movements. But a speed-increase brings the camera flying up out of sight of the bottom. A speed decrease tends to dip the camera in the mud.' The technique took two days of practice to work in harmony with the wind and the current, using her engines at dead slow, just to check the rate of drift. Once she was moored above a contact, the *Sea Salvor* was able to get within 6in of a target over a 200yd^2 area, simply by heaving in or paying out the wires.

The technicians watching the television screens then gave orders to the winch operators to make very fine or large alterations in the ship's position to get the grab exactly above the wreckage to secure it. On the first fine day of operations, the *Sea Salvor* made more than 200 move-ments up and down her moorings, only to find some old German mine cables left behind after the minefield had been cleared. Many mine sinkers also littered the seabed in a complicated zigzag of mine lanes covering most of the search area and proved to be a real nuisance throughout the whole of the operation. They often snagged the trawlers' lines, or were picked up on ASDIC as a possible target.

Later, Contact Charlie was covered with marine growth and proved to be an old Italian mine; Fox was simply 'non-Comet'. As the light was failing, sweeps were made over Contact George, but weather con-ditions deteriorated and the *Wakeful* returned to Porto Azzuro near Livorno, in northern Italy, for the night. Three days later, the *Barhill* laid the six moorings around George for the *Sea Salvor* to look at on her camera. Laying the moorings was no easy task. On the first attempt a normal two-point mooring was used, one each on her bow and stern, but the *Sea Salvor* still swung around too much. Then a four-point mooring also failed. Eventually a six-point mooring had to be secured for every location to ensure she did not move off site. This was crucial with a diving bell and cameras tethered to her main deck, as the slightest movement on the surface could wreak havoc 600ft below.

On 16 February 1954 Risdon Beazley's chief diver, John Galpin, was lowered down in the observation chamber for a closer look at Contact George, which looked on camera like it could be part of an aircraft. When the chamber was brought to the surface, relief diver Tom Bray took Galpin's place and went back to the seabed. On his word the *Sea Salvor* inched steadily towards the wreckage. Bray ordered the grab to be lowered slowly on to the wreckage and the eight-toothed jaws of the grab closed slowly over the twisted shards of metal. Forsberg added, 'For size it was not very considerable, but to us at that time it was an object almost of veneration.' Contact George was 'Comet'. After forty days and nights, Mountbatten's salvage operation was finally in business.

During the next week contact George yielded thirteen grabs, all from the rear end of the passenger cabin. For the next four weeks all the ASDIC contacts were examined and a great deal of Yoke Peter was recovered, including her four engines and undercarriage. By the end of March all the large portions of the aircraft had been found except the tail and wing sections. On 9 April both *Sea Salvor* and the *Barhill* were badly in need of minor repairs and were relieved of duty, as the trawlers were more than able to cope with the remaining wreckage. They could each lift one ton from the seabed, and the remaining pieces, including the tail section, weighed less than this.

Lieutenant Hooke replaced Fowke in April 1954 and was ordered to research the area in a specific pattern to confirm there was no more wreckage left. Forsberg marked out the one-square-mile crash site on a chart and before leaving he instructed Hooke to trawl the area thoroughly. Small pieces were found. Forsberg explained:

It was decided, therefore, to sweep the marked square mile rigorously, geometrically and precisely in at least four directions. This apparent quadruplication of effort was essential. It insured against holidays [areas missed] and against wreckage lying at such an angle as to escape the trawl in certain directions. The success of this method was proven when the tail unit was recovered in a spot at least four times trawled over before.

A small warship was used as a navigational leader to get the best out of the trawlers. Between April and September the Italian fishermen continued their sweeps and found a great deal more of the aircraft. Although the search went on until September, the key find occurred on 12 August when a piece of the fuselage, measuring 6ft by 3ft, containing the direction-finder aerial window was retrieved. This piece showed signs of fracture not likely to have been the result of a high-velocity impact.

Extraordinary efforts were being made to find the cause of the crash and the Royal Aircraft Establishment (RAE), Farnborough, was put in charge of the investigation. The RAE built a rig to pressurize repeatedly an entire Comet fuselage in order to simulate the cabin pressurization cycles of climb and descent. After some 3,000 'test flights' a crack caused by metal fatigue occurred at the corner of a cabin window. Metal fatigue begins with a microscopic fracture, which gets progressively worse as a plane is subjected to extremes in altitude and constant pressure changes. Some metals such as steel and titanium are not affected, but light alloys, such as aluminum, suffer greatly. Speed and altitude worsen the effect until the tiny crack reaches a critical mass, leading to the aircraft's rapid disintegration. The direction-finder window wreckage from Yoke Peter was proved to have suffered the same catastrophic pre-crash failure.

Although the Comet was built to specifications beyond those laid down by the Civil Aviation Authority, the early aircraft had big, square, picture windows to watch the world rush by. Their sharp corners meant that the metal began to expand and contract with each flight. The massive fluctuating pressure from 30,000ft to the ground and back acted like the bending and straightening of a spoon or fork until it cracks through. Other Comets were thought to have crashed through similar structural failure.

Nine months after Lennox-Boyd called Mountbatten from his bath on a cold English night, Forsberg wrote a lengthy report to the Commander-in-Chief Mediterranean. After reading what Forsberg had to say, Mountbatten concluded:

This must surely rank as one of the most remarkable operations in the history of salvage. The determination, ingenuity and endurance of all concerned stand out from the pages of the report. Particular credit is due to Commander E.G. Forsberg for his imaginative and successful leadership, which formed a queerly assorted mixture of RN officers and ratings, civil salvage experts, Maltese civilian seamen and Italian fishermen into a smoothly working team. More than 70 per cent of the total weight of the Comet has been recovered to date.

Forsberg felt the success of Operation Elba Isle lay elsewhere in his team. His report to Mountbatten concluded: 'The success of these recoveries was almost entirely due to Captain J.B. Polland, his boatswain-rigger and two divers. They showed themselves to be past-masters at this intricately complicated task.' Regardless of who should take the credit, the combined effort of all those involved broke every salvage record to recover Yoke Peter, and her vital clue that solved one of the biggest mysteries of early commercial jet travel. The fault was corrected by making the windows smaller and rounding the edges to spread the pressure – a design standard that is used in every jet airliner to this day.

The Comet was eventually redesigned as the Comet IV that inaugurated its first fare-paying transatlantic jet flights in 1958, largely achieved through evidence gathered from Wittingham's investigation and the salvaged wreckage. But the collateral, financial and human damage suffered in finding the answer to the loss of Yoke Peter is seen as a crucial episode in Britain losing her edge as the world leader in jet airliner production. Although Comets flew commercially until 1970, four-and-a-half vital years had been lost ten years earlier, allowing the Boeing 707 and McDonnell Douglas DC-7 to fill the vacuum, incorporating safety features learned through the forensic investigation and salvage of Yoke Peter. The Comet later gained a new lease of life as the Nimrod maritime reconnaissance aircraft, which is the backbone of the United Kingdom airborne AWACS (Airborne Warning and Control System) and anti-submarine capability – a fitting legacy to the Operation Elba Isle salvage team.

Chapter 16

Suez Crisis

During the Suez Canal's first hundred years of operation, sunken ships were used to render the 103-mile waterway useless three times, all within the same thirty-year period. Adolph Hitler ordered the Canal to be blocked in February 1941 when Luftwaffe bombers mined the waterway, sinking several large ships, including one liner. President Nasser seized control in 1956, and the Arab-Israeli Six-Day War forced the Canal to shut for seven years from 1967. Nasser's takeover bid was without a doubt the most significant. When Prime Minister Anthony Eden grossly miscalculated Nasser's motives, the Salvage Department became a political pawn in a much bigger game in which Britain lost her Premier and her influence in the Middle East, and Soviet President Nikita Khrushchev threatened to undermine world peace.

The glamorous and handsome young President Gamel Abdel Nasser dreamed of pulling Egypt out of her third-world status. He planned to build the biggest dam in the world, capable of spreading water throughout the country, giving new life to the many small farms and hydroelectric power to boost industry and the economy. The Aswan Dam would cost more than £100 million and he needed to borrow much of the capital from the United States, Britain and the World Bank to fulfil his goal. The ten-year building project began in 1952 and for four years the construction and loans continued. Meanwhile tension between Egypt and Israel had been smouldering for many years culminating with Nasser learning that his adversary was buying weapons from France, including Israel's first jet fighters.

Armed incursions into each other's territory and revenge attacks had been carrying on for some time, but to Nasser this latest development posed a much greater threat. In response he decided to rearm, and with Britain, the United States and France backing Israel he turned to the Soviet Union for help. In the mid 1950s the Cold War was at a peak where relations between East and West were bogged down in fear, ignorance and prejudice. Eden believed that the upstart leader must be a communist and as such a threat to democracy. In reality, as a practising Muslim, Nasser resented communist atheism and neither was he prepared to take orders from Khrushchev. Indeed, in Nasser's own country, communists could be imprisoned for their beliefs.

But Nasser had to be punished. Firstly a covert operation against the Middle East leader, called Operation Omega, was launched. This largely involved negative propaganda such as supplying false information to journalists and television networks. Then, under this smoke screen the United States slowed down her financing of the Aswan Dam. On 19 July 1956 Secretary of State John Foster Dulles called Egyptian Ambassador Ahmed Hussein to the State Department and informed him that the United States was formally cancelling her loan. Two days later Britain cancelled her funding and, as the World Bank loan depended on these two offers, its contribution was also stopped. As a final insult, Nasser only learned of the decision through Egyptian radio news.

He was left with two choices: accept the humiliation the West had inflicted; or fight. With earnings, Nasser claimed, of $100 million a year from Suez Canal tariffs he knew that the Aswan Dam could still be built if the shipping tolls went to Egypt instead. He therefore planned to seize control of the Suez Canal Company's four offices simultaneously. The whole mission depended on Nasser passing a codeword – 'Ferdinand de Lessops', the name of the Canal's builder – during a public speech. All four Army squads waited and listened to public broadcasts of Nasser's speech, but for one hour Nasser only gave a vivid account of all the humiliations Egypt had suffered under Western control. Another hour passed and still he failed to give the coded order. Then, innocently slipped into Nasser's rhetoric, the name Ferdinand de Lessops crackled through the soldiers' radio sets. Nasser repeated the codeword another thirteen times to ensure they did not miss their cue, but his men had already mobilized. Soldiers entered each office in a polite yet firm manner, informing the Company's staff that the Canal was now under Egyptian government control.

Before Nasser had finished his speech, he announced to the world what was happening to rapturous applause all across Egypt. Eden was informed while enjoying post-dinner drinks with government and Middle East officials, including King Feisal of Iraq. The Premier was furious, later saying, 'We all know this is how fascist governments behave and we all remember only too well what the cost can be in giving in to fascism.' Britain had the most to lose. She was a 45 per cent shareholder in the Canal and a third of all ships passing through (more than 14,000 each year) in the mid 1950s were British. Eden telegrammed United States President Eisenhower to say that force was the only way to get rid of Nasser. His justification was that Nasser was a Soviet puppet and a direct threat to British interests, especially her oil imports. Two thirds of the United Kingdom's supplies reached the country via the Suez Canal, more than 20 million tons each year.

Eden told Eisenhower, 'If we take a firm stand over this now, we shall have the support of all the maritime powers. If we do not, our influence and yours throughout the Middle East will, we are convinced, be finally destroyed.' Eisenhower preferred a more diplomatic approach. If Eden tried negotiating with Nasser, the world would see that he, at least, tried a more peaceful approach first. 'Public opinion here, and I am convinced, in most of the world,' he told Eden, 'would be outraged should there be a failure to make such efforts. Moreover, initial military success might be easy, but the eventual price might become far too heavy.' Eden did not want to take the dispute to the International Court, partly because the process was too slow and because Britain's legal position for such a hostile invasion into the Middle East was not entirely clear.

Eden consented to a twenty-two-strong member conference, representing the main countries using the Canal, but insisted that if negotiations failed, regardless of United Nations' approval, Britain would use force if a settlement could not be reached in a reasonable amount of time. The majority of the delegates did want a peaceful settlement and this was put to Nasser. He rejected the plan. Before the conference was finished a combined Anglo-French task force of 150 ships, including 75 requisitioned merchant ships, 4 aircraft carriers and 2 salvage vessels was being assembled, but to the world their actual combat deployment was still not a foregone conclusion. In Whitehall it most certainly was. The balance to invade was tipped when Israel launched a combined land and air attack on Egypt across the Sinai Desert. The Canal, and thus the West's most important trade route, came under a new threat.

Britain and France gave both sides twelve hours to cease firing or they would be compelled to intervene. Egypt and Israel refused, allowing the Anglo-French operation, in the eyes of the world, to use force legitimately to protect their interests. Operation Musketeer, the biggest air and seaborne invasion since D-Day, began on 31 October.

159

At first light, aircraft left the carriers' decks and bombed strategic targets, such as airfields throughout northern Egypt and the Gamil Bridge, which carried the main road from Port Said to Cairo across the Canal. Shortly afterwards British and French paratroopers landed in Port Said. Within one day they had advanced as far as El Cap, about 20 miles south, along the Canal. Eden insisted to the world that his actions were right, legal and morally sound. He later informed the British people, 'All my life I have been a man of peace, working for peace, striving for peace, negotiating for peace and I am still saying with the same conviction, same devotion to peace that I am utterly convinced that the action we have taken is right.'

Hundreds of civilians were killed, some crushed under advancing tanks, in the bitter street fighting that followed. Eden hoped that Nasser's people would rise up and overthrow their leader, but the effect was just the opposite. They all loved and stood by their Nasser, even forming local militias to retaliate against the invading French and British forces. To prevent Eden taking the Canal, Nasser ordered that the ships trapped in the waterway be sunk, including those in Port Said. As the crisis intensified Khrushchev prepared to send troops to help Nasser, which ultimately led to President Eisenhower forcing Eden to back down before the situation escalated into a much wider and more devastating conflict. Eden knew he had completely misread Nasser's power, the reaction of his people and world opinion. He had lost, strengthening Nasser's power and popularity. Sterling was dumped all over the world. Britain faced a massive oil shortage and winter was coming. Eden appealled to the United States for financial help. Eisenhower agreed, but only if the Prime Minister pulled his troops out. On 8 November 1956, Eden reluctantly called a ceasefire and the departing Anglo-French force were eventually hounded out of Port Said under a hail of small-arms and tracer fire.

The Salvage Service planned the Canal clearance operation while the exhausted Prime Minister left England for an extended holiday at Goldeneye in Jamaica, the house of his good friend Ian Fleming. The survey ship HMS *Dalrymple* located twenty-one wrecks in Port Said alone, ranging in size from 100 to 4,000 tons, all but one of the ships being sunk on or near the approaches to the Canal entrance. Some were completely submerged, or had only masts and superstructure above the water. Before salvage operations began, the wrecks were numbered from one to twenty-one, working backwards from the harbour entrance to the Canal itself. Aerial reconnaissance reported

160

another twenty-eight sunken vessels along the rest of the Canal from El Cap to Suez, and two demolished bridges, making fifty-one clearance jobs altogether. The same reconnaissance also showed that a south-bound convoy of fifteen mixed nationality ships, including Dutch, Russian, Liberian and British vessels, was trapped 40 miles into the Canal near Ismailia. Nasser was putting pressure on the crews to abandon their ships and create even more obstructions.

The two task force salvage ships were RFA *Sea Salvor*, which had been deployed for Operation Elba Isle, and the 950-ton Dispenser Class salvage vessel, HMS *Kingarth*. They entered Port Said the day after the *Dalrymple* completed her survey, and started clearing a channel for ships with a draught of 25ft to enter. Meanwhile, the Admiralty mobilized all available salvage craft and these arrived daily, including those from Risdon Beazley, Liverpool & Glasgow Salvage Association and Metal Industries. Many were salvage vessels that under the Phillips Report could be requisitioned in time of war. By mid November thirty-five mostly British and French vessels, including two large German lifting craft called the *Energie* and the *Ausdauer*, known colloquially as the two 'Ugly Sisters', were available to clear and open the Canal as soon as possible.

The first wreck raised was a pontoon crane with a deadweight of about 400 tons; the crane had detached when the pontoon sank after heavy charges were placed below her waterline. The crane was removed as well as the pontoon's pig-iron ballast, which took three divers at a rate of 20 tons each day. This was no mean task where the substantial weight was not the only problem, as the visibility was sometimes down to 4ft. Two lifting craft strung three pairs of 9in wires underneath the crane pontoon when she was light enough. The pontoon was raised off the seabed as the two lifting craft were pumped out and she was then towed gently to a pre-allocated shipping 'graveyard' for all those vessels deemed beyond economical repair. Several large tugboats had also been scuttled including the 235-ton *Garii*, lying across the Canal entrance. French salvage crews used two lifting craft to pass four 8in wires under the wreck to take two pairs of camels, tough inflatable pontoons capable of lifting tremendous weight. On 29 November air was forced into the camels, and the *Garii* was raised and towed into shallow water.

The biggest wreck was the 4,000-ton dredger *Paul Solente*, which had sunk on an even keel in the middle of the main channel, submerged right up to her bridge. To ensure she stayed where she was scuttled, eight charges had been detonated inside her hull, blasting outwards, creating eight jagged holes of 4ft across. Senior Salvage Officer Captain Thomas Podger recalled: 'The weight of the wreck was far beyond the capacity of the two lifting craft being towed to Port Said, so a combination of salvage methods would have to be used in removing the wreck.' Victor Campbell was in charge of salvage operations and he adopted the traditional techniques of shuttering with wood and pouring tons of concrete into the void, which was already reinforced with angle bars. The Metal Industries salvage vessel, *Salveda*, gained as much buoyancy as possible in the *Paul Solente*'s after end. With a combination of wires attached to lifting craft, the concrete patches and cofferdams leading to the deck area, the water within the *Paul Solente* was pumped or blown out of the wreck using compressed air, and she was beached well clear of the Canal entrance.

Although the Admiralty Salvage Service was still clearing Port Said, they had the ships ready to enter the remaining 90-mile Egyptian-held stretch of the Canal from El Cap to Suez. To remove the wrecks as expediently as possible, the Admiralty devised a sound three-point plan to work effectively in such narrow working conditions. Firstly a channel had to be cleared through the full length of the canal for ships with a draught of up to 25ft and a beam of 60ft. This meant immediately moving nine ships and the wreckage from the two bridges. Secondly, when this channel was cleared the remaining ships would be raised or demolished to allow bigger ships through. And finally, there would be a tidying-up operation to ensure there was no more debris left to snag or damage any vessel in transit. Small coastal salvage vessels were to be used owing to their manoeuvrability over the larger ocean-going vessels like the *Sea Salvor* and *Salveda*.

Some of the salvage ships were armed and many were flying the White Ensign. The *Dalrymple* carried four saluting guns. The two salvage vessels *Barhill* and *Brigand* had one Bofors each and two .303 machine guns. To enter this occupied area they had to come under United Nations control, which meant that all guns had to be removed, including small arms, and the Royal Navy flag had to be replaced with the Red Ensign or United Nations flag. Admiralty salvage crews might also have to be exchanged for Merchant Navy personnel, deeply concerning the Admiralty. A secret Minute said:

From the indications we have, however, it would be prudent to work for the time being on the assumption that our RN manned vessels will have to be civilianized. The First Lord [Quinton Hogg, Baron Hailsham of St Marylebone] has said that should this prove to be the case, he is willing to agree to the ships being 'disguised' by the Royal Navy crews wearing civilian clothes and the ships flying the UNO flag or the Red Ensign, but that he would not agree to the Royal Navy crews being replaced by Merchant Navy crews without his specific approval.

Details of this scheme had already been communicated to Commander-in-Chief Mediterranean, Earl Mountbatten of Burma, who would undertake the necessary 'disguise' should this be needed. Their concern was not without foundation. The secret Minute added:

> The point to be emphasized [to the UN] is that the Ministry of Transport will undoubtedly find great difficulty in obtaining Merchant Navy crews for the vessels concerned and those they are able to produce will probably be of only moderate to poor quality. From our point of view, therefore, the scheme has little to commend it since we should merely be replacing experienced men on a highly technical job with unqualified crews.

The salvage vessels were 'disguised', and some small arms were removed 'other than anti-shark weapons'.

Under Captain Thomas Podger, lifting and raising wrecks followed set patching and pumping procedures within Port Said until around mid November when the United Nations, and not the Admiralty, obtained permission to clear the rest of the Canal between El Cap and Suez. Nasser was adamant that under no circumstances would British and French salvage vessels work beyond El Cap. While Eden tried to relax at Goldeneye, it was left to Foreign Secretary Selwyn Lloyd to face the Parliamentary fire. On 3 December he gave a very lengthy speech, but one sentence caused a great deal of flack when he told the House of Commons that work south of El Cap would begin 'as soon as technically possible'.

Conservative MP for Yarmouth Anthony Fell jumped on the comment saying, 'Is it not a fact that it would have been "technically possible" by using British and French equipment, to have gone in days ago to start clearance of the rest of the Canal? Does "technically possible" mean waiting for Egyptian or other agreement to the using of our equipment by our people?'

163

Lloyd answered the question, simply stating that the United Nations was now in control, and all sides had agreed to that effect, but that at this time neither the British salvage force, nor the United Nations were clearing the Canal, which was proving costly to trade. Two days later an internal government memo reported:

> It seemed to us that the Foreign Secretary did his very best to cover this up in his statement 'it is planned to proceed with the greatest possible dispatch with the survey and diving operations which are a necessary preliminary, and that the actual work of clearance will begin as soon as technically possible.' This is obviously the only line which the Government can take with its backbenchers, but we need hardly emphasize that they are extremely vulnerable on this question.

Swedish-born United Nations Secretary-General Dag Hammarskjöld had tried repeatedly to convince Nasser to allow the British salvage fleet to at least finish work in Port Said, but by now Nasser wanted every semblance of the Anglo-French debacle off his land. British and French forces, armed or otherwise, must leave by the final withdrawal. Hammarskjöld appointed Lieutenant General (retired) Raymond 'Spec' Wheeler of the United States Engineer Corps as his special representative in charge of the salvage operation. Wheeler was known as a man of great patience and friendliness. He had no practical knowledge of marine salvage, but he had worked on the Panama Canal as an army engineer. He was seventy-one years of age and very energetic, his staff finding it hard to keep up with him. Wheeler's appointment clearly went against the grain of the British government which, as a matter of prestige, wanted *their* salvage ships to clear *their* canal.

Wheeler expected to be in full charge of all clearing operations, but Head of Egyptian Canal Administration Colonel Mahamoud Younis told him very firmly that he [Younis] was in charge, and that the position of the United Nations salvage organization was to help as directed by Egypt. Podger wrote of Wheeler, 'He keenly felt the way in which Younis treated him in the typical Egyptian official's manner of superficial courtesy but making it clear that he regarded him as a subordinate, keeping him standing and demanding most detailed reports and explanations. A man of less character than General Wheeler would, I think, have found it impossible to continue.' Wheeler did report to the Egyptian government that that he wanted three ships

164

from the Anglo-French salvage fleet to continue clearing the channel in Port Said, and a further six vessels to help beyond El Cap.

By 21 December the thirty-five-strong Anglo-French salvage fleet was cut to eleven ships. Nasser eventually granted three of the eleven vessels, the Royal Navy's *Sea Salvor*, Metal Industries' *Salveda* and the French vessel *LCT 525* to re-enter Port Said while the other eight were idle. The others remained at anchor in the outer harbour. The salvage men often worked only 100yds from high waterfront buildings where snipers, or the apprehension of them, made working conditions intolerable and many wanted to be repatriated. First Lord Quinton Hogg flew out to Port Said to help persuade the crews to stay. But they were adamant they would not remain without 'White Ensign' protection.

He said that after the first few days, the situation would naturally calm down, but their fears were further fuelled after the BBC reported that the Egyptian Foreign Minister had stated his country would not allow any British or French salvage crews to take part in the clearance, and that it would not be safe for them to remain. Repeated small-arms fire continued while they tried to work and other forms of attack were not uncommon. On Christmas day 1956 a French Roman Catholic priest gave Holy Communion aboard the vessel, HMS *Striker*, and then again for the next two Sundays. Nasser had the priest expelled from Egypt for associating with the Anglo-French salvage personnel. A sick crew member was arrested upon reaching the shore for treatment and was about to be imprisoned when Wheeler told the Egyptian police that they would have to take him in as well. The case was dropped.

In a bid to allow the Anglo-French salvage fleet to operate south of El Cap, Secretary-General Hammarskjöld sent his deputy, Andrew Wellington Cordier, on a special mission to Egypt to persuade Nasser to rescind his order. For Britain, at least, the sooner the Canal was open the quicker essential imports such as oil could be resumed. Winter was biting and petrol was already rationed. Cordier had a strong argument. If all salvage resources were deployed, including French, British and United Nations, the Egyptian-held stretch could be cleared in seven weeks. If only United Nation's vessels were used, the clearance operation would extend to three and a half months. Nasser would not compromise on allowing the Admiralty salvage vessels into the main Canal, and Podger knew it. He later said, 'When Cordier arrived, I think General Wheeler did not continue to press for the six ships to work further south because he was by then convinced Nasser would never accept them.' Cordier only managed to secure the Anglo-French salvage fleet continuing to deal with the wrecks that they had already started in Port Said.

Having been given one extension after another, Hammarskjöld left General Wheeler to tell the Admiralty Salvage Service that enough really was enough and it was now time to go. Wheeler told Podger quite plainly that he would no longer support any further extensions, and that the United Nations wanted them to go as soon as possible. Personally, Wheeler regarded the Admiralty Salvage Service as a responsibility which tied him to Port Said and prevented his giving full attention to the more important work further south. Podger said, 'In view of the situation as I saw it from here, it seemed to me that we should lose prestige and gain nothing by further argument, and I proposed to the Commander-in-Chief [Mountbatten] that the Salvage Fleet should be withdrawn on or about 24th January.'

Nasser lost no opportunity for one final snub at the departing salvage fleet, really the last remnants of Eden's failed invasion. Podger realized that he would need an extra tug to tow one of the lifting craft out of the harbour, so he asked Wheeler for one last favour to try to obtain permission from Colonel Younis for an Admiralty tug to enter. 'This was refused,' recalled Podger, 'with the comment that if we could not transfer the tow outside, Younis would lend us two Egyptian pilots to do it for us.' Metal Industries salvage vessel, *Salveda,* eventually took the tow, as the Anglo-French salvage vessels slipped out of Port Said, mostly for Malta and Algiers.

Although Wheeler could be seen as abandoning the Admiralty's cause to remain, Podger still held the General in great esteem. Podger wrote to Mountbatten:

He regarded his first duty to UKSU [United Kingdom Salvage Unit] to be to ensure our protection against any attack or annoyance, and I was informed by Mr Martinez-Cabanas, Deputy Director-General of the Technical Assistance Administration of the United Nations, that the General had several moments of considerable anxiety on this score. Had he not shown such firmness and watchfulness in this respect, I am sure that the Egyptians would have made our position intolerable and we should never have achieved the results we did.

The Anglo-French salvage team still managed to raise thirteen ships from Port Said, including the biggest ship sunk throughout the whole Canal, the 4,000-ton dredger *Paul Solente*.

The final cost of clearing the Canal was £3 million. The United Nations footed the bill, made up with advances from the eleven countries which used the Canal the most. The United Nations, in turn, recovered the full amount by charging 3 per cent on the toll for all ships using the waterway. The British government was not too keen on the proposal. Eden's private secretary Sir John Pierson Dixon said:

> I suppose if we can be recognized as a creditor this might go all right politically at home. But I am afraid of an uproar at the idea that shippers and ship-owners should pay rather than the Egyptians themselves. On the other hand, if we take up the view too strongly that the Egyptians should pay, it might end in a resolution by the United Nations that the French and we should pay the whole bill. I assume that we would take no notice of such a resolution but it would (a) damage our position; (b) annoy the other people who have put up some money; (c) complicate the difficult issue now looming ahead of paying for UNEF [United Nations Emergency Force]. It might also be an undesirable precedent for Egypt's war damage claims against us.

The government tried to coerce British shipowners to pay the surcharge out of their own profits, but the shipowners regarded the whole scheme as a poor return for their loyal co-operation throughout the Suez crisis. However, eventually the shipowners did agree to pay – provided the government reimbursed them in full. After months of flatly refusing to do so, the government admitted to having 'no powers to compel the United Kingdom shipowners to pay the surcharge and so, in the absence of any satisfactory alternative method of raising the money for the United Nations, Her Majesty's Government have decided in principal to reimburse the owners of ships registered in the United Kingdom and Colonies'.

Russian writer Anton Chekhov once said that if a loaded gun appears in the first act of a play, it must go off by the last. Eden's loaded gun was clearly waved before the public when he entered Suez to *protect* the Canal from the invading Israeli Army. However, unlike Chekhov's analogy of a single shot, Eden's gun going off was closer to a semi-automatic burst, culminating in his downfall and the end of Britain's foothold in the Middle East. He was unable to convince the British public that an invasion was the right and proper way to treat a supposed communist dictator; nor was he able to enlist United Nations' support for the attack; then he lied to Parliament. On 14 October 1956, French Acting Foreign Minister Albert Gazier and General Maurice Challe arrived at Chequers for a meeting with Eden. The French formulated the plan for Israel's attack on Egypt, allowing Britain to invade a Middle East country with an ulterior motive. Eden liked the plan. He would not only be able to seize the Canal, but also overthrow Nasser. The British, French and Israeli governments finalized the plot in the Paris suburb of Sèvres.

On 30 October 1956, before actually invading Egypt, he told the House of Commons, 'Five days ago news was received that the Israel Government were taking certain measures of mobilization. Her Majesty's Government at once instructed Her Majesty's Ambassador at Tel Aviv to make enquiries of the Israel Minister of Foreign Affairs and to urge restraint.' The Sèvres Protocol, as it became known, had already been signed. Eden's strong belief that Nasser was a communist pawn had relied on intelligence gathered by an MI6 operative known only as 'Lucky Break'. The data showed Eden what he wanted to know, such as the Egyptian people welcoming Nasser's overthrow. It is likely some of the intelligence was inaccurate, or Eden selected the parts that suited his political agenda. Either way this chilling echo from history would not be the last time a British premier claimed he relied on faulty MI6 Intelligence to drag Britain into another Middle East conflict, with no clearly defined boundaries.

Chapter 17

Operation Rosario

Former Prime Minster Margaret Thatcher wrote of the Suez crisis:

> As I came to know more about it, I drew four lessons from this sad episode. First, we should not get into a military operation unless we were determined and able to finish it. Second, we should never again find ourselves on the opposite side to the United States in a major international crisis affecting Britain's interests. Third, we should ensure that our actions were in accord with international law. And finally, he who hesitates is lost.

Three years into her first term of office the 'Iron Lady' was forced to put these lessons to the test after a major conflict was triggered by – of all people – a group of salvage workers.

On 11 March 1982, the 3,828-ton Argentine naval fleet transport vessel *Bahia Buen Suceso* sailed from Buenos Aires, carrying forty-one men and supplies for a four-month expedition to salvage the scrap metal from a derelict whaling station near Leith, South Georgia, about 800 miles south-east of the Falklands. Argentine scrap-metal dealer Constantino Davidoff had been slowly breaking up the station since the late 1970s and this looked like just another working party fulfilling a salvage contract. However, although the *Bahia Buen Suceso* had British clearance, suspicions were alerted after she maintained constant radio silence throughout the eight-day voyage, bypassing South Georgia's immigration stop at King Edward Point, about half a mile from Grytviken, and heading directly to Leith, where her crew raised an Argentine flag. A British Antarctic Survey (BAS) station nearby went to investigate and found a mixture of men in both civilian clothes and military uniforms, who appeared to be unloading steel boxes that may or may nor have contained arms. They informed the *Bahia Buen Suceso*'s captain that he must return to South Georgia's principal settlement, Grytviken, as his stay was illegal.

169

Three days later the *Bahia Buen Suceso* did sail, but not all of her company were aboard. The BAS team noticed that about eleven men were still in Leith. All representations to Argentina to have them removed failed. Britain saw their presence as an illegal occupation of her territory, while Argentina insisted the men were only there to conduct salvage operations. The British response was to send the ice patrol vessel *Endurance* with her two Wasp helicopters and twenty-three Marines to South Georgia to deport the men. The move was met with strong opposition from Argentina's military junta who were adamant that the salvage workers were allowed to be there. Argentina threatened to remove the BAS team and sent the 9,600-ton icebreaker *Bahia Paraiso* to prevent the *Endurance* removing their nationals. She carried two helicopters (an Army Puma and an Alouette) as well as more stores.

Both sides refused to back down and what began as a minor incident escalated into Britain deploying the two nuclear submarines, HMS *Splendid* and *Spartan*, as well as the *Endurance*. Argentina sent the 950-ton corvette *Guerrico* to support the *Bahia Paraiso*. She had Exocet capability and about 100 Marines on board; these landed on 25 March. A week later *Endurance* landed her Marine detachment at nearby King Edward Point to defend the island. The incident was clearly becoming one of sovereignty rather than illegal immigration, bringing to a head more than 200 years of disputed ownership over the Falkland Islands. Britain's hard line approach only fuelled the junta's increasing resolve to take all the Islands by force. On 2 April, Argentina launched Operation Rosario, and invaded Port Stanley in the Falkland Islands. Argentine forces secured the capital in barely two hours; Government House finally surrendered eighty-five minutes later and the 'Islas Malvinas' were then under Argentine rule.

The following day, the Argentine Puma aboard the *Bahia Paraiso* landed its first twenty Marines near King Edward Point and the Battle for Grytviken commenced. After initial fierce resistance from the British Marines, who managed to shoot down the Puma, they finally surrendered to the overwhelming Argentine presence.

About 8,000 miles away in London, Whitehall had long thought that to launch a military campaign so far from the United Kingdom was fraught with logistical difficulties. The Falklands' rough terrain meant that troops could not be landed in heavy transport planes, that is, if permission was granted from one of Argentina's border countries to allow flights in the first place. Deploying a task force of military and merchant ships from the United Kingdom and Gibraltar was therefore the only option. Three days after Argentina took Port Stanley, Operation Corporate was launched to retake the Falklands and its dependencies. The aircraft carriers HMS *Hermes* and *Invincible* led the Task Force, which would eventually comprise eight destroyers, fifteen frigates, two landing ships, ten tankers, five minesweepers, five supply ships, six logistical support ships and eighteen merchant vessels, ranging from hastily converted luxury liners like the *Queen Elizabeth II* and the *Canberra* to cross-Channel ferries, which were referred to as 'STUFT' vessels (Ships Taken Up From Trade). Altogether, Task Force 317 was Britain's biggest amphibious assault since Suez, and the second only since D-Day, finally involving more than eighty ships.

Amid the first wave of southbound vessels were three salvage ships requisitioned from the Hull-based firm, United Towing Limited. The Department of Trade first requisitioned United Towing's most powerful salvage vessel, the 1,568-ton *Salvageman* on 6 April 1982. She was fitted with extra salvage plant and satellite communications equipment before anchoring off Ascension on 20 April and arriving in the Falklands on 5 May. The much smaller 689-ton *Irishman* was requisitioned on 7 April. She was hastily fitted with satellite communications equipment as well as a HIAB hydraulic crane of 6-ton capacity and a new inflatable workboat before arriving in theatre on 9 May. Her sister ship, the *Yorkshireman*, was requisitioned on the same day as the *Irishman* and also arrived in the South Atlantic on 9 May.

However, sufficient time had elapsed between the end of the Second World War and the Suez crisis for the role of salvage in a deployed task group to slip into the background of military planning. Chief Salvage and Mooring Officer Morgyn Davies OBE was then third officer aboard the tanker RFA *Olna* during the conflict and witnessed some of the salvage operations in the area. He said:

> It was not the Iceland Faeroes Gap conflict envisioned in a rapidly heating Cold War scenario that we had always anticipated. The Falklands was expeditionary littoral conflict like that experienced during the Second World War, which was not what the military machine had anticipated other than to reinforce Norway as required by the 'Cold War' scenarios. No one really thought that British ships would actually be attacked, damaged and sunk in such large numbers.

171

The salvage element in Task Force 317 was really an add-on, primarily to lay essential moorings for the dozens of inbound ships once the Falklands were back in British hands. Davies continued:

> Two major salvage problems were never addressed. There are tugs that can tow an aircraft carrier at 12kts and it can still launch aircraft, but you have to build that into the thinking and that was not built into the Falklands conflict battle plans. Neither was the sort of thinking in place that, if we have a ship that is burning, we can run it up the beach. Perhaps we can even take it out into deep water, scuttle it and it is gone forever, or at the very least very difficult to get at. But it was a case of 'they lie where they fall'. When I came to the [salvage] Unit I reflected on this and wondered why we had not been better prepared to deliver salvage capability.

British ships were attacked four days before the *Yorkshireman* arrived. Although HMS *Alacrity*, *Arrow* and *Glamorgan* were all slightly damaged on the same day, they were all still operational, but the Royal Navy's luck soon ran out. On Tuesday, 4 May an Argentine Super Etendard fighter-bomber fired a French-built Exocet missile, propelling 165kg of Hexolite high explosive at about 800mph into the guided-missile destroyer HMS *Sheffield*. 'Exocet' is an apt name for the medium-range anti-ship missile. The French word means 'flying fish' which, by their very nature, skip across the sea, only to land on the decks of low-freeboard vessels. The warhead failed to detonate, which would be a pattern for Argentine ordnance throughout the rest of the conflict, but the missile's unspent solid-fuel mass ignited the warship, eventually burning her out with the loss of twenty lives.

When the *Sheffield*'s remains refused to sink the decision was taken to tow her back to the United Kingdom. The Rothesay Class frigate HMS *Yarmouth* was initially deployed for the operation. However, on 10 May the *Sheffield* slowly filled up through her many holes and was allowed to sink, making her the first British warship lost in action since the Second World War. But this created another problem. 'The challenge then,' continued Davies, 'was that after the conflict the Salvage Department had to go back and remove equipment.' Barely a fortnight later, three ships were attacked in one day. HMS *Broadsword* was extremely lucky when a bomb dropped from an Argentine A-4B Skyhawk passed through her stern and landed in the open sea without detonating. The two other ships were not so fortunate. The 14,950-ton

Cunard container ship, *Atlantic Conveyor*, was acting as a carrier supply ship with eleven assorted Wessex and Chinook helicopters to fly the British troops into Stanley to retake the island, as well as six Sea Harriers.

Two Super Etendards attacked her simultaneously, firing two Exocet missiles, one slamming into her accommodation block. Although there is no way to confirm whether the missile detonated, its unspent solid fuel ignited and, as in the *Sheffield*, fire spread rapidly through the vessel. All except one of the helicopters were incinerated and twelve men, including some of her crew members and Royal Navy personnel, were killed. Fortunately one Chinook and all the Harriers had already left but, as the fire spread, it became patently obvious that drastic action was needed to beach her quickly and save as much of her cargo as possible.

The *Atlantic Conveyor* was the only heavily damaged ship where salvage was attempted while she was still in theatre and still burning, for which several salvage men were decorated. The *Irishman* was deployed to aid the burning container ship and although this was the 1980s, what followed played out like a salvage attempt during the Battle of the Atlantic forty years earlier. The *Irishman*'s crew managed to get her alongside, from where two men boarded the burning vessel to secure a towline. They did succeed, but the line parted. A second attempt also failed.

The container ship was now an inferno with flames and black, acrid smoke billowing all around her and the *Irishman*. No further attempt could be made until the fire died down two days later as the salvage tugs were not fully fitted for fire-fighting support (even today fire-fighting aboard a container ship is notoriously difficult). Although a line was finally secured, the *Atlantic Conveyor* sank while being towed and before a full inventory of what had survived the fire could take place. Two of her crew members were awarded the BEM for twice boarding the burning ship, and the *Irishman* received a brass plaque from the Royal Navy in recognition of outstanding bravery during the Falklands conflict. Whereas the *Sheffield* was the first warship lost in action since the Second World War, the *Atlantic Conveyor* was the first British merchant ship to sink the same way.

Although the conflict only lasted ten weeks British collateral losses were large. Twenty-two ships were attacked with seven either seriously damaged or sunk. Had at least 50 per cent more of the Argentine ordnance actually detonated, especially the bombs, the losses could have been as many as thirteen more ships. This would have seriously compromised Task Force 317's ability to engage Argentina, and win back the Falklands and all her dependencies. The real salvage engagement took place after the conflict. This fell into two areas: firstly, removing classified material from sunken warships, such as the *Sheffield* and her sister ship, HMS *Coventry*, which was bombed and sunk on 25 May (there is currently no information available on what classified equipment was removed); secondly, good old-fashioned patch-and-pump, and port clearance of those ships sunk in very shallow water. The various salvage operations continued from 1982 to the summer of 1985.

The 3,270-ton RFA (Royal Fleet Auxiliary) supply ship *Sir Galahad* and the much larger 6,407-ton *Sir Tristram* were unloading stores in Fitzroy about 20 miles south-west of Port Stanley. The *Sir Tristram* had almost completed her work while the crowded *Sir Galahad* still had a number of Welsh Guardsmen on board waiting to disembark. Without any warning Argentine A-4B Skyhawk jets flew in low over Fitzroy and attacked the two ships. The *Sir Galahad* took two or three direct hits, while the *Sir Tristram* was strafed before she, too, was bombed. Both suffered severe damage and were abandoned, the *Sir Galahad* being by far the worst hit, suffering 146 casualties with forty-eight men killed.

Saving the *Sir Galahad* was not an option, largely due to her damaged condition as well as unexploded ammunition on board and considerable loss of life associated with the casualty. The RMAS (Royal Maritime Auxiliary Service) ocean-going tug *Typhoon* towed her out to sea to be scuttled as a war grave. The Oberon Class submarine HMS *Onyx* was tasked with the delicate operation. The quickest method was to use torpedoes, but almost immediately the *Onyx* encountered one major problem. Due to the ship's construction she failed to go down easily. Her main tank deck was considerably higher above the waterline than for a conventional car ferry as she had been designed to land on a beach with, and survive, severe bottom damage. The *Onyx* had to fire a number of torpedoes into the *Sir Galahad* before she eventually disappeared beneath the South Atlantic.

The *Sir Tristram* was also virtually unsinkable but much less damaged, so she was towed round to Port Stanley. After a preliminary patch-and-pump operation she was used as a depot ship for the Salvage and Mooring team to store the myriad equipment needed to place and maintain the many moorings around the Falklands. Her engine room was still fully functional, meaning that her deck cranes and all generators were also able to be worked, although rats became a significant problem.

The *Sir Tristram* finally returned to the United Kingdom on 10 August 1984 aboard the heavy-lift salvage vessel *Dan Lifter*, a salvage process that has become increasingly used ever since. Tyne Shipyard was contracted to repair and modify the ship. Her length was increased by 29ft and a bigger flight deck was also added. Exactly 364 days later the *Sir Tristram* was recommissioned to greater effectiveness, becoming the only severely damaged ship salvaged during the Falklands conflict that was returned to active service. She has since been deployed in both Gulf Wars as well as the Balkans in the early 1990s, and in support of British troops in Sierra Leone. The *Sir Tristram*, after giving a further twenty-three years of continuous naval support, was finally decommissioned on 17 December 2005.

One of the biggest and most complex post-conflict salvage operations was not to raise a British ship, but an Argentine submarine packed with a full war load of arms and ammunition destined for the Argentine occupying forces on South Georgia. The 1,526-ton ex-American Guppy Class submarine *Santa Fe* was spotted on the surface off Cumberland Bay, South Georgia, on 25 April. Unfortunately for the *Santa Fe*, British forces were mounting Operation Paraquat to retake the island later that day. Five helicopters from the nearby warships HMS *Antrim*, *Plymouth* and *Brilliant*, the last two deploying from the *Endurance*, were already in the area and shot 1,600 small arms rounds into the submarine, two Mk11 depth charges, one Mk46 homing torpedo and deployed nine AS12 missiles.

The damage sustained included her port after ballast tank, which was ruptured during the depth-charge attack. One fuel tank was split open and another fracture occurred in her pressure hull. Her stern gland seal, where the propeller shaft meets the open sea, was also breached. The final air strike badly damaged the periscope, radio aerials and snorkel. On fire and sinking, she made for King Edward Point jetty about half a mile from Grytviken where her crew abandoned her alongside the jetty. Operation Paraquat commenced later that day and after initial resistance, the Argentine garrison surrendered South Georgia to the British forces.

Two days after her attack the *Santa Fe*'s captain, Horacio Bicain, and some of her original crew, under Royal Marine guard, moved her to a new location on a nearby, disused pier. Bicain and his crew, including Petty Officer Felix Artuso, blew her tanks to reduce the submarine's trim to only 5°. The *Santa Fe* got underway and was moving along well when suddenly she quivered and lurched much further to port. Speed was now everything if they were going to save her, and themselves. As the tension rose in her control room, Bicain ordered Artuso to blow the tanks once more. As he bolted across the control room a Royal Marine guard took Artuso's actions as a hostile intent to scuttle the *Santa Fe* and shot him dead where he stood. An inquiry into the shooting was held, but its findings have not been made public.

The *Santa Fe* eventually moored alongside the old jetty and slowly settled 70ft down, in a mixture of rotting whalebone and thick micro life that reduced visibility to zero. As the conflict was still ongoing, her rudder was blown off to prevent enemy salvage, should she be re-captured. She spent the rest of the conflict sinking into the soft seabed as all available salvage resources were tied up elsewhere in the South Atlantic theatre. After ten weeks that saw some of the most savage close-order fighting and maritime loss since the Second World War, Argentina surrendered the Islas Malvinas back to British control on 14 June.

Most of the post salvage clean-up was centred around the main Falkland Islands' group, but the *Santa Fe* was not only blocking a jetty urgently needed for the many ships visiting the only truly sheltered anchorage, but was becoming an unstable time bomb. The only option was to scuttle the submarine deep in the South Atlantic where her ordnance could do no harm. The theory of salvaging the *Santa Fe* was no different to raising a sunken vessel during the Second World War; bullet and shell holes needed to be plugged and leaks in air tanks sealed. But her salvage operation was still considered unique, due to its remoteness and lack of base support.

Three attempts under the most trying conditions had to be made before she was finally recovered. The first was in late May 1982. The *Typhoon, Endurance* and *Salvageman* were deployed, but mechanical problems and constant reassignments to assist other vessels entering and leaving the area dogged the operation. On 28 June the three vessels, plus the *Yorkshireman* and *Stenna Inspector*, gained enough buoyancy for a lift. Two weeks later she was taken off the berth and beached safely out of the way of visiting ships.

By 1983 she had to be removed because of her unstable war load. The first stage was to blow air into her saddle tanks once the *Salvage-*

man was alongside, but strong gales halted the progress when she veered in the swell and listed to 45°. Both salvage ships, along with the *Santa Fe*, were secured to a mooring buoy in King Edward Cove to ride the storm. In 1999, Salvage Officer, the late Mike Cobbold, reported: 'Three minutes later a loud crack was heard, the submarine rolled too quickly to port and settled by the stern assuming a trim by the stern of 30°.' Compressed air was pumped into the submarine's ballast tanks all afternoon to correct the fault, but to no avail. The decision was taken to tow her anyway, but, no sooner had the tow restarted than the *Santa Fe* fouled a mooring buoy and sank like a stone.

Divers conducted a survey once the storm had abated. Cobbold continued:

[The survey] revealed that she had sunk in the mud with only the port side of the fin and a small part of the bilge being visible to the divers, 95 per cent of the submarine having been swallowed up by the mud. The wreck was fouling a first class mooring in the cove and had become a major salvage task; the project was abandoned and the *Salvageman* and party sailed for Port Stanley on 27 March 1983.

Under the code name, Operation Okehampton, the final salvage attempt sailed from the United Kingdom in late autumn 1984 under the then Chief Salvage Officer, Ferris Morton. The mooring and salvage vessel RMAS *Goosander* and the Falklands veteran, *Salvageman*, were deployed for the task. Five weeks later the small expedition arrived in King Edward Cove in early November to find the shore under several inches of snow and half the cove frozen over with snow-covered ice. Each diver wore a tailor-made neoprene dry suit to cope with descending so deep into the freezing mass. A four-point mooring, similar to that used for the de Havilland Comet operation, was laid over the *Santa Fe* for the *Goosander* to remain rigid over the wreck site where she was to remain for more than three months.

The first job was to survey the *Santa Fe* again, both externally and internally this time. She lay with a 25° list with her stern driven about 15ft into the mud and her conning tower hatch open. Entering the submarine was necessary to close as many of the transverse bulkhead doors as possible to break up the longitudinal free surface effect of so much moving water. The divers carried hand-held underwater television cameras fitted with a floodlight, controllable from the monitor's position on the ship. The camera resolution was six times greater than the human eye, allowing the diving supervisor and salvage officer to guide the 'blind' diver through the live explosives as he progressed in his tasks. This provided a very useful morale booster to the divers and relieved their supervisor of much worry, as each knew the other was in constant video as well as voice contact.

A great many bullet holes still had to be patched, using small plates welded over them, or bolted, using high-pressure Cox bolt guns that dated back to the 1920s. All the time, the divers walked totally blind along a submarine packed with volatile explosives. The first few entries were made with a great deal of trepidation. As their internal knowledge grew, so did their confidence and eventually divers were working up to 60ft away from the access hatch, through her engine rooms and bulkhead doors.

Her flooded dead weight was calculated at 2,500 tons. Cobbold explained: 'The plan called for a combination of recovered buoyancy, added buoyancy and a mechanical lift provided by RMAS *Goosander* whose lifting capacity over the bow was 200 tons.' A 7in wire was placed around the *Santa Fe*'s fore end, just behind her diving planes, where ten lifting bags were attached and inflated. A 9in wire was placed around her 'A' frame above the propeller shafts and up to the *Goosander* to break the submarine's suction from the seabed.

When the pressure hull was tested for leaks there was another problem. Some of the air was leaking into the fuel tanks. This was never corrected and it had to be taken into account when the final raise was done. Davies explained: 'The use of compressed air to de-water a submarine's hull is restricted by the fact that all hatches, valves and seals are designed to withstand external pressure. Very careful application of internal pressures is necessary to avoid starting seals, which, if sympathetically loaded, will usually hold, but once a leak develops, it is extremely difficult to reseal.'

Divers had fitted thirty-one compressed-air hoses along the sides of the saddle tanks and pressure hull. They were then led into the *Goosander* and fitted to a ring main, which controlled the distribution of compressed air throughout the submarine. The first move was on 8 February 1985. Three days later she surfaced and was beached while final preparations were made before she would be towed and scuttled in 1,000 fathoms.

On 20 February the *Salvageman* lay alongside the *Santa Fe* and made fast. She was then gently eased off the beach, across King Edward Cove to where the *Salvageman* took her in a stern tow down

Cumberland Bay. She listed to starboard and three hours later she was sinking by the stern. The submarine was clearly not going to make her designated wreck site, so she was scuttled just clear of Cumberland Bay in only 196 fathoms where she still lies today. Altogether Operation Okehampton needed 868 dives in freezing water to recover the *Santa Fe*, including forty-two inside the submarine.

For the past twenty years most of the work in the Falklands has been to establish moorings in Port Stanley, including accommodation and store ships, and small moorings for barges. Secure moorings were also needed in San Carlos Waters, Bonners Bay and South Georgia. Sometimes salvage personnel were posted ashore in one of the many camps around the Falkland Islands where a few moorings had to be secured on land.

Mike Cobbold spent some time in 'Navy Point' camp and gave some insight into what life was like for the armed forces stationed on the Falklands after the conflict:

On the whole the camp was very good, few home comforts, but adequate meal times were always an adventure. As you stood in line, wondering what culinary delight was waiting at the end of the queue; whatever it was the smell of petrol dominated every other smell. The next obstacle was to get back to the mess with your dinner still on the plate having negotiated the muddy pot-holes and the catwalk, avoided the sheep and fended off the seagulls, only to find the fearsome ever-present wind had blown your dinner away.

The large British military force in the Falkland Islands, as well as a continuous Mooring and Salvage presence on station, has now been there since 1982. Although twenty-five years have passed since Operation Rosario failed, Argentina still claims the sole legal ownership of the Islas Malvinas.

Chapter 18

The New Admiralty Salvage

The end of the Cold War threat led to many naval auxiliary marine services being put out to tender and subsequent contractor delivery – all, that is, except for the salvage service. The Admiralty still wanted to maintain control and design of moorings, and the ability to salvage warships during peace and war. Chief Salvage and Mooring Officer Morgyn Davies said, 'In a sense that decision to retain a salvage element was based on the documentation provided by the Salvage Service on the lessons learned during the First and Second World Wars as the Phillips Report had addressed.' Although the new service has grown significantly since the Cold War era, its expansion was in personnel and expertise rather than equipment. The advantages were considerable. Today there are no salvage vessels within S&MO (Salvage and Mooring Operations), the last three of the RMAS 'R' Ocean Class tugboats being paid off in 1994 when the service underwent a major overhaul. Each ship required a crew of up to twenty-six personnel to operate, at a unit cost of £1.4 million per year. This did not include all the salvage equipment that needed regular servicing and renewal.

As warships evolve to meet new perceived threats, so salvage equipment must also change. Davies added, 'We are now going away from small-scale multi-compartmented ships with lots of water-tight doors back to big ships with big spaces, big compartments and big issues.' To meet this need, the MoD still retain that backbone of marine salvage – an array of specialist pumps. Two types are used mostly, hydraulic and electric. Both are submersible, an important prerequisite first pioneered by Frederick Young nearly ninety years ago, during the *Asturias* salvage. The hydraulic type is heavier and for general-purpose work, whereas electric pumps are used more for removing non-flammable fluids. Each pump will take about 300 tons per hour. One of the more recent changes is that many of these units are now air portable for speed and delivery to a casualty.

S&MO currently operates with a permanent Integrated Project Team, or IPT, of sixty-four people controlled from its offices at the MoD establishment in Bath, Avon. About forty-six personnel are technical experts, who are all qualified divers, and include marine engineers and naval architects. Historically, salvage officers were all Merchant Navy deck officers with master's certificates, but in recent years this has been changed to increase the skill mix. Davies explained, 'By the end of the Second World War we had a very good salvage organization. Those getting the best success were the technical men who had operated in a maritime environment for five years and could dive. So why try to re-invent the wheel?'

Within the specialist personnel are two teams. The first, known as R0, is at permanent six hours' notice to deploy to any embarkation point for a job anywhere in the world. The second team is at R4, meaning they are at forty-eight hours' notice. Their main role is to spearhead an operation and determine the equipment and personnel requirement of any given operation. This is basically the same philosophy as during the two world wars when a report was delivered to the Admiralty, either in writing or by telephone, illustrating the state of a casualty, and how best to fix it. Today's organization ensures that such essential early stability can now be delivered on a worldwide basis. The core operation costs barely £3 million each year to manage, less than the amount of the running costs of the last three R Class tugs alone, back in the early 1990s.

S&MO deals with about twelve operations a year, outside a combat scenario, with every operation being individually assessed and priced to the best possible advantage. There are always a variety of different operations, such as warships running aground, like the Type 42 Destroyer HMS *Nottingham* that ran aground on Wolf Rock, Lord Howe Island, in March 2002. A surprisingly large number of military aircraft crashes have also occurred – in the past fifteen years nearly fifty have been recovered, fifteen of which were Tornados. Recovery may well involve drawing on salvage vessels and specialists from the private sector. 'It is basically a matrix,' explained Davies. 'We look at the problem. We look at the availability of people, what combination of personnel will give the best fit for the solution. What is the location? What is the best available combination of assets available? Is it Army, plus United States support, plus a contractor?' The end result is a tailor-made and a very cost-effective solution.'

As the unit cost of each warship is so high, and numbers so limited, every possible means to save a vessel will be used. An increasingly relevant sub-component of salvage is the security issue. Fighting in a marine environment used to mean leaving equipment aboard a sunken vessel, but this is now not possible, as today there is no seabed in the world that cannot be reached with the right equipment. This was demonstrated during the Falklands conflict clean-up and in aircraft recovery operations that have been conducted in depths of more than 13,000ft.

S&MO has been deployed in a number of peacetime and combat operations during the past decade. Rarely do they now recover merchant vessels but, as in the two world wars, they still have the right to claim. The necessary vessels would still have to be chartered from the private sector even if a Royal Navy vessel was in the area, as it is uneconomical to deploy a £400 million warship to salvage a £2 million cargo ship, where perhaps the award will be only 10 per cent of the salved value. This does not mean that S&MO specialists are not called upon for more unusual work within the mercantile sector.

One salvage operation solved the mystery surrounding the loss of Britain's largest ever merchant ship to have ever been lost at sea, for which Salvage Officer James Ward was eventually awarded the MBE. On 9 September 1980, the MV *Derbyshire* was en route from Canada to Japan with 157,446 tons of iron ore. About 200 miles off Japan, Typhoon Orchid, reaching winds of 95mph, engulfed her with waves thought to have been as high as 80ft. All forty-four personnel, including two officers' wives, vanished along with the ship. No distress call was ever heard, and after an extensive air and sea search, not one piece of the 90,000-ton ship, or her crew, could be found. Her disappearance remained something of a mystery for more than fourteen years.

The British government refused to hold an enquiry into her loss, as there was no evidence whatsoever on which to base an investigation. Six years later the *Derbyshire*'s sister ship, the *Kowloon Bridge*, broke in half after suffering severe cracking just forward of her accommodation block. Her loss forced the government to hold a formal enquiry into the *Derbyshire*, but after ten months its findings were still inconclusive. Her remains were 2½ miles down and her exact position might never be known. Constant pressure, mainly from the families of those who had been lost, led to a small expedition to locate the wreckage during the summer of 1994. The International Transport Federation funded the operation and the support vessel *Shin Kai Maru*, using side-scan sonar, was chartered for the search. The approximate location of a large oil patch spotted by an air-sea-rescue helicopter back in 1980 was the only clue of her whereabouts. An area of more than 200 square miles needed to be searched, but a small amount of wreckage was located after only twenty-three hours. Once she was found, the site was recorded until a much more extensive expedition could be organized to find the main wreck site and hopefully discover what really happened.

Three years later S&MO was tasked by the Department of Transport with putting together an expedition on behalf of the British government to conduct a broad photographic forensic survey, then a more detailed examination. Initially S&MO was asked to bring back some of the shattered metal, but at the depth she lay this would have been very challenging. The model adapted was used for finding the USS *Thresher* and was ideally suited to find the *Derbyshire*. In April 1963 the 3,540-ton nuclear submarine, USS *Thresher*, had disappeared about 220 miles east of Cape Cod, Massachusetts. After a lengthy search, her shattered remains were located more than 1½ miles down, using deep-sea cameras that showed she had broken into six large pieces. The surprisingly clear monochrome images, along with small pieces of debris, allowed the Court of Enquiry to determine that the *Thresher* sank through construction failure when a joint in a salt-water piping system failed as she tried to surface.

The search method was very efficient for locating and determining an abyssal wreck, and with underwater technology having moved forward considerably in thirty years, S&MO put together a technical package using equipment from the United States, mobilized from Guam and Okinawa, and the United Kingdom. The first phase was to confirm the location and identity of the wreck, using an ocean survey vessel that was working in the area. Once this had been achieved the 3,250-ton survey vessel *Thomas G. Thomson*, together with the Woods Hole Oceanographic Institute (who found the *Titanic* and *Bismarck* during the 1980s), was charted for the mapping mission. She carried two Remote Operating Vehicles, or ROVs, to map the wreck site. The ROV *Argo* was used for general imagery while *Jason* was deployed for a more detailed survey.

Both ROVs had to undergo alterations before they could be lowered to the bottom of the Pacific. This work mostly involved installing high-definition video cameras with enhanced telemetry for their operation and recording ability. Another important upgrade was to improve the system of tiling images together, or mosaicing, for a much wider understanding of what had happened. On 9 March 1997 the *Thomas G. Thomson* sailed from Guam. Aboard was a thirteen-man team from Woods Hole, to collate the data and operate the ROVs, and fifteen British assessors. For the next fifty-two days the *Thomas G. Thomson* covered in detail 125 square miles of ocean with sonar, video and still images. The more detailed forensic survey revealed a startling picture.

The team expected to find a wreck that was perhaps cracked in half just forward of her accommodation block, and the mystery would be solved. What they actually found could not have been more surreal. All that is left of the *Derbyshire* is an intact bow and stern. Her accommodation block is upside-down and over to one side with the bridge wings torn off, while the engine is in a big crater nearby where it literally fell out of the ship. The rest of the *Derbyshire* is scattered across the seabed in small fragments, closely resembling an aircraft crash site rather than a massive shipwreck. Whatever happened in her final minutes was catastrophic; and certainly not the result of a crack near to her accommodation block. With no easy way of getting large metal samples to the surface for analysis, *Argo*'s, and especially *Jason*'s, cameras became invaluable.

The advanced camera equipment and a lighting system, with variable frequency, showed the various fractures in great detail. Through a 30,000ft fibre-optic cable, at thirty-two frames per second, the cameras could zoom in from several feet right into the metal's crystalline structure and failure faces. After the expedition had finished, more than 2,500 individual parts of the *Derbyshire* had been captured with 135,000 digital images, many being collated to form much bigger pictures. More than 200 hours of video footage had also been shot. From these images it was possible to discover what probably happened.

Closer analysis of the fragmented wreckage showed why her bridge watch did not have time to send a Mayday. For several days the Pacific had been crashing over her bow with colossal force. Hundreds of tons of water swamped the bow until pressure in her Number One Hold became too great and its hatch top burst open. Water poured in so fast that she went down within minutes, but this would not explain such a large fragmented debris field of a once 90,000-ton ship.

The sheer speed of her descent meant that the air trapped in her first hold could not escape, and the *Derbyshire*'s other eight holds were also sealed, some with cargo and some without. As the water flooded each hold, pressurizing the air in the watertight spaces, a deadly energy release of about two tons of TNT per hold was reached. The deeper she sank, the more the air pressurized and the greater the devastation. Many tests were carried out to prove a theory called 'implosion-explosion' to show how each sealed compartment was blown outwards or very badly cracked before being compressed inwards by the increasing outer water pressure. As the bubble migrated through the ship, trying to reach the surface, it pulled out the *Derbyshire*'s welds and ripped the Grade A mild steel to pieces like paper. It took about one hour for all the fragments to reach the seabed. The theory of the *Derbyshire*'s disintegration and loss was accepted, but the outcome of the new public inquiry based on the new evidence became extremely controversial.

Three assessors were appointed to analyse the data and to conclude, at last, what might have triggered such a catastrophic chain of events, and in March 1998 they finally published their findings after eleven months. One photograph showed that the forward rope locker hatch was open. At first glance the image does seem to indicate that this was crew error. The forward rope locker hatch *is* open, and a mooring rope *is* trailing out and across the fore end. Crew error was formally and finally accepted.

Later that same year, Deputy Prime Minister John Prescott ordered another inquiry. In 2000, after analysing the same data, and sitting for only fifty-four days, the second inquiry concluded that the locker was forced open after an impact from perhaps a heavy windlass being ripped out of the deck, or the foremast collapsing. A closer look at this frame does show a massive crushing impact on its leading edge, and the hatch lugs are torn off directly opposite. The dead crewmen were finally vindicated and the blame for her loss was put down to poor design. At the time of her sinking, about seventeen bulk carriers were disappearing each year, mostly due to structural failure. Recommendations put forward in the report have led to a considerable reduction in bulk carrier loss, and the crews who sail in them. And, as in the recovery of the de Havilland Comet Yoke Peter, this operation had far-reaching implications for future design decisions.

A more recent salvage operation was the first of its kind, but it set a precedent that will alter the way shipping losses will be investigated worldwide. On 3 February 2006, the 12,000-ton car ferry *Al-Salaam*

Boccaccio 98 was en route from Duba, Saudi Arabia, to Safaga in southern Egypt. About 60 miles into her voyage the car ferry sank in bad weather, dragging 1,408 passengers and crew half a mile to the bottom of the Red Sea where she finally settled in an upright position. Survivors reported a fire on the car deck where perhaps the immense quantity of water needed to extinguish the blaze caused her to capsize, but the definitive cause was still not clear. The *Al-Salaam* was unique in modern maritime salvage practice being one of the first casualties worldwide to carry a purpose-built marine 'black box' data recorder, or to give it its common maritime name, a 'voyage recorder'.

Installing the device was one thing, recovering the equipment was quite another, especially when some parties displayed a degree of reluctance to pursue the search. The International Maritime Organization (IMO) requested the British government's help to recover the recorder. On the advice of the Air Accident Investigation Branch, the United Kingdom Marine Accident Investigation Branch requested the assistance of S&MO, who regularly recover black boxes from military aircraft crashed at sea. S&MO accepted the job. Davies said, 'We did find the data recorder, which was fitted to a mounting on the upper bridge deck.' Under a strong Egyptian military presence, the recorder was brought inboard and a later inquiry, using the evidence it provided, showed that the captain was negligent in not sending out a distress signal before his ship went down. As of December 2006, the ultimate cause for her loss is still under investigation, but is believed to have been due to flooding of the car deck following a fire. Ironically she was the sister ship of the *Herald of Free Enterprise* that also suddenly capsized and sank after catastrophic flooding of her car deck off Zeebrugge, Belgium, on 6 March 1987, with the loss of 194 lives. New maritime legislation requires that all ships of more than 3,500 tons must carry a voyage recorder by 2008, so it is probable that this will be a growth area for future salvage activity.

One military salvage operation has been ongoing since 1998, and was first approached by Thomas McKenzie in October 1939. S&MO has been working on the sunken battleship, *Royal Oak*, in Scapa Flow to remove her many tons of fuel that had been leaking steadily out of the hulk for many years. The chance of a catastrophic leak was always present and so far more than 900 tons of fuel oil have been 'hot tapped' out of the battleship without mishap, often after reaching internal spaces obscured by many tons of live ordnance.

As with every major conflict since 1914, a salvage element was also necessary to accompany the Coalition forces during Gulf War II in 2003, S&MO's most recent combat deployment. For the first time since D-Day and the Allied advance across Europe, salvage during the current Gulf War was shared between Britain and the United States. During the preparations for Operation Telic (or Op Telic), Britain's code name for Gulf War II, S&MO chartered the Singapore-based 1,957-ton anchor and supply handling vessel *Pacific Commodore* and the much smaller Dubai-based 949-ton tug, *Seabulk Harrier*. They were known as Action Salvage Vessels, or ASVs, and the 2,260-ton American salvage vessel, USNS *Catawba* covered the American contribution. She was no stranger to attending casualties in the Middle East, having helped to recover the guided missile destroyer USS *Cole* in Aden two-and-a-half years earlier after the warship was nearly lost after a major terrorist attack.

The main salvage role during Gulf War II was to assist surface casualties like the 28,000-ton aircraft-training vessel RFA *Argus*. Her hydraulic lift failed on the plane flight deck, jamming it in the 'down' position, rendering a large deck area useless. S&MO personnel utilized a merchant ship that was delivering cargo at the time. She was moored alongside *Argus*, de-ballasted to make her as high in the water as possible, and her forward heavy-lift derrick literally pulled the broken platform back up to the main deck level where the platform was welded in position.

One of the most tragic operations involved the recovery of two Sea King helicopters, call signs XV650 and XV704, deployed from HMS *Ark Royal* on early warning and electronic surveillance duties. Before sunrise on 22 March 2003, one of the Sea Kings was returning from its mission while the other had deployed to relieve it. Crew members aboard the aircraft carrier witnessed a massive explosion and fireball fall from about 200ft into the sea about 5 miles away shortly after take-off. The helicopters had collided, killing all six personnel and one American officer observer. The initial salvage operation was only to recover the dead. Davies said, 'It was an evolution in combat fighting and we have had to evolve with it. It was driven by the human, and the moral, component.'

Very shortly afterwards the task was refocused as a full salvage mission, but all three ships were not configured to conduct a successful underwater aircraft recovery. Davies' colleague, Salvage Officer

Christopher John Miners, was heavily involved in the operation. He explained that the mission went ahead:

despite pre-war 'contention' that aircraft recovery would not be necessary during time of conflict. This stance impacted on the type of support vessels charted (and readily available) and on the type and levels of equipment carried by S&MO and US Sup. Salv. units alike. The ASV was selected against criteria of surface support and as such was not best suited as a diving platform. However, it was on charter, on site and was therefore pressed into service as an effectively cost neutral option.

The bulk of the wreckage was within an area approximately 650ft × 500ft, about 60ft down, and was largely centred around two craters dug into the hard, sandy bottom where the two aircraft impacted. Divers from the *Catawba* were first on scene and located the cab of XV650 using hand-held sonar equipment and retrieved the first body. As all three salvage vessels had no secure means of transmission, recovery and identification of the dead was communicated by phonetic alphabet coding over an open radio. *Pacific Commodore* entered a three-point mooring over XV704 to both locate crew members and avionics instruments that could show how and why the mid-air collision happened. Some essential equipment was recovered, but there was no sign of the missing crew member. The next three-point mooring was over XV650 where a diver found, by touch alone, the Mission Recorder that was buried in the seabed. S&MO's own ROV, the *Falcon*, was also deployed and proved an invaluable asset for recovering key debris.

The two largest pieces of wreckage identified were the shattered hulks of both aircraft, but none of the three salvage vessels were capable of retrieving them. A barge was chartered from Kuwait and a normal road crane was also hired and welded to the barge's deck to solve the problem. Its hook could then be lowered down, the wreckage stropped and then eased up onto the barge. Various pieces of wreckage were then selected to assist the investigation, including the Mission Recorder for XV704. Six of the seven crew members were found. One of the last dives to the wreck site was to lay a memorial plaque, from the crew of HMS *Ark Royal*, to the missing crew member.

Both the USNS *Catawba* and *Seabulk Harrier* towed the laden barge to Bahrain from where the wreckage was sent to RNAS Yeovilton for further investigation. In a repeat of the D-Day salvage co-operation between British and United States teams on Utah and Omaha, Miners concluded, 'Neither salvage organization was 'initially' ideally configured for a protracted aircraft salvage operation of this nature. However, each successive priority was addressed in turn by all resources available at the crash site. It is a credit to the team 'ethos' displayed by disparate units that such significant results were achieved within a relatively short time scale.'

Although the salvage vessels were unarmed and working well within a defined war zone limit, with protection from a warship in the vicinity, there was still every chance of being attacked. Towards the end of the operation, while the *Pacific Commodore* was secured firmly within a three-point moor, an Iranian dhow approached very closely. Miners recalled, 'The ship was powerless to prevent their actions. On this occasion their objective was merely to seek assistance for engine repair. However, had their motive been more sinister the Coalition warship was 6 miles off, hidden in a sandstorm at the far end of its patrol area, and could not have prevented any attempt at boarding.' Another indication that salvage men still work unarmed in the thick of conflict occurred on the first day of operations when a cruise missile fired from a United States Navy warship was photographed from the *Pacific Commodore* as it arced through the sky.

S&MO's involvement in Gulf War II is still ongoing. In 2005 a small team was deployed to Basra after the British Army captured one of Saddam Hussein's many palaces. The property backed on to a river. The Army had no water-borne barrier between them and a highly likely riverine enemy attack. S&MO flew a team out to Basra aboard a Hercules with a boom-defence system, which was secured in the river with the assistance of Army engineers. 'Problem solving in a maritime component is really what it is all about,' said Davies. 'And it is becoming more and more that kind of activity, not just raw salvage.'

Two more changes are currently affecting Admiralty salvage as it moves into its second century. Throughout August and September 2006, S&MO was heavily involved with moving three derelict nuclear-powered Russian submarines for final break-up, an operation that was both technically and historically very important. Admiral Phillips's findings that the Soviet Union was unwilling to allow British salvage personnel into her territorial waters remained unaltered from the end of the Second World War until 2004. After three years of talks, between the Foreign Office, the environmental organization, Arctic

Military Environmental Cooperation Programme (AMEC) and British salvage officers, the Russian government finally allowed Western salvage teams to enter some of their secret military establishments, although this was not without several years of objection from the Russian military machine.

The Russian dispersal pattern for their laid-up submarines and the fight for funding for scrapping and removal is very complex because each time a submarine is cut up the military lose funding, while the commercial sector makes a profit. This attitude crippled the safe disposal of disused Soviet nuclear-powered submarines for many years, until their decay represented too great a hazard. Still, their disposal was delayed until a tragedy forced action.

In 2003 the badly decayed November Class nuclear-powered submarine *K-159* sank while being towed from the Northern Fleet Gremikha base to be dismantled in the Polyarny shipyard on the Kola Peninsular. The only way to keep her afloat was to secure four rusting steel salvage pontoons, made in the 1940s, to her rotting hull. The pontoons constantly leaked, requiring ten men to keep blowing compressed air into them for the journey. Two days into the Barents Sea the *K-159* hit a bad storm, some of the pontoons were ripped off and she sank by the stern in about 800ft of water. Nine out of her ten transit crew were lost. Carrying personnel aboard a submarine while being towed was against common sense, let alone standard Russian naval regulations. In a warship the reserve buoyancy is about 120 per cent, leaving plenty of leeway to carry extra personnel for special duties, but aboard a November Class submarine the reserve buoyancy is only about 13 per cent, meaning there is little chance to save personnel, and if something goes wrong it happens very quickly. The *K-159* had been laid up for more than a decade. The three submarines that S&MO was about to remove had been laid up for fifteen years.

Raising and moving submarines has been taking place since the First World War, but from a technical point of view, never has an operation like this been attempted before. Nuclear-powered submarines have been towed in the West with no great environmental threat, however, the three Russian vessels were not only nuclear-powered, none of them had been de-fuelled. Their crews basically switched off the engines, jammed all the levers into the 'shut' position and walked away, leaving their reactors intact. The *K-159* is still on the seabed with more than 800kg of spent nuclear fuel aboard.

Towing these three vessels and risking another major loss was not an option. This would be the first time ever that a derelict, fuelled, nuclear submarine was recovered and moved, let alone three, so another method of removing the submarines had to be found. The 26,547-ton Dutch ship *Transshelf* was chartered from the heavy-lift firm Dockwise for the actual lift. She can carry 34,000 tons of deadweight on her 16,000ft^2 deck, more than enough to lift a dead 4,000-ton nuclear submarine. Unlike a conventional salvage and towage operation, the *Transshelf* floods her many water tanks, similar to a submarine, to submerge below a casualty. As the tanks are blown the *Transshelf* surfaces and the casualty is raised clear of the sea. It again harks back to the lessons learned during the recovery of the *Sir Tristram* after the Falklands conflict and shows how, although the type of casualty might change, salvage officers constantly build on previous experience to achieve a successful recovery.

The two Victor-1 Class vessels, *K-147* and *K-370*, dating back to the 1960s, were the first to be moved in late August 2006. They were raised from their moorings in the Polyarny shipyard and taken in turn to the Zvezdochka shipyard in Severodvinsk, northern Russia. Once each vessel had been loaded, it was supported in a tight steel cradle, angled at 45° all the way around to limit any movement. In early September 2006, the 6,000-ton November Class submarine, *K-60*, was lifted and carried in the opposite direction to Polyarny, from the closed city of Gremikha, arriving five days ahead of schedule.

Internationally the operation was also a complete co-operative success. The project began with the Russian view that *no* foreign salvage ship was to come within 200 miles of the Russian coast, and ended with the West taking a commercial salvage ship into previously 'closed' cities with full Russian co-operation. It has opened a lot of doors and built a lot of confidence between the West and the former Soviet Union. As well as establishing good East-West relations, the value of removing the submarines went beyond ensuring the limiting of radioactive contamination, especially for the United Kingdom. Davies explained, 'This will help us, as now that we have our own nuclear submarines operating east of Suez, there is always the chance that one might have to be brought home, fully fuelled. So the Russian expedition gave us invaluable experience in case such an incident arises.'

As Admiralty salvage moves into its second century, the recovery of exotic materials such as composite-built warships and helicopters, is becoming the next challenge. A crash site such as Yoke Peter or the two downed Gulf War Sea Kings was to some degree easier. Once the wreckage was located, it remained in place. This is not necessarily the case with this new generation of ships and aircraft because very little is known about the effects of long-term saltwater exposure to such materials. One composite-built Merlin helicopter has already crashed and been recovered from the sea. This limited experience has shown that some wreckage will sink, but a great deal will float away, creating an ever-changing debris field. A relatively small aircraft is one thing, but what if it was a new composite-built warship? 'I will be fascinated to see how designers will manage damage control with some of these materials,' Davies concluded. 'They investigate the engineering failure mode, but nobody really investigates their disaster and failure characteristics. I will watch with interest to see how these developments are carried forward.'

Admiralty Salvage has had a continuous involvement within twentieth-century human conflict from the First World War to the present day. It has learnt from forgotten men like Captain Frederick Young, whose practical experience galvanized the Admiralty into firm action, and John Polland, who realized and corrected such a major flaw in the Phoenix Units just prior to the D-Day landings. Thomas McKenzie's skill and leadership achieved so much during the Battle of the Atlantic and from D-Day onwards. In time of peace, Commander Guybon Damant made his record-breaking gold salvage from the *Laurentic*. Gerald Forsberg's experience, using television to recover Yoke Peter has been applied to many underwater operations ever since. These are just a few of the past chief salvage officers who have laid the foundations from which S&MO can operate today. Wider recognition of these exceptional men, and the importance of salvage within strategic military planning, is long overdue. This is especially so today as once more the United Kingdom is gearing its maritime military machine to deal with the 'new' concept of deployed warfare in the foreign coastal zone. When it gets there it will find the salvage teams waiting for them, trained and ready, for the expeditionary littoral that has always been their home ground.

Bibliography

Ambrose, Stephen E., *D-Day, June 6, 1944, The Climactic Battle of World War II*, Pocket Books, London 2002.

A Narrative of the Loss of the Royal George at Spithead, August 1782, published by S. Horsey Sen., Portsea 1840.

British Vessels Lost at Sea, His Majesty's Stationery Office, London, 1919.

Davis, R.H., *Deep Diving & Submarine Operations*, Siebe Gorman, Eighth Edition, Gwent, Wales, 1981.

Freedman, Sir Lawrence, *The Official History of the Falklands Campaign, Volume I: The Origins of the Falklands War*, Routledge, London, 2005.

——, *The Official History of the Falklands Campaign, Volume II: War and Diplomacy*, Routledge, London, 2005.

Holger, Herwig H., *Total Rhetoric, Limited War: Germany's U-boat Campaign 1917–1918*, University of Calgary, 1998.

Hough, Richard, *The Great War at Sea*, Oxford University Press, Oxford, 1983.

Journal of Hygiene, Publication 16, Volume VIII, 1925.

Lipsomb, Commander Frank W., OBE, RN, *Up She Rises*, Hutchinson, London, 1966.

Lloyd's Ship Losses 1939–1945.

Lycett, Andrew, *Ian Fleming*, Weidenfield & Nicolson, London, 1995.

Macintyre, Donald, *U-boat killer*, Cassell Military, London, 1999.

Masters, David, *Epics of Salvage*, Cassell & Company, London, 1953.

Newbolt, Henry, *Naval Operations, History of the Great War Based on Official Documents, Volume V*, The Naval & Military Press Ltd, Sussex, and The Imperial War Museum, London, 2003.

Rodger, N.A.M., *The Wooden World: An Anatomy of the Georgian Navy*, Collins, London, 1986.

Sowdon, David, *Admiralty Coast Salvage Vessels*, World Ship Society, Windsor, 2005.

Thatcher, Margaret, *The Path to Power*, HarperCollins, London, 1995.

Thomas, Hugh, *The Suez Affair*, Weidenfield & Nicolson, London, 1966.

Young, Desmond, *Ship Ashore, Adventures in Salvage*, Jonathan Cape, London, 1932.

——, *Try Anything Twice*, Hamish Hamilton, London 1963.

Wynne, Deane Stuart, *Recollections from 'Below the Mast'*, Penzance, Cornwall, 2002.

Ziegler, Philip, *Mountbatten, The Official Biography*, Fontana, London, 1986.

National Archive, Kew

ADM 116/1505, Salvage of Zeppelin *L.15*.

ADM 116/1585B, Index of ships salvaged 1916–1921 (at front of file).

ADM 116/1586, Salvage of hospital ship *Asturia*s.

ADM 116/1553, Loss of *Laurentic*, 1917.

ADM 116/1740, *Laurentic*, salvage of bullion.

ADM 116/1858, Salvage of liner/troopship *Oriana*, 1918.

ADM 116/2730, Salvage Regulations 1929–34.

ADM 116/1639, Salvage of liner/troopship *Aeneas*.

ADM 116/334, Preparation for Admiralty Salvage Section, 1914–1916.

ADM 116/4545, Admiralty agreement with Metal Industries.

ADM 116/6006, Salvage of Comet aircraft Yoke Peter off Elba.

ADM 116/6111, Suez Canal clearance operations 1956–57.

ADM 1/10099, Admiralty Salvage Scheme: proposals for implementation.

ADM 1/10099, Proposals for Implementing salvage agreements.

ADM 1/11095, Salvage agreement with Risdon Beazley.

ADM 1/11237, Institution of a Director of Salvage and Deputy Director.

ADM 1/15521, Salvage of SS *Coulmore*.

ADM 1/15523, Salvage organization for Operation Overlord.

ADM 1/15529, Second World War port clearance and salvage.

ADM 1/15548, Administration of Rescue Tug Service.

ADM 1/15632, Salvage vessels required for Operation Overlord.

ADM 1/17046, Salvage and tug markings for Operation Overlord.

ADM 1/17274, Ships salvaged during initial assault and advance in Europe.

ADM 1/20327, Peacetime policy for salvage and deep-sea rescue work.

ADM 1/20328, Admiralty salvage function, 1942.

ADM 1/22403, Recovery and salvage from SS *Laurentic*.

ADM 1/26760, Suez Canal: UK Salvage and support of UN Salvage Team.

ADM 1/29724, Awards to officers of *Lady Brassey* and *Lady Duncannon*.

ADM 1/30024, Awards to salvage personnel during D-Day assault.

ADM 1/30204, Awards for services on Sword Beach.

ADM 1/30379, Awards to salvage officers in France & North-west Europe.

ADM 1/8483/53, Salvage cases. Various questions and decisions, 1917.

ADM 1/8496/187, New form of salvage agreement, 1914–17.

ADM 1/8453/76A, Bill to amend the merchant Shipping Salvage Act 1894.

ADM 1/8500/227, Salvage of SS *Tanfield*, 1917.

ADM 1/8506/268, Parliamentary questions as to future operations, 1917.

ADM 1/8694/1, *Laurentic* salvage, notes by G.C.C. Damant (1).

ADM 1/8706/200, *Laurentic* salvage, notes by G.C.C. Damant (2).

ADM 1/9598, Blister or bulge protection of warships, 1915–34.

ADM 1/9703, Salvage of SS *Valverda* and Lords judgement.

ADM 199/2165, History and development of Rescue Tug Service.

ADM 1/9986, Importance of salvage vessel *Zelo* for U-boat recovery.

ADM 121/105, Report on salvage operations on Comet Yoke Peter.

ADM 131/96, Salvage of SS *Riversdale*.

ADM 137/3496, Loss of salvage vessel *Dalkeith* and HM *Tug Moose*.

ADM 156/201, Loss of Rescue Tug *Salvage King*.

ADM 179/395, Disguise of Phoenix Units in Selsey area.

ADM 204/2383, Underwater television use for Comet Yoke Peter salvage.

BT 220/101, Accident to Comet G-ALYP on 10 January 1954, Medical Aspects.

CAB 120/408, Cabinet Minutes on Salvage actions.

MT 23/491, SS *Harmatris* loss, and salvage operations.

MT 25/23, Appointment of Assistant DNE 1916.

MT 23/364, Torpedoing of *Asturias*, 1915.

MT 23/585, Further refinement of Salvage Organization, 1916.

MT 25/7, Salvage and repair of British tonnage at home and abroad.

MT 25/23, Wrecks and derelicts on British coast after Armistice.

MT 25/24, Reorganization of Admiralty Salvage Section, 1918.

MT 59/1394, Salvage in North-west Europe, 1944–1947.
PREM 3/324/9, Salvage August 1940–May 1941.
PREM 11/2286, Payment for clearing Suez Canal.
TS 32/121, Salvage operations: proposed Admiralty control, 1940–41.
TS 32/447, Liverpool & Glasgow Salvage Association agreement.

Ministry of Defence, Foxhill, Bath
Directorate of Marine Services (Naval) Marine Salvage Asset Study 11 November–20 December 1991.
Faulkner, Douglas, 'Implosion-Explosion Actions and Analyses'. Appendix 9 of the investigation into the loss of the MV *Derbyshire*.
Government Salvage – Who Does It and Why (report into 1990s salvage practice).
Polland, John B., 'Marine Salvage in War', three lectures by Captain J.B. Polland RNVR, Deputy Director, Admiralty Salvage Department.
Report on the Policy for Salvage and Deep-sea Rescue Work, Vice Admiral H.C. Phillips KBE, CB, 1946.
Salvage and Marine Operations IPT Salvage of Sea Kings XV650 & XV704, Arabian Gulf 2003, report by Salvage Officer C.J. Miners.
And finally the notes compiled by Salvage Officer, the late Michael Cobbold.

Other
Economic History Services
Imperial War Museum
ITN Archive
ITN Archive/Stills
National Oceanic and Atmospheric Administration Photo Library
Orkney Library & Archive
Parliamentary Archives:
  Merchant Shipping (Salvage) Bill, 10 August 1916 (House of Commons)
  Merchant Shipping (Salvage) Bill, 16 August 1916 (House of Commons)
  Merchant Shipping (Salvage) Bill, 3 July 1940 (House of Commons)
  Merchant Shipping (Salvage) Bill, 16 July 1940 (House of Lords)
  Emergency Powers (Defence) Act 1939
  Compensation (Defence) Act 1939
The *Orcadian*, newspaper, Orkney

Index

198

Eden, Sir Anthony: appeals to United States for financial help, 160; calls ceasefire, 160; Eisenhower warns of invasion consequences, 159; forced to back down, 160; grossly miscalculates Nasser's motives, 157–8; hopes Nasser's people will overthrow him, 160; informed that Suez Canal was seized, 158; insists invasion was right, 160; lies to people, 167–8; Nasser block Canal to prevent Eden taking it, 160; private secretary's concerns about salvage costs, 167; realizes he misread situation, 160; reluctant to take matter to International Court, 159; salvage force last part of failed invasion, 166; takes holiday at Goldeneye, 163; telegrammed Eisenhower, 158
Edgar Class, Cruiser, 21
Edwards, Captain, 47
Eisenhower, Dwight D., 127, 129, 131–2, 159–60
Elba, xiv, 149, 151–2, 156, 161
El Cap, Egypt, 160, 162–3, 165
Emergency Powers (Defence) Act 1939, 95
Eminent, HMT, 114, 116–20
Empire Lough, SS, xi–xiii
Employers' Federation, 98
Endurance, HMS, 170, 175–6
Energie, heavy-lift craft, 161
English Channel, 16, 41, 45
Enigma machine, 113–14
Escort, tugboat, 16
Essential Work (General Provision) Order 1941, 107
Excellent, HMS, 9–10
Exocet, missile, 170, 172–3

Falcon, ROV, 188
Falklands conflict, xiv, 172–3, 175, 182, 191
Fall of Gondolin, 39
Falmouth, Devon, 56
Falmouth, HMS, 28
Farnborough, Hampshire, 155
Fastnet, Ireland, 27
Feisal, King, 158

Feldkirchner, Kapitänleutnant Johannes, 16
Fell, Anthony, 163
First World War: Admiralty does not accept convoy system until late in, 20; accurate salvage records kept during, 136; affect of London Declaration on, 10; bad time for merchant ships, xiii; changes to salvage during, 92; Commander Kay excelled himself during, 133; description of sinking ship during, 28; first British casualty during, 16; first use of hydrophones during, 41; French base ports used for, 22; futility of battles during, 40; Hog Islanders built during, 140; importance of salvage during, 79; lack of salvage information known about during, 42; length of time Admiralty salvage has existed since, 192; more ships raised during D-Day than during, 136; most salvage decorations during, 80; number of hospital ships attacked during, 38; salvage begins as legitimate naval arm during, xv; spreads to the Mediterranean, 50
Fitzroy, Falkland Islands, 174
Fladda, Scotland, 119
Flamborough Head, Yorkshire, 91
Fleming, Ian, 160
Fleuriot, Chief Engineer Ernest, 61, 66
Flintshire, Admiralty tugboat, 45–6
Flower Class, 113, 119
Folkestone, Kent, 134
Force Mulberry, 130
Foreign Office, 144, 189
Forsberg, Commander E.G., 150, 153–6, 192
Fortitude, Admiralty tugboat, 45–7
Fowke, Lieutenant Commander M.G., 152, 154
Fowler, Lieutenant Commander G.D., 114, 119
Frobisher, HMS, 93
Furlong, Engineer R., 52, 54

Galpin, diver J., 154
Galtier, Renoux and Brizard, 25–6

get vessels out from and along main Canal, 165; biggest ship raised is from, 167; Gamil Bridge runs from, 160; General Wheeler feels tied to, 166; has ships ready to enter main Canal from, 162; Hogg flies out to in bid to persuade salvage men to stay at, 165; paratroopers land at, 160; some salvage vessels allowed to re-enter port, 165; standard salvage operations begin at, 163; try to finish work at, 164; twenty-one wrecks located at, 160; salvage teams enter, 161

Port Stanley, Falklands, 170–1, 174, 177, 179

Portsmouth, Hampshire, 4–6, 9, 11, 150

Position Z (see also Piccadilly Circus, English Channel), 130

Prawle Point, Devon, 31, 56

Prescott, Deputy Prime Minister John, 185

Pridham-Wippell, Admiral H.D., xiii

Princes Dock, Glasgow, 73

Privy Council, 95

Puma, helicopter, 170

Pye, 151–3

Q ship, 17

Queen Elizabeth II, MV, 171

Racer, salvage vessel, 16, 69, 88–9, 160

Ramsey, Sir B.H., 125

Ranger, salvage vessel: Admiralty enquire about chartering, 14, 16; attends *Asturias*, 32; divers to investigate *Asturias* from, 33; feeding steam power into *Asturias* from, 35; finally arrives at *Asturias*, 33; in urgent need of overhaul, 37–8; moored in Scapa Flow, 33; powerful pumping capacity on, 16; pumps lowered into *Asturias* from, 33; Salvage Section grown much since she was charted, 69; steel cover made for *Asturias* aboard, 35; used on Belgian coast after First World War, 73

Redpath, A., 66

Red Sea, 186

Reindeer, salvage ship, 69

Rennard, N., 52–4

Rennew, drifter, 58

Renown, HMS, 21

Repulse, HMS, 21

Rescue Tug Service, xiv, 105, 144

Revenge Class, battleship, 103

Rhinoceros, salvage lifting craft, 69

Ringdove, salvage vessel, 16, 69

Risdon Beazley, 97, 126, 151, 154, 161

Riversdale, SS, 56–8

River Schelde, Holland, 138, 140

River Seine, France, 138, 41

River Thames, England, 8

Robertson, J., 96, 98

Robinson, 'Bill' W., 121–2

Roman Empire, 20

Rome, Italy, 146

Rommel, Erwin, 100, 134

Rothesay Bay, Scotland, 119

Rothesay Class, frigate, 172

Rouen, France, 100, 141

Rousso, C., 55

Rover, tugboat, 57–8

Rowand, Commander, 24–5

Royal Aircraft Establishment, RAE, 155

Royal Artillery, 8

Royal Fleet Auxiliary, RFA, 161, 171, 174, 187

Royal Engineers, 8–9, 124

Royal Mail, 29

Royal Maritime Auxiliary Service, RMAS, 174, 177–8, 180

Royal Military Academy, Woolwich, 8

Royal Naval Reserve, RNR, 33, 96

Royal Oak, HMS, 21, 103, 186

Russo-Japanese War, 11

Safaga, Egypt, 186

Salcombe, Devon, 31–2, 58

Salvage and Mooring Operations, S&MO: deals with about twelve casualties a year, 181; deployed to Gulf War II, 187; involved in *Derbyshire* forensic survey, 182–3; long wealth of experience of value today, 192; no salvage vessels owned by today, 180; operates with Integrated Project Team, 181; provides secure barrier on river in

Salvage Officer Kay acts as his assistant, 32; concerned *Asturias* might sink before reaching dry dock, 37; concerned at lack of qualified staff, 15; concerned at salvage plant tied up on *Laurentic*, 86–7; concerns make Admiralty act, 15, 192; damns condition of equipment, 15; deals with eight salvage operations simultaneously, 80; dies three days before seventieth birthday, 77; ex-Admiralty diver, 12; finally raises *Asturias*, 37; finally opts for brute force to lift *Asturias*, 37; form S 1317 created so he can make quick decision on wreck salvage, 19; gives salvage advice, 30; goes to Salcombe to begin *Asturias* salvage operations, 32–3; happy with *Asturias* salvage progress, 34–5; in 1938 the state of Admiralty Salvage worse than his report in 1914, 90; invents 'Standard Patch' for rapid ship recovery, 69; Kay's leave short to join on *Asturias* operation, 33; knighted, 76; *Laurentic* mined during, xiv; lent to Admiralty during First World War, 14; Liverpool Salvage Association lend clerical staff, as well as, 71; made Naval Salvage Advisor, 18; meets Kay in Scapa Flow, 33; ordered to raise *Asturias*, 30; original contract never altered, 77; personal philosophy stretched in bid to raise *Asturias*, 37; promoted to Head of Salvage Section, 72; promoted to Commodore, 76; realization of the importance of pumps still recognized today, 180; realizes full power of pumps to raise ships, 38; realizes use of pumps critical in saving *Asturias*, 33; refuses legal pay-out, 77; sceptical of post-war salvage boom, 77–8; similar damning report of made on state of Salvage Sections accounts, 71; son, Desmond, joins him on salvage operations, 12; strength and size of Salvage Section grows under, 69; stretched to limit shortly after Salvage Section formed, 19; successfully deploys firefighting tug on Belgian coast, 75; successfully rights HMS *Gladiator*, 14; test lifts *Asturias* made, 36; tries conventional methods in Belgium, but do not work, 75; tries to get water low enough to use *Asturias*'s own pumping system, 36; undertakes salvage equipment survey, 15; wants *Laurentic* operation cancelled permanently, 87; weather causes delay raising *Asturias*, 34; writes book on salvage practice, 11